Praise for *The Biggest Bluff*

One of *The New York Times'* 100 Notable Books of 2020
One of *The Washington Post's* 50 best nonfiction books of 2020
One of *Wired's* Most Fascinating Books of 2020
One of *Behavioral Scientist's* Notable Books of 2020

———

"[*The Biggest Bluff*] will inspire readers as much as it entertains them."
—*The Washington Post*

"Fascinating . . . Konnikova is like your smart friend who instantly contextualizes everything by sharing the latest data and sharpest insight, whom you come to quote too often. . . . Konnikova keeps the lines so clean and even, so steady and unshowy that she might be the Charlie Watts of prose: While the backbeat never ceases and the narrative propels along, it's her curiosity that proliferates. In fact, one of the biggest bluffs of *The Biggest Bluff* may be that Konnikova hasn't written a book about her success with cards and chips exactly, but bet the house on the power of her mind to synthesize big philosophical ideas and psychological insights at a time when we, too, find ourselves questioning our fortunes, hoping to master our fates and playing much bigger odds than ever before." —*The New York Times Book Review*

"There has never been a more pressing need for digestible and coherent literature on rational decision-making. Enter *The Biggest Bluff*, psychologist Maria Konnikova's depiction of her journey into professional poker. What at first seems a lighthearted story about a curious academic dipping her toe into shark-infested waters delivers a crucial lesson in how to thrive in an increasingly misleading world. . . . As someone who has read almost every piece of literature on poker, I can say that *The Biggest Bluff* is the best depiction yet of the game I love, and the invaluable thinking skills it teaches. . . . Konnikova's is an uplifting zero-to-hero journey that will raise a smile in these trying times." —*Nature*

"*The Biggest Bluff* is a great read if you play poker. But it's also a great read for those, like me, who don't play poker. For us, the game provides the backdrop for a fascinating look at human nature, at attention and focus, at game theory (applied much more broadly than just to games), and at making better decisions. And how to better deal with the outcomes of those decisions—and not just learn, but keep moving forward. . . . [A] must-read for most entrepreneurs." —*Inc.*

"An inspired investigation of 'the struggle for balance on the spectrum of luck and control in the lives we lead, and the decisions we make,' partway between memoir, primer on the psychology of decision-making, and playbook for life." —Maria Popova, *Brain Pickings*

"*The Biggest Bluff* is a brilliant book, mostly because Konnikova is a brilliant writer, but also because she is a brilliant observer of the weird world she has immersed herself into. . . . The most enthralling parts of the book are when she takes the reader inside the cockpit and talks through some of the high-stakes plays she finds herself involved in." —*Daily Telegraph* (London)

"A smart and subtle delight—highly recommended for fans of cards and brain-hacking alike." —*Kirkus Reviews* (starred review)

"I absolutely love this book. The story is fantastically gripping, and offers lessons about decision-making, luck, risk—and, most important, how to play at life like a cool-headed pro. This is one of my favorite books of the year." —Charles Duhigg, author of bestsellers *The Power of Habit* and *Smarter Faster Better*

"*The Biggest Bluff* is an exhilarating and often hilarious personal journey. What's most exciting, though, is the probing sociological analysis by the brilliant and eternally curious Maria Konnikova."
—Jesse Eisenberg, author of *Bream Gives Me Hiccups*

"The narrative is so gripping that you might get halfway through *The Biggest Bluff* before you even notice that you're getting a master class in learning, focus, and decision-making. I tore through it in two sittings, and haven't stopped thinking about it since." —David Epstein, author of *Range*

"One of the most extraordinary outcomes of any experiment in participatory journalism. This is a book not just about the game of poker, but about the meaning of luck, the science of skill, and the psychology of outsmarting your competitors."

—Joshua Foer, author of *Moonwalking with Einstein* and founder of Atlas Obscura

"This book probably won't turn you into an international poker champ overnight, and it definitely won't make you as smart as Maria Konnikova. But it will do something just as valuable: it will teach you to think more like her. It's rare enough to find a memoir this transfixing or a behavioral science book this insightful. To have them combined in one place—by a psychologist who mastered one of the most competitive games on earth—is a real treat."

—Adam Grant, *New York Times* bestselling author of *Originals* and *Give and Take*, and host of the chart-topping TED podcast *WorkLife*

"Maria Konnikova has penned a page-turning memoir about going from journalist-curious-about-poker to professional-gambler-raking-in-hundreds-of-thousands. The fascinating portrait of her Buddha, Erik Seidel—the ultimate poker studmuffin and all-around Renaissance man—puts this whole tale on a par with the best nonfiction by that czar of the form John McPhee. A must read!"

—Mary Karr, author *The Liars' Club*, *Lit*, and *The Art of Memoir*

"I love it. Not only did *The Biggest Bluff* lead me into a complex and charismatic new world, it made me think about my own life and my own self-deceptions about control—and taught me to pay more attention to my own opponents, mine being of the tennis sort. The narrative is deftly crafted, and the journey—the self-examination, the oddball characters, the awful misogyny, the Aggros, the notion of tilt—accumulates in a seamless and satisfying way. I read this in what for me was record time."

—Erik Larson, #1 *New York Times* bestselling author of *The Splendid and the Vile*

"*The Biggest Bluff* is a flat-out classic. It's a ripping good story—with an underdog heroine, a Yoda-like mentor, and a cast of wild characters. It's a sophisticated meditation on the relative importance of deep skill and dumb luck. And it's a primer on how to pay attention, think objectively, and make better decisions. Reading this book is like drawing a straight flush. You won't believe your good fortune—and you'll remember it for a long, long time."   —Daniel H. Pink, #1 *New York Times* bestselling author of *When*, *Drive*, and *To Sell Is Human*

"We're all searching for greater self-knowledge—and Maria Konnikova found it through poker. She set out to make herself a champion, and along the way, she learned far more than the game. In lessons we can use ourselves, poker taught her greater emotional and physical regulation, tolerance for risk and uncertainty, more intelligent decision-making, a grasp of the intertwined roles of chance and skill, and sheer confidence. As she explains, 'This book isn't about how to play poker. It's about how to play the world.'"
—Gretchen Rubin, author of *The Happiness Project* and *Better Than Before*

"There are a lot of great books about psychology. And there are even *some* great books about poker. There isn't any book like *The Biggest Bluff*. Maria's journey from a novice into a world-class poker player is a page-turning adventure that you'll enjoy whether you're a seasoned pro or someone who doesn't know a busted draw from a full house. But what makes *The Biggest Bluff* so unique is its honesty and humility. It understands the importance of luck and uncertainty in our lives—and how different they can look when we're suddenly facing high-stakes, life-altering decisions. I can't think of a better guide for navigating these subjects than Maria, and I highly recommend this book."
—Nate Silver, founder and editor-in-chief, *FiveThirtyEight*

PENGUIN BOOKS

THE BIGGEST BLUFF

Maria Konnikova is the author of *Mastermind* and *The Confidence Game*. She is a regular contributing writer for *The New Yorker*, and has written for *The Atlantic*, *The New York Times*, *Slate*, *The New Republic*, *The Paris Review*, *The Wall Street Journal*, *Salon*, *The Boston Globe*, *Scientific American*, *Wired*, and *Smithsonian*, among many other publications. Her writing has won numerous awards, including the 2019 Excellence in Science Journalism Award from the Society of Personality and Social Psychology. While researching *The Biggest Bluff*, Maria became an international poker champion and the winner of over $300,000 in tournament earnings. Maria also hosts the podcast *The Grift* from Panoply Media and is currently a visiting fellow at NYU's School of Journalism. Her podcasting work earned her a National Magazine Award nomination in 2019. Maria graduated from Harvard University and received her PhD in Psychology from Columbia University.

ALSO BY MARIA KONNIKOVA

The Confidence Game

Mastermind

The
Biggest Bluff

How I Learned to Pay Attention,
Master Myself, and Win

MARIA KONNIKOVA

PENGUIN BOOKS

PENGUIN BOOKS
An imprint of Penguin Random House LLC
penguinrandomhouse.com

First published in the United States of America by Penguin Press,
an imprint of Penguin Random House LLC, 2020
Published in Penguin Books 2021

ISBN 9780525522645 (paperback)

THE LIBRARY OF CONGRESS HAS CATALOGED THE HARDCOVER EDITION AS FOLLOWS
Names: Konnikova, Maria, author.
Title: The biggest bluff : how I learned to pay attention,
master the odds, and win / Maria Konnikova.
Description: New York : Penguin Press, 2020. | Includes index.
Identifiers: LCCN 2020002627 (print) | LCCN 2020002628 (ebook) |
ISBN 9780525522621 (hardcover) | ISBN 9780525522638 (ebook)
Subjects: LCSH: Konnikova, Maria. | Seidel, Erik, 1959- |
Poker players—United States—Biography. |
Women poker players—United States—Biography. | Poker players—
Psychology. | Poker—Psychological aspects. | Human behavior.
Classification: LCC GV1250.2.K66 A3 2020 (print) |
LCC GV1250.2.K66 (ebook) | DDC 795.412—dc23
LC record available at https://lccn.loc.gov/2020002627
LC ebook record available at https://lccn.loc.gov/2020002628

Printed in the United States of America
2nd Printing

Book design by Claire Vaccaro

In memory of Walter Mischel.
I still haven't published my dissertation,
as I promised you I would, but at least there is this.
May we always have the clarity to know
what we can control
and what we can't.

And to my family,
for being there
no matter what.

Пусть все будут здоровы.

"Life's single lesson: that there is more accident to it than a man can ever admit to in a lifetime and stay sane."

FAUSTO MAIJSTRAL, IN THOMAS PYNCHON'S *V.*

"I wish you luck, because what lies ahead is no picnic for the prepared and the unprepared alike, and you'll need luck. Still, I believe you'll manage."

JOSEPH BRODSKY, "SPEECH AT THE STADIUM"

"But once in a while the odd thing happens,
Once in a while the dream comes true,
And the whole pattern of life is altered,
Once in a while the Moon turns Blue."

W. H. AUDEN, LIBRETTO FOR *PAUL BUNYAN*

Contents

A Prelude

The room is a sea of people. Bent heads, pensive faces, many obscured by sunglasses, hats, hoodies, massive headphones. It's difficult to discern where the bodies end and the green of the card tables begins. Thousands of bodies sit in seeming disarray on chairs straight out of a seventies dining room catalogue—orange-and-mustard patterned upholstery, gold legs, vaguely square frame. Garish neon lights suspended on makeshift beams make the place look like the inside of a hospital that's trying a bit too hard to appear festive. Everything is a bit worn, a bit out-of-date, a bit frayed. The only hints of deeper purpose are the color-coded numbers hanging on strings from the ceiling. There's the orange group, the yellow group, the white group. Each placard has a number and, beneath it, a picture of a single poker chip. The smell of stale casino air fills the room—old carpet; powder; a sweet, faintly sickly perfume; cold fried food and flat beer; and the unmistakable metallic tang of several thousand exhausted bodies that have been sharing the same space since morning.

Amid the sensory assault, it's hard at first to pinpoint why something seems off. And then it comes to you: it is eerily quiet. If this was a real party, you would expect the din of countless voices, shifting chairs, echoing footsteps. But all there is is nervous energy. You can smell, hear, taste, the tension. And you can certainly feel it making a nest in your stomach. There's just one sound left in the room, reminiscent of a full-throated courting ritual of summer cicadas. It's the sound of poker chips.

It's the first day of the biggest poker tournament of the year, the Main Event of the World Series of Poker. This is the World Cup, the Masters, the Super Bowl—except you don't need to be a superhero athlete to compete. This championship is open to the everyman. For a neat ten grand, anyone in the world can enter and take their shot at poker glory: the title of world champion and a prize that has been known to top $9 million. If you happen to be British or Australian, you even get it tax-free. For professional poker players and amateurs alike, this is the career pinnacle. If you can win the Main Event, you have guaranteed yourself a place in poker history. Sit down with the best and have a chance at the most prestigious, richest prize in the poker world. Some people in the room have been saving for years to take their one shot.

It's near the end of the day. Of the several thousand people who've entered today's starting flight—so many want to play that starting days have to be staggered into flights to accommodate everyone; the dream is expensive, but it's awfully alluring—many are now out, having gone bust, in poker speak. The ones who remain are concentrated on making it through to the second day. You don't want to play the whole day only to find yourself walking out with minutes until the end and nothing to show for it. Everyone is gunning for the magic bag, a clear plastic glorified ziplock into which those lucky enough to have made the next day of a multiday tournament can place their chips. You write your name, country of origin, and chip count in excited capitals on the outside before tugging on the dubiously functioning adhesive strip to seal the damn thing up. You then take the requisite photograph for social media with the requisite chip count and add the #WSOP hashtag. And then you collapse, exhausted, into some anonymous hotel bed.

But we're not yet at the bagging and tagging stage of the day. There are still two more hours to go. Two whole hours. A lot can happen in two hours. Which is why one table stands out from the rest. Eight players are sitting as players should, receiving their cards and doing whatever it is poker players do with them. But one lone chair in the middle of the table, seat six, remains empty. That wouldn't be remarkable in the least under normal circumstances—empty chairs are what happens when a player busts out and no new player has yet arrived to take their place. Except in this case, there has been no bust-out. On the green felt in front of the empty chair sit several neat piles of chips, arranged from highest to lowest denomination, color-coded from left to right. And with each hand dealt, the dealer reaches over to take a precious ante—the forced amount that everyone at the table must pay each hand to see the cards—before depositing two cards that are then unceremoniously placed into the muck, or discard pile, seeing as there's no one there to play them. With each round, the neat piles of chips grow slightly smaller. And still the chair remains empty. What kind of an idiot pays $10,000 to enter the most prestigious poker event in the world and then fails to show up to play? What kind of a dunce do you have to be to let yourself blind down (the term for letting your chips dwindle by not playing any hands) in the middle of the Main Event?

The genius, I regret to say, was your author. While everyone at the table idly speculated about my likely fate, I was huddled in fetal position on the bathroom floor of the Rio Hotel and Casino and, for lack of a more refined term, barfing my brains out. Could it have been food poisoning from the guacamole I knew I shouldn't have eaten at the Mexican place just down the hallway during dinner break? A bad stress reaction? Delayed onset of stomach flu? Who knows. But my money was on migraine.

I had prepped endlessly. I had planned for all the contingencies—including, of course, migraine. I'm a lifelong sufferer, and I wasn't about to leave anything to chance. I'd taken preventive Advil. I'd done yoga in the morning for relaxation. I'd meditated. I'd slept a full nine hours. I'd even eaten over dinner break, even though my nerves were telling me to avoid all sustenance. And still here it was.

That's the thing about life: You can do what you do but in the end, some things remain stubbornly outside your control. You can't calculate for dumb bad luck. As they say, man plans, God laughs. I could definitely detect a slight cackle.

My reasons for getting into poker in the first place were to better understand that line between skill and luck, to learn what I could control and what I couldn't, and here was a strongly-worded lesson if ever there were: you can't bluff chance. Poker didn't care about my reasons for being on the floor. There was no one to whom I could direct a complaint, a plaintive "But it's the Main Event!" The *why* didn't matter. Nerves or stress, migraine or food poisoning, the cards would keep getting dealt. The message was clear. I could plan all I wanted, but the X factor could still always get me. The outcome would be what it would be. All I could do was my best with what I could control—and the rest, well, the rest wasn't up to me.

As I contemplated the merits of dying right there versus first mustering the energy to bribe someone to bag up what measly chips I had left for me, before crawling off to die somewhere a bit less sticky and odiferous than this stall, I heard the telltale sound of my phone's text message alert. It was my coach, Erik Seidel. "How's it going?" the message read. Simple enough. He wanted to see how his student was faring in this, her biggest quest. The cackling from above was definitely growing stronger. I gathered my remaining willpower to text back.

"Fine. A little below average in chips." Which was true as far as I knew. "Hanging in there." Slightly less true, but hey, I'm ever the optimist.

"k, good luck" came the reply. Oh, Erik, you have no idea how much I need exactly that. A good infusion of old-fashioned luck.

Ante Up

New York, Late Summer 2016

"But for its costliness and dangers, no better education for life among men could be devised than the gambling table—especially the poker table."

CLEMENS FRANCE, *THE GAMBLING IMPULSE*, 1902

From across the room, I see Erik Seidel's signature baseball cap lying on the banquette by his side. I know it's his signature because I've been studying him carefully from afar. I've charted his personality—or at least what seems like his personality—from the sidelines. He isn't like most of the limelight-seeking top professionals, the players who love the camera, love the audience, love their shtick, whatever that shtick happens to be—temper tantrums, crazy aggression, incessant table chatter. He is quiet. Reserved. Determinedly attentive. He seems to play with deliberation and precision. And he is a winner: multiple World Series of Poker bracelets, the World Poker Tour title, tens of millions in winnings. I have chosen with care. I am, after all, about to ask him to spend the next year of his life with me—a marriage proposal, if you will, right off a first date. It was crucial I do my research well.

For the first time in a while, I'm nervous—*really* nervous. I chose my outfit with care—sophisticated but not stuffy, serious but not overly so. The kind of person you could trust and depend on, but who would also be fun to hang around with over drinks. It's going to be a complicated seduction.

We're meeting at a Hollywood version of what a French café should rightly look like. I'm early, but he's even earlier. There he is, in the far right corner of the room, folded into a bistro table that seems too small for his lanky limbs and six-and-a-half-foot body. He's wearing a dark T-shirt that offsets a pale, intent face, and is reading a magazine. To my great relief, it looks like a *New Yorker*, the late August edition—the one with the muted watercolors of Sempé's ocean landscape. A poker player who reads the *New Yorker* is my kind of poker player. Gingerly, a hound on the scent, afraid to scare off the prey in its sights, I approach the table.

ERIK SEIDEL IS SURELY the most self-effacing poker champion in the world. Apart from his poker accolades, he stands out from other players for his longevity: he still contends for number one, as he has since his career first started, in the late eighties. That takes some doing: the game has changed a lot in the last thirty years. As with so many facets of modern life, the qualitative elements of poker have been passed over in favor of the quantitative. Measurement presides over intuition. Statistics over observation. Game theory over "feel." We've seen the trend play out in areas as far afield as psychology—social psychology giving way to neuroscience—and music, with algorithms and experts quantifying not just what we listen to but how, to the fraction of a second, a song should be structured for maximum pop. Poker is no different. Caltech PhDs line the tables. Printouts of stats columns are a common sight. A conversation rarely goes for more than a beat without the offhand dropping of GTO (game theory optimal) or +EV (positive expected value). Talk of frequencies trumps talk of feelings. But despite predictions that his style of play—a psychological one, based less on mathematical outputs and more on understanding the human element—would render him a dinosaur, Erik stays on top. In the bombastic, testosterone- and expletive-filled, ego-driven world of professional poker, Erik is atypical in more than his unassuming manner. He may be the only poker pro to boast a membership to the Brooklyn Academy of Music, a willingness to fly cross-country to see Dave Chappelle do stand-up, or a near encyclopedic knowledge of the latest in the culinary scene from Los Angeles to Manila. He's certainly the only pro who prefers New York to Vegas—and has a part-time residence on the Upper West Side of Manhattan, the same area where he grew up, and not just the usual Vegas abode. His curiosity is genuine and boundless, his enthusiasm for life entirely contagious.

"Do you know Julia and Angus Stone?" he asks offhand the first time we meet.

Who? I don't even know which bucket those names fit into. Authors I've never heard of? Actors I'm woefully unaware of? Random New Yorkers Erik thinks I should know? Musicians, it turns out. I hope I am not losing his interest, that I'm sophisticated enough to pass his litmus test. My nervousness is going nowhere fast.

"They're really something special. A brother-sister duo from Australia. I've heard them play many times."

"Something special" is a phrase I'll come to know well. Birbigs: something special. The new production of *Othello*: something special. An offbeat, tiny sushi bar tucked far from the strip in Vegas, where we go for dinner during my first trip out to the city of sin: something special. A professional poker player named LuckyChewy: something special. I'm his junior by a quarter century, but I realize talking to him that I've forgotten what it feels like to enjoy new experiences. I get lazy. I feel jaded. I want to curl up and stay in rather than see the latest talk at the 92Y or an obscure musical act from Canada playing at Joe's Pub. (Erik drags me to both, and each time, he is right. Over the coming months, my playlist will be overhauled with his recommendations, much like my stand-up predilections, Netflix queue, and list of theater shows that I "absolutely have to see" that I will of course never make it to. He's a one-man Goings On About Town.) My ideal evening: dinner at home, some wine, some tea, a book or a movie in bed. His reply: You're in New York City, the greatest city in the world! Look at what you're missing.

He approaches poker with the same passion and constant inquisitiveness. He loves to follow the up-and-coming players, is hip to the latest apps and programs, never assumes that he's learned all there is. He refuses to plateau. If I had to assign him a life motto, it would be this: life is too short for complacency. Indeed, when I inevitably ask him the question he gets asked most frequently—what his single piece of advice would be to aspiring poker players—his answer is two words long: pay attention. Two simple words that we simply ignore more often than not. Presence is far more difficult than the path of least resistance.

I first encountered Erik the way I imagine most poker newbies do: in the 1998 movie *Rounders*. In many ways, *Rounders* brought poker to the masses—a story of a brilliant law student (Matt Damon) who pays his way through school with his poker prowess, in the end quitting law altogether to play full-time. And the one game that most inspires Damon's character, playing in the background and analyzed ad infinitum throughout the film, is the 1988 WSOP final table showdown, between Erik Seidel and Johnny Chan. Johnny fuckin' Chan, the master, the commentators repeat over and over. And Erik Seidel—the kid doesn't know what hit him. The most famous poker match in the non-poker world. Seidel's queens falling to Chan's straight—an expert trap for an unwitting victim.

Chan was the reigning world champion. Seidel was at his first ever major tournament. He'd made it past 165 other contenders to be there, at the final table, the last man standing save one. It was an incredible feat, and the start of an incredible career.

The movie was a hit on college campuses. It came out in the late nineties, and by the early aughts, every kid was contemplating a life of paying their way through school by poker prowess. I didn't care about poker at the time—I had no idea what a straight was, or why Chan had "trapped" Seidel with it, or any of it; it was a foreign language I had little interest in learning. But when I finally watched the film, some years later, a line uttered by Matt Damon as he contemplated Seidel and Chan's matchup struck me: It wasn't about playing the cards. It was about playing the man. A cliché, true—but one that got to the heart of my interests, that captured much of what I'd been thinking about the world. Psychology. Self-control. Being willing to check your straight all the way to the end, as Chan did—sitting on the best hand possible so stealthily that you rope along your opponents, tricking them into thinking they are winning when you've had them beat the whole time. You didn't have to know what a straight was to see the appeal and the strategic beauty.

And here was the man himself: the kid turned master. One of the walking legends of the poker world. And I was here to persuade him to take me on as a student of poker for the next year of his life—even though, as far as I knew, he'd never taken a student in the past, and I had never even played a single game of poker. I wanted Erik to teach me—to train me for the ultimate poker championship, the World Series of Poker, or WSOP. The one that, so many years ago, had first made him an unwitting poker legend. Through that journey, I hoped to learn how to make the best decisions I possibly could, not just at the card table but in the world. Through poker, I wanted to tame luck—to learn to make a difference even when the deck seemed stacked against me.

IT WAS SUPPOSED TO be a year. Neat. Controllable. Digestible. I had a plan. I'd approach Erik, we'd team up, I'd play the Main Event at the World Series of Poker. And I'd live to tell the tale.

Coming up with a time limit was the easy part. A year is definable. It's finite. It sells—because everyone can imagine doing something for a year. My year of this, my year of that, my year of trying on a new role that has a definite expiration date. No one wants to hear about my three and a half years of not-quite-making-it. Who has that kind of time? A year is manageable, pretty. A year is a neat antidote to the messiness of life.

But life had other ideas. A plan shifted. A framework disappeared and was replaced by something unforeseen. Man plans, God laughs, indeed. Whatever I may think about God, I believe in randomness. In the noise of the universe that chugs along caring nothing about us, our plans, our desires, our motivations, our actions. The noise that will be there regardless of what we choose or don't choose to do. Variance. Chance. That thing we can't control no matter how we may try. But can you really blame us for trying?

. . . . .

THE STRUGGLE FOR BALANCE on the spectrum of luck and control in the lives we lead, and the decisions we make, is one I have been grappling with for many years. As a child, I had perhaps the greatest luck of my life: my parents left the Soviet Union, opening to me a world of opportunity I would never otherwise have had. As a teen, I used every ounce of skill I had to excel academically and become part of the first generation in my family to make it to college in the United States. As an adult, I wanted to disentangle just how much of where I'd ended up had been my own doing as opposed to a twist of fate—like so many before me, I wanted to know how much of my life I could take credit for and how much was just stupid luck. In *All Said and Done*, Simone de Beauvoir says of her life that the "penetration of that particular ovum by that particular spermatozoon, with its implications of the meeting of my parents and before that of their birth and the births of all their forebears, had not one chance in hundreds of millions of coming about." Such was the role that chance had played in the whole trajectory of her existence. "And it was chance, a chance quite unpredictable in the present state of science, that caused me to be born a woman. From that point on, it seems to me that a thousand different futures might have stemmed from every single movement of my past: I might have fallen ill and broken off my studies; I might not have met Sartre; anything at all might have happened." How could you ever hope to separate the random from the intentional?

It was a philosophical query as much as anything else. And I tried to pursue it in the best way I knew how. I went to grad school. I posed the question. I developed some studies. How often are we actually in control, I wondered? And how does the perception of being in control in situations where luck is queen actually play out in our decision making? How do people respond when placed in uncertain situations, with incomplete information?

Over the course of five years, as part of my doctoral research at Columbia, I asked thousands of people to play a simulated stock market game, under time pressure. They would have to "invest" a certain amount of their money—real money; how they performed would translate directly into how much they were paid, and the range was vast, from one dollar to over seventy-five dollars—in one of two stocks, or in a bond, and do so over hundreds of trials. The bond always paid safely, and it always paid little—one dollar, to be exact. The stocks, however, mimicked the behavior of actual stocks in the market. They might earn you far more money—up to ten dollars a turn. But they could also be losers, wiping out ten dollars from your gains in the click of a mouse. In each round of the game, the two stocks (creatively titled "A" and "B") were randomly assigned to be either "good" or "bad." Choose the good stock, and you'd have a 50 percent chance of getting ten dollars, a quarter chance of making nothing, and a quarter chance of losing ten dollars. Choose the bad one, and your winning chances fell to 25 percent, while your losing chances jumped to 50. Here's what I was interested in: What strategy would people follow in their choices—and how quickly would they learn which of the stocks was the winning one? (Optimal investment strategy would have you quickly gravitate to the good stock, as your overall earnings would be highest despite the intermittent losses.)

What I found was something completely unexpected. Over and over, people would overestimate the degree of control they had over events—smart people, people who excelled at many things, people who should have known better. Not only would they decide ahead of time how they were going to divide their investments, but they would decide based on incredibly limited information which stock was "good" and stick to their guns—even as they started losing money. The more they overestimated their own skill relative to luck, the less they learned from what the environment was trying to tell them, and the worse their decisions became: the participants grew increasingly less likely to switch to winning stocks, instead doubling down on losers or gravitating entirely toward bonds. Because they thought they knew more than they did, they ignored any signs to the contrary—especially when, as inevitably happens in real stock markets, winners became losers and vice versa. In other words, the illusion of control is what prevented real control over the game from emerging—and before long, the quality of people's decisions deteriorated. They did what worked in the past, or what they had decided would work—and failed to grasp that the circumstances had shifted so that a previously successful strategy was no longer so. People failed to see what the world was telling them when that message wasn't one they wanted to hear. They liked being the rulers of their environment. When the environment knew more than they did—well, that was no good at all. Here was the cruel truth: we humans too often think ourselves in firm control when we are really playing by the rules of chance.

The problem stayed with me. But what was its solution? How could you use that theoretical knowledge to make better choices, practically speaking?

It's a tough ask, for one main reason: the equation of luck and skill is, at its heart, probabilistic. And a basic shortcoming of our neural wiring is that we can't quite grasp probabilities. Statistics are completely counterintuitive: our brains are simply not cut out, evolutionarily, to understand that inherent uncertainty. There were no numbers or calculations in our early environment—just personal experience and anecdote. We didn't learn to deal with information presented in an abstract fashion, such as *tigers are incredibly rare in this part of the country, and you have a 2 percent chance of encountering one, and an even lower chance of being attacked*; we learned instead to deal with brute emotions such as *last night there was a tiger here and it looked pretty damn scary*.

Millennia later, the shortcoming persists. It's called the description-experience gap. In study after study, people fail to internalize numeric rules, making decisions based on things like "gut feeling" and "intuition" and "what feels right" rather than based on the data they are shown. We need to train ourselves to see the world in a probabilistic light—and even then, we often ignore the numbers in favor of our own experience. We believe what we want to see, not what research shows. Take something that's on plenty of minds in recent times: disaster preparedness. What do you do to prepare for the extreme weather events—hurricanes, floods, earthquakes—that are increasing in frequency as the earth warms? What about nuclear war or a terrorist attack—do you need to worry about that? There are statistics to help you reach an answer, like whether you need special insurance for your home or if you should even be buying property in certain areas—just like there are probability charts that inform you of the risk of your being the victim of terrorism as opposed to, say, slipping in your shower and suffering a fatal or debilitating fall. But here's what psychologists find, over and over: you can show people all the charts you want, but that won't change their perceptions of the risks or their resulting decisions. What will change their minds? Going through an event themselves, or knowing someone who has. If you were in New York City during Hurricane Sandy, for instance, you are far more likely to purchase flood insurance. If you weren't, you may invest in a beach-front property in Malibu even though the numbers say your beach will be gone soon, and your house along with it. If you lived through 9/11, your fear of terrorism will be vastly overblown. In all cases, the reaction isn't in line with the statistics. Not every house in New York needs flood insurance—you've overcompensated because you went through a bad experience. Beachfront properties are an awful long-term investment—you've undercompensated because the statistics haven't ever affected you personally. Your likelihood of slipping in a shower is orders of magnitude larger than your likelihood of being in a terrorist attack—but just try convincing someone of that, especially if they knew someone who died in the Twin Towers.

Our experiences trump everything else, but mostly, those experiences are incredibly skewed: they teach us, but they don't teach us *well*. It's why disentangling chance from skill is so difficult in everyday decisions: it's a statistical undertaking, and one we are not normally equipped to deal with. Which brings me to poker: Used in the right way, experience can be a powerful ally in helping to understand probabilistic scenarios. The experience just can't be a one-off, haphazard event. It has to be a systematic learning process—much like the environment you encounter at the table. And the correct systematic learning process can help you unravel chance from everything else in a way that no amount of cramming numbers or studying theory ever will.

Several years after I left academia, the problem of skill versus chance became more personally pressing. 2015 was not a good year for the Konnikova clan. The first week of January, my mother—my role model in most every way—lost her job of almost twenty years, summarily downsized in a private equity acquisition. Her coworkers cried. Her boss cried. They petitioned to hire her back. She was good at what she did: computer programming. I thought she'd be back on her feet in no time. Instead, she hit upon a harsh reality of Silicon Valley: ageism is alive and thriving, especially for women. She's in her fifties—too old for the young set, not old enough to retire. A year later, she was still jobless. *Life is so unfair* was my first thought—but if there's anything Mom taught me, it's that life has no concept of fairness. It's just tough luck. Deal with it.

A few months later, my vivacious, healthy, living-on-her-own grandmother slipped in the night. The edge of a metal bed frame. Hard linoleum floor. No extra pair of ears to hear anything amiss. The neighbors found her in the morning, alerted by a light that shouldn't have been turned on. Two days later, she was dead. We never said goodbye. I don't even remember our last conversation—it was that banal, the same phrases, the same intonations, no, nothing new to report on either end.

She probably asked when the first copies of my new book would be ready. She wouldn't be able to read it—she'd have to wait for the Russian translation—but she couldn't wait to hold it. It's a safe bet that question came up. She asked me that every time we spoke. And every time, I'd berate her: stop asking; I'll let you know when. I'd grow frustrated. She'd raise her voice and inform me that she was never going to ask me anything about anything ever again. I should have been kinder. But hindsight always sees most clearly. To the end, she signed off her voicemails to me with a short phrase: "This is Grandma." As if there could be some confusion. And to the end, I never called back quite quickly enough. She'd been through World War II, survived Stalin, Khrushchev, Gorbachev, and was defeated by a slippery floor and one misplaced foot. Unfair. Or rather, unlucky. One surer step and she'd still be here.

My husband lost his job next. The startup he'd joined failed to start up as planned, and with that, I momentarily found myself in a position I hadn't been in for years: supporting my family on a freelance writer's income. We left our beautiful West Village apartment. We changed our habits. We did our best to adjust. And on top of it all, I found my health suddenly failing. I'd recently been diagnosed with a bizarre autoimmune condition. No one knew quite what it was, but my hormone levels had declared insanity, and I was suddenly allergic to just about everything. Sometimes, I couldn't even leave the apartment: my skin broke out in hives whenever anything touched it, and it was winter outside. I sat huddled with my laptop, draped in an old, loose T-shirt, hoping for the best. I went from expert to expert, steroid regime to steroid regime, only to be told the same thing: idiopathic. Doctor speak for "We don't have a clue." That idiopathy (root word: idiocy) was expensive. Unfair. Bum luck. But was it? Maybe it had been my fault for failing to listen to my mother and sneaking out to play on the balcony so many years ago. I was born in

Russia, after all, and was there for Chernobyl; her admonition to stay inside had its reasons. Maybe my two-year-old self was to blame. I sat reading James Salter—"We cannot imagine these diseases, they are called idiopathic, spontaneous in origin, but we know instinctively there must be something more, some invisible weakness they are exploiting. It is impossible to think they fall at random, it is unbearable to think it"—and I found myself nodding in recognition. Whether it was pure chance or not, it sucked.

It's a familiar pattern of thought. Luck surrounds us, everywhere—from something as mundane as walking to work and getting there safely to the other extreme, like surviving a war or a terrorist attack when others mere inches away weren't as fortunate. But we only notice it when things don't go our way. We don't often question the role of chance in the moments it protects us from others and ourselves. When chance is on our side, we disregard it: it is invisible. But when it breaks against us, we wake to its power. We begin to reason about its whys and hows.

Some of us find comfort in pure numbers. We call it what it is: pure, high-school-math chance. As Sir Ronald Aylmer Fisher, a twentieth-century statistician and geneticist, pointed out in 1966, "The 'one chance in a million' will undoubtedly occur with no less and no more than its appropriate frequency, however surprised we may be that it should occur to *us*." Consider the 7.5 billion people who currently make up the world's population and you can be sure that the highly improbable is happening with regular frequency. The "one chance in a million" takes place every second. Someone close to you will die in a freak accident. Someone will lose a job. Someone will fall ill with a mysterious disease. Someone will win the lottery. It is probability, it is pure statistics, and it is part of life, neither good nor bad. If bizarre coincidences and one-off events didn't happen—well, that would be the truly remarkable thing.

Some of us imbue probability with emotion. It becomes luck: chance that has suddenly acquired a valence, positive or negative, fortuitous or unfortunate. Good or bad luck. A lucky or unlucky break. Some of us invest luck with meaning, direction, and intent. It becomes fate, karma, kismet—chance with an agenda. It was meant to be. Some even go a step further: predestination. It was always meant to be, and any sense of control or free will we may think we have is pure illusion.

So how exactly does poker fit into all this? Until I began this journey, I'd never been a card player. I'd never played poker in my life. I'd never even seen a real game. Poker was a nonentity in my mind. But faced with event after event breaking the wrong way, I did what I always do when I try to understand something. I read. Anything that could help shed light on what was happening, that would allow me to regain some semblance of control. And in my reading frenzy, I came across John von Neumann's *Theory of Games and Economic Behavior*.

Von Neumann was one of the greatest mathematical and strategic minds of the twentieth century: he invented that little machine we all carry around with us, the computer (back then, it wasn't so little), crafted the technology behind the hydrogen bomb, and is the father of game theory. *Theory of Games* is his foundational text, and here's what I learned within its pages: the entire theory was inspired by a single game—poker. "Real life consists of bluffing, of little tactics of deception, of asking yourself what is the other man going to think I mean to do," von Neumann wrote. "And that is what games are about in my theory."

Von Neumann did not care for most card games. They were, he thought, as boring as the people who wasted their lives playing them, trying to coax mastery—impossibly—out of pure chance. Games of pure chance, though, were to his mind not much worse than those at the opposite end: games like chess, where all the information could theoretically be gleaned, where every move could be mathematically accounted for in advance. There was one exception to his distrust of gaming: poker. He loved it. To him, it represented that ineffable balance between skill and chance that governs life—enough skill to make playing worthwhile, enough chance that the challenge was there for the taking. He was a god-awful player by every account, but that never stopped him. Poker was the ultimate puzzle: he wanted to understand it, to unravel it—to, in the end, beat it. If he could figure out how to disentangle the chance from the skill, how to maximize the role of the latter and learn to minimize the malice of the former, he believed he would hold the solution to some of life's greatest decision challenges.

For poker, unlike quite any other game, mirrors life. It isn't the roulette wheel of pure chance, nor is it the chess of mathematical elegance and perfect information. Like the world we inhabit, it consists of an inextricable joining of the two. Poker stands at the fulcrum that balances two oppositional forces in our lives—chance and control. Anyone can get lucky—or unlucky—at a single hand, a single game, a single tournament. One turn and you're on top of the world—another, you are cast out, no matter your skill, training, preparation, aptitude. In the end, though, luck is a short-term friend or foe. Skill shines through over the longer time horizon.

Poker has a mathematical foundation, but with a dose of human intention, interaction, psychology—nuance, deception, little tricks that don't quite reflect reality but help you gain an edge over others. Humans aren't rational. Information isn't open to all. There are no "rules" of behavior, only norms and suggestions—and within certain broad constraints, anyone might break those norms at any point. The games that interested von Neumann are the ones that, like life, can't ever be mapped cleanly. Real life is based on making the best decisions you can from information that can never be complete: you never know someone else's mind, just like you can never know any poker hand but your own. Real life is not just about modeling the mathematically optimal decisions. It's about discerning the hidden, the uniquely human. It's about realizing that no amount of formal modeling will ever be able to capture the vagaries and surprises of human nature.

When I read von Neumann's rationale for choosing poker above all else to explore the most important strategic decisions in the world—he was advising the US military, after all—something clicked. Poker wasn't theoretical, the way the research I'd done and the studies I'd run had been. Poker was practical. Poker was experiential. Poker embodied the way the human mind learns best, and it wasn't a one-off event: it was a systematic process. It was, in other words, perfect for what I had in mind.

Poker isn't a homogeneous game; there are multiple varieties of play, with names like Stud, Omaha, Razz, Badugi, and HORSE. Each has its own unique set of rules, but in any style of poker, the basic parameters are essentially the same: Some cards are dealt faceup, visible to all—these are the community cards—and some facedown, so that only the person to whom they are dealt can see them. You make bets based on how strong your hand is and how strong you think others' hands are. Because the only other cards you know for sure are your own, you are in a game of incomplete information: you must make the best decision you can, given the little you know. The last player left standing at the end of the final round of betting takes the pot, or the sum of money that has been bet up to now.

But the style I've chosen to pursue is one particular variant of the game, which happens to be the most popular. No Limit Texas Hold'em. How no limit hold'em differs from other forms of poker is twofold. The first is in the precise amount of information that is held in common versus in private. Each player is dealt two cards facedown: the hole cards.

This is privileged information. I can try to guess what you have based on how you act, but I can't know for sure. The only information I'll have is your betting patterns once the public information—the cards dealt to the middle of the table, faceup—is known. In hold'em, there are three stages of dealing the middle cards: the first three cards, called the "flop," are dealt at the same time; the fourth card, the "turn," is dealt after another round of betting; and the fifth, the "river," is dealt after yet another round. In total, then, you have two cards in your hand, known only to you, five cards in the middle, known to everyone, and four "streets," or betting rounds, in which to make your best guess as to how the cards you can't see stack up against your own.

Where some forms of poker assume too many unknown variables (one form gives each player five cards facedown, for instance), making skill less of a factor, and others leave too little unknown (one hole card), reducing the guesswork too greatly, the amount of incomplete information in Texas hold'em creates a particularly useful balance between skill and chance. Two hole cards is just about as practical a ratio as you can have: enough unknown to make the game a good simulation of life, but not so much that it becomes a total crapshoot.

The second thing that distinguishes this particular playing style is the concept of no limit—von Neumann's own preferred style. "The power of the pure bluff is restricted in a game of limit," explains Amarillo Slim, one of the best poker players of his day, who, in 1972, won the third ever WSOP title. When there's a limit, it means that the exact amount you bet has a ceiling on it. Sometimes, the ceiling is set by the house rules—an arbitrary number above which you can't go. Sometimes, in what's known as "pot limit," it's set by the total amount in play: your bet cannot exceed what's in the pot. Either way, your range of action is artificially restricted. In no limit, you can bet everything you have, at any point. You can "shove" or "jam"—that is, make an all-in bet, placing every chip you have into the pot. And that's when the game gets *really* interesting. Limit is for people who have "the guts of an earthworm or make [their] living as an accountant," Slim says. "If you can't 'move in' on someone—meaning bet everything you've got in front of you—then it's not real poker."

And that's what makes this game a particularly strong metaphor for our daily decision making. Because in life, there is never a limit: there's no external restriction to betting everything you have on any given decision. What's to stop you from risking all your money, your reputation, your heart, even your life at any point you choose? Nothing. There are no rules, at the end of the day, save some internal calculus that only you are privy to. And everyone around you has to know that when they make *their* decisions: knowing you can go all the way, how much should they themselves invest? It's the endless game of brinkmanship, popularized by another giant of game theory, the Nobel-winning economist Thomas Schelling, that plays out everywhere in our lives. Who will say "I love you" first, moving "all in" in the relationship—and if you say it, will you be left out, so to speak? Who will walk away from the business negotiation? Who will wage war? The ability to go all in—and the knowledge that going all in is an option for everyone around us—is the crucial variable that makes so many decisions so very difficult.

And, of course, there's the emotional element. Be it at the poker table or out in the real world, there is no risk quite like the risk of the shove: at its best, it can let you "double through"—that is, win the maximum amount possible, doubling your stack—but it can also end your game. You can emerge with the deal of a lifetime, or a life partner—or you can find yourself bankrupt or emotionally devastated. Like life, no limit poker is high risk and high reward. It's no coincidence that the WSOP champion is determined by No Limit Texas Hold'em. And it's no coincidence that that is the style of play I have chosen to learn. If you're trying to make the best decisions, you might as well go with the best proxy.

Once you've chosen your game, there's one more choice to make: cash or tournament? In a cash game, every chip has a cash value. You buy in to a game for a certain amount, say, $100, and you get that exact amount in chips placed in front of you. At any point, you can choose to add more money to your stack by paying the requisite amount in cash. At any point, you can get up and walk away. And if you ever go bust, you can always choose to rebuy and start over for another shot. What's more, the structure will remain constant. If you bought in to a $1/$2 game—a game where the blinds, or forced bets that you have to post into the pot before seeing your cards, are one dollar for the small blind and two dollars for the big blind—it will always be a $1/$2 game. You won't turn around and find you're suddenly forced to pay five dollars when it's your turn in the big blind.

In a tournament, chips have value only relative to other players': they are a way of keeping score. A $100 buy-in might get you ten thousand chips or two hundred; it doesn't really matter. Everyone gets the same amount, and your goal is to accumulate as many of them as possible, with the eventual winner holding all the chips. If you start losing, that's too bad; there's no option to call someone over and pay another $100 for another stack of chips. And once you bust, you're out of there. You're playing for your tournament life. As for the blinds, those go up on a predetermined schedule. So, while you might start at 1/2, you will find that in a half hour or forty-five minutes or whatever the structure says, they rise to 2/4, 4/8, and so on. Suddenly, your chips aren't worth as much as they were and the pressure is on to start winning more pots. Otherwise, in short order you'll blind out—that is, spend all your chips paying the forced bets, or blinds—and find yourself with nothing.

Those two setups create rather different dynamics. Cash games are *War and Peace*. You're a thousand pages in and still no closer to finding out how the battle resolved itself. You can try to flip ahead, but events will unfold at whatever pace they choose. Tournaments are far more Shakespearean in nature. You've barely hit act three and half the cast is already dead. If you want an overview of life at warp speed, tournament poker is the way to go. That's what I choose.

After spending the several months following my von Neumann revelation poring over books on poker, watching videos of the best pros playing and listening to the commentary, I began to genuinely wonder if, in poker, I could finally find a way to overcome my all-too-human inability to disentangle chance from skill in the morass of daily life, and instead learn to master it. Could poker help my husband figure out his next career move, and when it was right to just start playing again as opposed to waiting for the perfect cards? Could it help me think through when to give up with the medical consultations, or how to deal with the fallout of the bills in planning our financial future? Could it help my mother leverage an unfavorable table environment, so to speak, in her favor? Could it help me plan my own career moves in a way that would maximize my wins and minimize the losses? I decided to try my hand at finding out.

WHICH BRINGS US BACK to my meeting with Erik Seidel, for whom the challenge of poker is slightly different. For over three decades, he has led the poker world. He holds eight WSOP bracelets (only five players in the tournament's history have more) and a World Poker Tour title. He is in the Poker Hall of Fame, one of just thirty-two living members. He boasts the fourth-highest tournament career winnings in the entire history of the game (for many years he was number one), and is fourth in the number of times he cashed in the WSOP (114). Over the years, he has spent fifteen weeks ranked first in the Global Poker Index, and many consider him the GOAT—the greatest of all time.

Why on earth would a professional poker player—*the* professional poker player—agree to let a random journalist follow him around like an overeager toddler, asking the most basic questions about how the world works? He doesn't care for fame, so I can't play the journalism card all that well. He doesn't like to share his tactics. He's notoriously reticent.

"I wouldn't actually *be* in the book, would I?" Erik asks back at the West Village bistro as I lay out my proposal. He shifts around on the bench and hunches over a little more, as if deflecting attention from his presence as much as he possibly can.

"Well . . ." This isn't going quite as anticipated.

"I don't know if I can take anything on. You know I've never coached anyone. And my travel schedule . . ."

I cut him off. This is going nowhere fast. "I may not know how many cards are in a deck—"

"Wait, you're serious?" He cuts me off. His eyebrows have shot up. At least I've managed to surprise him.

"Absolutely. I'm not going to be the typical student."

What I do have, I continue, is my background.

"I have a PhD in psychology. I studied decision making—the sort of stuff you do every day, but from a theoretical perspective."

"A psychologist. Now that's interesting. That could be really helpful in poker." He leans over the table, lanky elbows framing his egg-white omelet. "I think you're approaching it from the area of most value, especially of most differentiated value. All the other guys are very math-based, very data-based. This area is way more open. Actually, of the great players, the ones who are some of the most exploitable are the ones who are really into math."

"Oh, good." I'm happy to have struck a chord after the false start. "I haven't done any math since high school," I admit.

"My math skills are not particularly great, either, and that's not unusual," Erik says, putting me at ease. "It doesn't hurt, but it's no barrier to playing well. The basic math is so basic that a six-year-old could do it."

I'm relieved. But I should probably omit the part where I tell him that I usually count on my fingers.

"It's all about thinking well. The real question is, can good thinking and hard work get you there? And I think it can," Erik says. In a way it's good, he goes on, that I'm an outsider. I can bring fresh eyes, perspective—and some of the skills players don't typically have. I might not have the narrow expertise of knowing what a "range" is or why I'd want one that's polarized or merged, but I do have the broad expertise of knowing how to learn, how to think, how people work. In *Range*, David Epstein reflects on the nature of the outsider: "Switchers are winners," he writes. Perhaps, as a switcher, I'll be able to get beyond the myopia that often comes with an insider's perspective, bring what psychologist Jonathan Baron calls "active open-mindedness." Not all experience is created equal, of course, but mine might be particularly well suited here.

Erik is especially intrigued by my language ability.

"You can speak how many languages?" he asks.

"Well, only two completely fluently, English and Russian. But I've been fluent in French and Spanish in the past, and pretty good in Italian," I continue. "I used to take Persian, but I've really forgotten all of it."

"I think that's going to be really helpful," Erik says. "Do you know Phil Ivey?"

I nod. He's one of the only poker names that is on my radar.

"There was an argument for him being the best at all of these different poker games at one point," he explains. I can think of each game like a different language that needs to be mastered. "And what's extra fascinating about that to me is that his sister is a linguist. And she speaks fifteen languages or something."

I'm impressed. My abilities look meager in comparison.

"How many people do you get that have that kind of a brain or interests?" Erik continues. "It seems as if Phil and his sister have a very similar brain that functions in a way that they pick up languages in some incredible way. It's nice to hear that you do have obviously some abilities to pick up languages quickly or to adapt to different languages, because that's essentially what the challenge is."

It makes a certain amount of sense. In many ways, poker does resemble language learning. After all, there is a new grammar, a new vocabulary, a new way of relating to the world. But there is one big difference that I can see. Humans have built-in language-learning ability. Some are better at it than others, true, but we all learn our native language fairly effortlessly—the brain seems to come equipped with a road map for discerning meaning out of sounds and figuring out rules without ever being taught them explicitly. Not so poker: no matter how psychologically you want to play, much of the game is about statistics. You need to understand odds, how good your hand is, how good it is relative to others', how likely it is to improve, and so on. Each of these requires a certain amount of statistical calculation. How well I'll fare there is another story.

"You know, psychology really is the most fascinating part of the game," Erik says, interrupting my thought process. "What specifically about decision making did you study? Like Kahneman?"

"Actually, my graduate adviser was Walter Mischel—you know, the marshmallow guy?"

"Oh wow. That's exciting. Self-control is huge in the game."

So Mr. Seidel knows the marshmallow guy, too. I seem to have picked well.

"I figured it might be," I reply. "I mean, I've obviously never played. But here's what I can tell you: I'm willing to bet I've read more about all of this than anyone else at the poker table. I've done studies on stress and decision making. Emotional stuff. Time pressure stuff. All sorts of things that I think are going to be super relevant. And—and . . ." I'm on a roll and don't want him to interrupt. I need him to agree to take me on. "Look at this paper I found." I fish out my ace in the hole—a paper I've tracked down on poker tells that, as far as I know, never made it out of academia. *And* it's based on a WSOP final table analysis. The real deal.

Erik reads carefully. He's all concentration. And then he starts laughing.

"Wow. OK. Just don't show this to anyone else."

I promise him I won't. And with that, a partnership is born.

I HAVE A RARE opportunity here: hardly ever do we have a chance to learn an entirely new skill, to immerse ourselves in novicedom, not only with the guidance of the best expert in the world but in an area, where the skill-chance continuum is so balanced, so redolent of life, as poker. Erik Seidel doesn't actually care about whether I win any given game. He just wants to see how far we can go—how far psychology, people reading, and emotional nuance can get me. If you are starting from scratch, can a deep understanding of the human mind win out over the mathematics and statistical wunderkinds of the poker table? In a way, it's as much a test of life philosophy as anything else. The qualitative side of things versus the measurable. The human versus the algorithmic. I will be on one extreme of a dynamic that is at the center of a paradigm shift in this country. And the ultimate test will be the World Series Main Event. The tournament has never in its history had a female champion—and only one woman has ever made the final table. Erik isn't just training me to play. He's training me to win: that's how much he believes that this way of doing things can ultimately succeed. And I will do everything I can to make the journey count.

For me, this isn't *just* a test of a philosophy—though that is central. It's also personal. I don't want to let Erik down. His faith is, in part, confidence in my ability and his approach, but is also an expression of boundless generosity: to his friends and the people he trusts or respects, Erik is the most giving person I have encountered in a long time. He isn't just giving me his time. He is giving me his trust, his energy, his mind, his reputation. All I can think is, *I better not fuck this up.*

IT WAS SUPPOSED TO be a year. It became a new life. From novice, I turned champion. From amateur, I went pro. And all along the way, I watched with a mix of wonder and pride as my life changed for the better. This book is the result of that journey. It is not an exhaustive exploration of the game, how to play it, how to win at it, how to excel. It is no guide. That has been covered by experts far greater than I. It is a picking up of von Neumann's challenge: poker as a lens into the most difficult and important life decisions we have to make, an exploration of chance and skill in life—and an attempt to learn to navigate it and optimize it to the best of our potential.

What I will offer throughout is insight into decision making far removed from poker, a translation of what I'm learning in the casino to the decisions I make on a daily basis—and the crucial decisions that I make only rarely, but that carry particular import. From managing emotion, to reading other people, to cutting your losses and maximizing your gains, to psyching yourself up into the best version of yourself so that you can not only catch the bluffs of others but bluff successfully yourself, poker is endlessly applicable and revelatory. The mixture of chance and skill at the table is a mirror to that same mixture in our daily lives—and a way of learning to play within those parameters in superior fashion. Poker teaches you how and when you can take true control—and how you can deal with the elements of pure luck—in a way no other environment I've encountered has quite been able to do. What's more, in an age of omnipresent distraction, poker reminds us just how critical close observation and presence are to achievement and success. How important it is to immerse yourself and to learn new things, truly. As Erik told me that first day, lesson one: pay attention. This book isn't about how to play poker. It's about how to play the world.

The Birth
of a Gambler

Boston, Fall 2016

"If we consider games of chance immoral, then every pursuit of human industry is immoral; for there is not a single one that is not subject to chance, not one wherein you do not risk a loss for the chance of some gain."

THOMAS JEFFERSON, "THOUGHTS ON LOTTERIES," 1826

Y ou are going to be a *gambler*?"

That's my grandmother Baba Anya speaking. My other grandmother, my last living grandparent. I've come to Boston for a family visit, nearly bouncing with excitement at my new project, and she is not impressed. To call her lukewarm would be the understatement of the hour. She has a way of setting her jaw that makes it jut out like it's about to slice through stone. The chiseled expression of a conquering hero atop a pedestaled horse. A conquering hero—or an angry general. I can feel the full brunt of grandmotherly disappointment gather on my shoulders. She's almost (though not quite) come to forgive me for not wanting kids after over a decade of my persistent explanations, but this—this is a new low. If you think you know the kind of disappointment a five-foot-some-odd ninety-two-year-old is capable of, think again. She was a

Soviet-era schoolteacher. She's had more practice than an army drill sergeant.

She shakes her head.

"Masha," she says—my Russian nickname. "Masha." The word is laden with so much sadness, so much regret for the life I'm about to throw away. In a single word, she has managed to convey that I'm on the brink of ruin, about to make a decision so momentously bad that it is beyond comprehension.

I can see the visions of Dostoyevsky's gambler dancing through Baba Anya's head, throwing away his life in the fictional Roulettenburg. Dostoyevsky knew of what he wrote. On a trip to Baden-Baden with his twenty-two-year-old lover, Polina Suslova, he developed a passion for roulette and "lost absolutely everything." That didn't stop him from wanting more: even though the game would eventually lead to the end of his affair, the near-end of his second marriage, and financial ruin, the tables held an irresistible draw. "I go to the bottom line in everything," he wrote in one of his letters, "and throughout my entire life, I have crossed this bottom line."

This is the fate I can clearly see written all over my grandmother's face. A Harvard education and this, *this*, is what I'm choosing to do?

"Masha," she repeats. "You are going to be a *gambler*?"

My grandmother's reaction may be extreme—nothing is quite as personal as your grandchildren heading out to ruin on your watch; you have to throw your body in the breach—but it is far from atypical. In the coming months, I'll be accused of being responsible for a society-wide "sin slide" for advocating for poker as a teaching tool. I'll be called a moral degenerate by strangers. A group of highly intelligent people at a retreat will tell me playing poker is all well and good, but how do I feel about encouraging people—children even!—to *lie*?

The world of poker is laden with misconceptions. And first among them is the very one I'm seeing from a stricken Baba Anya: equating poker with gambling. I'd been ready to go, gearing up to get started. To my mind, the journey was well motivated as it was: *of course* people would understand that poker was an important way to learn about decision making. I mean, think of von Neumann! Let's get to the tables! But looking at Baba Anya, I realize that the battle for support—and the justification for poker as not just a learning tool, but as one of the best tools there is for making decisions that have nothing to do with the game itself—is going to take a bit more fighting. I'm going to be explaining this over and over, so I may as well get it right.

POKER, TO THE UNTRAINED eye, is easy. Just like everyone who meets me seems to have "a book in them," which they'll write just as soon as they get a chance—everyone can use words, after all—so everyone who meets Erik thinks they are just a hop away from becoming a poker pro or, at the very least, a badass poker bro. Most of us underestimate the skill involved. It just seems so simple: get good cards and rake in the dough. Or bluff everyone blind and rake in the dough once more. Either way, you're raking it in. It seems like every time I talk to Erik he has a new story of a bartender or server or Uber driver who recognizes him and offers up the wisdom that he could play just as well; he's just never gotten the chance to do so. That "lucky break" simply hasn't manifested itself. But maybe if Erik just stakes him for that big game . . .

And poker does have an element of chance, to be sure—but what doesn't? Are poker professionals "gamblers" any more than the man signing away his life on a professional football contract, who may or may not be injured the next week, or find himself summarily dropped from the team in a year because he failed to live up to his promise? We judge the poker player for gambling; we respect the stockbroker for doing the same thing with far less information. In some ways, poker players gamble less than most. After all, even if they lose an arm, they can still play.

But the misperception is ingrained in the popular mind for one simple reason. Unlike, say, Go or chess, poker involves betting. And betting involves money. And as soon as that enters the picture, you might as well be playing craps or baccarat—games that truly are gambling. And so I tell my grandmother the words that I've come to repeat so often they are like my own private mantra: in poker, you can win with the worst hand and you can lose with the best hand. In every other game in a casino—and in games of perfect information like chess and Go—you simply must have the best of it to win. No other way is possible. And that, in a nutshell, is why poker is a skilled endeavor rather than a gambling one.

Imagine two players at a table. The cards are dealt. Each player must look at her cards and decide whether or not the cards on their own are good enough to bet. If she wishes to play, she must at minimum "call" the big blind—that is, place as much into the pot as the highest bet that already exists. She may also choose to fold (throw out her cards and sit this hand out) or raise (bet more than the big blind). But who knows what factors she's using to make her decision? Maybe she has a premium hand. Maybe she has a mediocre hand but thinks she can outplay her opponent and so chooses to engage anyway. Maybe she has observed that the other player views her as conservative because she doesn't play many hands, and she's taking advantage of that image by opening up with worse cards than normal. Or maybe she's just bored out of her mind. Her reasoning, like her cards, is known only to her.

The other player observes the action and reacts accordingly: if she bets big, she may have a great hand—or be bluffing with a bad one. If she simply calls, is it because her hand is mediocre, or because she's a generally passive player, or because she wants to do what's known as "slow playing"—masking an excellent hand by playing it in a restrained fashion, as Johnny Chan did in that 1988 WSOP matchup with Erik Seidel? Each decision throws off signals, and the good player must learn to read them. It's a constant back-and-forth interpretive dance: How do I react to you? How do you react to me? More often than not, it's not the best hand that wins. It's the best player. This nuance, this back-and-forth: this is why von Neumann saw the answer to military strategy in the cards. Not because everyone is a gambler, but because to be a winning player, you have to have superior skill, in a very human sense.

Indeed, when the economist Ingo Fiedler analyzed hundreds of thousands of hands played on several online poker sites over a six-month period, he found that the actual best hand won, on average, only 12 percent of the time and that less than a third of hands went to showdown (meaning that players were skillful enough to persuade others to let go of their cards prior to the end of the hand). In mid-stakes games, with blinds of 1/2 and 5/10, there were some players who were consistent winners, and as stakes went to nosebleed—50/100 and up—the variability in skill went down significantly. That is, the higher the amount of money for which people played, the greater their actual skill edge. When Chicago economists Steven Levitt and Thomas Miles looked at live play and compared the ROI, or return on investment, for two groups of players at the 2010 WSOP, they found that recreational players lost, on average, over 15 percent of their buy-ins (roughly $400), while professionals won over 30 percent (roughly $1,200). They write, "The observed differences in ROIs are highly statistically significant and far larger in magnitude than those observed in financial markets where fees charged by the money managers viewed as being most talented can run as high as three percent of assets under management and thirty percent of annual returns." Success in poker, in other words, implies far more skill than success in that far more respectable profession, investing.

Of course, the rationale goes much deeper. Betting—that bête noire that seems to be such a stumbling block for even rational minds when you try to explain the skilled nature of poker—is actually at the heart of what makes it superior to almost any other game of skill: betting on uncertainty is one of the best ways of understanding it. And it is one of the best ways of conquering the pitfalls of our decision processes in just about any endeavor. It doesn't take a gambler to understand why. In his *Critique of Pure Reason*, the German philosopher Immanuel Kant proposes betting as an antidote to one of the great ills of society: false confidence bred from an ignorance of the probabilistic nature of the world, from a desire to see black and white where we should rightly see gray. From a misplaced faith in certainty, the fact that to our minds, 99 percent, even 90 percent, basically means 100 percent—even though it doesn't, not really. Kant offers the example of a doctor asked to make a diagnosis. The doctor reaches a verdict on the patient's malady to the best of his knowledge—but that conclusion isn't necessarily correct. It's just the best he can do given the information he has and his experience in this particular area. But will he tell the patient he's unsure? Maybe. But more likely, if his certainty reaches a specific threshold—a different one for different doctors, to be sure—he will just state his diagnosis as fact.

But what if he had to bet on it? "It frequently happens that a man delivers his opinions with such boldness and assurance that he appears to be under no apprehension as to the possibility of his being in error," Kant writes. "The offer of a bet startles him, and makes him pause." Now that he has something real at stake, he has to reevaluate just how sure of a sure thing his opinion really is. "Sometimes it turns out that his persuasion may be valued at a ducat, but not at ten," Kant continues. "If it is proposed to stake ten, he immediately becomes aware of the possibility of his being mistaken."

And what if the bet is even higher? Suddenly, we have a corrective for many of the follies of human reason. "If we imagine to ourselves that we have to stake the happiness of our whole life on the truth of any proposition, our judgment drops its air of triumph, we take the alarm, and discover the actual strength of our belief," says Kant. Would you bet your entire net worth on an opinion that you've just spent hours confidently offering on social media, broaching no possibility of being mistaken? Would you bet your marriage? Your health? Even our deep convictions suddenly seem a lot less certain when put in that light.

Of course, it's a long way between betting on your own opinions and judging someone else. When we err, we are much more tolerant than when we think someone else has gone astray. Think of the 2016 presidential election. Every media source had polls showing Hillary Clinton winning—and every media source was wrong. No one was on the receiving end of the subsequent ire more than Nate Silver. He had done such an accurate job forecasting past elections that he was practically pilloried for being so "wrong" this time around. But what exactly did Silver say? In his final poll, on November 8, 2016, he gave Clinton a 71 percent chance of winning—and Trump a 29 percent chance. Twenty-nine percent. That's a whole lot of percent. That's nearly a third. And yet most people saw the 71 and read it as certain. The complexity of the alternative is just too taxing to take into account every time we make a judgment. To the vast majority, 71 is synonymous with 100. Clinton is winning.

But what if you had to bet, given Silver's estimates? Would you bet on a 71 percent certainty the same way as if it were 100 percent, place the same amount of money on each proposition? Or would you then realize that there was a more than notable margin of error? It turns out that the odds of Trump winning are roughly the same as the odds of flopping a pair in hold'em—and you only have to play once or twice to realize that the odds of flopping a pair are a far cry from zero.

Nate Silver is a poker player. In fact, once upon a time he made quite a tidy living playing online. And poker has taught him something fundamental about the nature of the world that most of us simply never bother to grasp. Poker is such a powerful window into probabilistic thinking not in spite of, but because of, the betting involved: the betting in poker isn't incidental. It's integral to the learning process. Our minds learn when we have a stake, a real stake, in the outcome of our learning. It's why kids learn so much better—and remember what they've learned—if they know exactly how or when they'll apply the knowledge. This is the partner element to learning probabilities from experience: not only do we understand what 29 percent feels like; we now retain that knowledge because if we don't learn, it hurts us. If we keep betting the wrong amount, we will be punished. If we keep saying "I think I'm good here" without quantifying how often we're actually good, we'll lose all our money.

But in life, we normally do just that without a single thought. Why did I buy that stock? Another investor said it was good over lunch. Why did I sell that? Well, he shorted that one and that sounds right to me. We react emotionally rather than looking at the statistics: traders sell winning stocks to lock in the wins—it feels good, even though the numbers say that winners continue to go up in the short term; they hold on to losers to avoid locking in the losses—that would feel bad, even though the numbers say you should cut and run. In fact, numerous studies show that professional investors have a remarkable ability to ignore statistical information for their own gut and intuition—and that they'd often be better served not trading at all as a result.

"For a large majority of fund managers, the selection of stocks is more like rolling dice than like playing poker," says Daniel Kahneman, the Nobel-winning economist. Not only do most funds underperform the market, but the correlation in year-to-year performance is incredibly low. Kahneman continues, "The successful funds in any given year are mostly lucky; they have a good roll of the dice. There is general agreement among researchers that nearly all stock pickers, whether they know it or not—and few of them do—are playing a game of chance."

It's a difficult lesson to internalize outside the poker table. Even people who seem like they suffer consequences, like stock traders, are often loath to admit that they were wrong in their certainties. Because the world is much messier than the poker table, it's far easier to blame something else. It's easy to have an illusion of skill when you're not immediately called out on it through feedback. Poker rids you of the habit in a way nothing else quite does—and in so doing, it improves decisions far afield from the game itself.

When I'd just started dating my husband, he would often fact-check me mid-conversation. I've never invested anything in my life, but I did in the past have a habit of investing my statements with perhaps a bit more certainty than they warranted. "Are you sure?" he'd ask, endearingly. "I think I might want to check that." And he would pull out his phone or a book to do just that. I got better, but I could never quite kick it. It wasn't until I entered the world of poker that the process really sank in. I hadn't been playing long before I found myself saying things like "Well, I'm about seventy-five percent sure." I'd experienced the consequences of improper certainty a few too many times in my bank account—and knew that I had been the only one to blame for my bad play.

That personal accountability, without the possibility of deflecting onto someone else, is key. One specific class of lawyer, in fact, actually fares far better at probabilistic thinking than financial professionals whose jobs are more explicitly tied to probabilities: the lawyers who take cases for a percentage of the eventual settlement. You have a far higher personal stake in calibrating correctly, and so you learn to do just that. Likewise, meteorologists and horse-race handicappers: their calibration of risk is accurate because they not only deal explicitly in percentages but have immediate feedback on their performance—and no one else to blame if their estimate is incorrect.

Outside the realm of games, accurate probabilistic thinking is a rare skill. Dan Harrington, one of the greats of the poker world, left poker some years ago to start a real estate business that has performed very well. He told me the story of one hire that hadn't gone according to plan. He'd seemed nice and qualified, but his judgment ended up leaving something to be desired; it wasn't nearly as sharp as it had seemed during the interview process. There was a key difference between him and other employees: he had a traditional finance background; the others were connections from the poker and backgammon worlds. "My partner said to me, 'Dan, in the future if we hire a nonprofessional gambler, just give me a swift kick in the ass,'" Dan remembers. "The successful hires understood equity and they understood the decision tree matrix that that involves, and they don't get involved in it personally. And that comes from gambling. It's invaluable for life." They never hired someone who hadn't spent some time in the world of gaming ever again.

I'd wager it's no coincidence that the father of probability—the first person who we know of to go beyond a vision of chance as some sort of unknowable goddess, or otherwise in the purview of the supernatural—was a gambler. Girolamo Cardano was a doctor, a mathematician, a philosopher. He was part of the group responsible for the advent of higher algebra and was known for his thought-provoking prose (Shakespeare, it seems, was a fan, and it has been claimed that Cardano's *Consolation* was the book originally held by Hamlet in the "To be or not to be?" scene). He also made much of his money through gambling—but gambling in a way that was foreign to his contemporaries.

Cardano had little patience for the prevailing divination methods of the day. Astrologers may claim to see the future in the stars, but, Cardano wrote, "I have never seen an astrologer who was lucky at gambling, nor were those lucky who took their advice." Likewise, geomancy, which he called "an unstable vanity and dangerous." (I had to look up the meaning of "geomancy." It is divination from markings on the ground or soil.) In 1526 this was quite the outlier opinion. Remember, we're talking about a time when people were sometimes burned to death for saying that the earth wasn't the center of the universe. Astrology seemed like cutting-edge science.

Trusting in luck as a vague sort of higher power, Cardano realized, was a losing enterprise. It was pointless to try to divine whether there was a god or spirit or other guiding force at play. He offered another way: prediction through probabilities. He remembers the moment he realized he could make certain plays based on specific frequencies being in his favor. He'd lost a lot of money to a man who had lured him into a game with marked cards. In contemplating how to regain his belongings (he'd also lost many of his clothes and personal effects), a more mathematically minded approach came to him. He not only won back his opponent's ill-gotten bounty but published his thoughts in the first known book on probability, *The Book on Games of Chance*. (It was published in 1663, long after his death.)

It just so happens that, in musing on the ways to calculate dice throws and card distributions, Cardano also wrote a description of what many take to be the earliest form of poker, primero. It wasn't played with a full deck, and the rules of betting were somewhat convoluted, but the essence was similar to the games we have now: some cards private, some in common, and a complex interplay between representing the hand you may or may not have and interpreting the signals of your fellow card players. Primero traveled across Europe, variably termed *primiera*, *la prime*, and eventually *pochen*, a German name derived from the verb "to bluff." The French took *pochen* and made it *poqué*—and soon, the game would morph into a new form.

No one knows quite when it made its way across the ocean, but it seems to have taken root, as so many national pastimes, in the muggy heat of a boring summer. It was 1803, and some Frenchmen in Louisiana had grown listless aboard a slow-moving steamship bound for New Orleans. They started up a game of *poqué*, which would soon spread gradually by steamboat throughout the new country, eventually becoming poker. And in a sense the theory of probability traveled apace with the game.

Cardano lamented one thing, though. Understanding probability wasn't enough to tame the luck factor. Unless you cheated—and he spent quite some time describing how that would be possible, with crooked dice and marked cards—you had no way of winning consistently. His findings "contribute a great deal to understanding but hardly anything to practical play," he reflected. Not entirely true, but you can see the sentiment: if you want to improve your odds, understand probabilities; if you want a sure thing, rig the deck.

Poker isn't just about calibrating the strength of your beliefs. It's also about becoming comfortable with the fact that there's no such thing as a sure thing—ever. You will never have all the information you want, and you will have to act all the same. Leave your certainty at the door.

BABA ANYA IS NOT convinced. Poker may teach you that nothing is certain, but she is still positive I'm going over to the dark side. I realize that nothing I say will change her mind. She waves away all my talk of skill with a dismissive hand. She has more arguments in mind.

"But this isn't serious," she says. Skill or no skill, there is one other element of this whole thing that bothers her. "It's only a game. How can you be serious about a *game*?" She wants me to be a professor—now that's serious business. A real job. A skilled job.

Until it isn't. The more I think about it, the more I start doubting just how much of a gamble-free endeavor it could be. Imagine me going down the academic path. What did I choose to study? Social psychology. Ah, but neuroscience is having a moment. I may have followed my interest, but not the job market. With whom did I study? Good luck to me getting a job in any psychology department where the Big Five personality traits are still big—I studied with Walter Mischel, and he and the Big Five are not on speaking terms. What about academic publications? Who might get assigned to review my manuscript—someone with a sympathetic ear or someone who thought my research was so much hogwash? I'm not going to get kicked out of a poker tournament for choosing a style of play that goes counter to the strategy of the bigwigs of the day and may challenge their ascendance. But if I were to go against the head of a department or hiring committee—or even one of the celebrity hotshot professors? Bye-bye, job prospects.

In many ways, poker is the skilled endeavor. The job market is the gamble. How did my job talk go? Where did I go to college? To grad school? Did I rub someone the wrong way in an interview? These details, all subject to a big dose of chance, can make or break me. At the table, I play how I play. And I rise or fall on my own merits.

"BUT WHY COULDN'T YOU have maybe played chess instead?" My grandmother talking again. "Now that's a respectable game."

I let out a final sigh. How I wish I could take her on a walk to Washington Square Park so she can see the actual chess players. Between the hustle and the side hustle, it's some of the most intense betting I've ever witnessed. "I feel a connection to these people," Erik tells me once, during a walk in Washington Square. "Because they're games players. They hang out, play chess, sometimes backgammon. They get it."

But I'm out of energy. I don't dive into my lecture about chess being a game of perfect information and life being a game of uncertainty. And I don't mention Washington Square. I'll just have to get on with it and hope to prove myself along the way.

The Art of Losing

New York, Fall 2016

"If you can make one heap of all your winnings
And risk it on one turn of pitch and toss,
And lose, and start again at your beginnings
And never breathe a word about your loss . . ."
RUDYARD KIPLING, "IF—," CIRCA 1895

I wake up bleary-eyed, my tail decidedly un-bushy, to the sound of the harp alarm on my phone. It was chosen to be less jarring than the alternatives; instead, it makes me hate harps with unhealthy fervor. It's six in the morning—not a time a self-employed writer usually sees unless she has stayed up all night writing. But I need to get from Brooklyn to the Upper West Side by eight. Erik, it turns out, is an early bird. Eight was the compromise time, not the opening bid.

The lesson begins, as all New York lessons must, with lox and bagels. We're sitting at the Fairway Market Café, and Erik is eager to hear about my progress, which has, thus far, been admittedly theoretical.

"How was the meeting with Dan?" he asks.

Dan is Dan Harrington, or Action Dan as he's often called with a wink, for his seemingly conservative playing style. He and Erik go way back, to the days when Erik still played backgammon and the Mayfair

Club was still a private poker club in New York where many of the future greats cut their teeth. It was 1979, and Erik had come up to Boston, across the river from Harrington's hometown, for a backgammon tournament. Dan had been around the backgammon scene for some time; Erik was the newcomer, "this nineteen-year-old whiz kid," Dan recalls. They made it to the end of the tournament: it was down to the old stalwart and the young whiz.

Dan won. "I played well," he tells me, "and Erik just said, 'Who the hell are you? I never heard of you before.' Because he's from New York, and New Yorkers have this attitude that nothing exists outside of New York."

Erik figured out who the hell Dan was, Dan became interested in poker, and six years later they met a second time, at the Mayfair. It was the start of a lifelong friendship. Dan is now retired from the poker world—"I got too old," he says. "This is a young person's game, believe it or not. A miracle is someone like Erik. The fact that he continues to do this at this age is just absolutely astounding. I did it at his age, but it was a much weaker field." But his accomplishments include the one thing everyone covets, the title of World Series of Poker Main Event champion. He can also boast a record four Main Event final tables, including a third-place finish in the year made famous by an accountant, Chris Money-maker, winning the top prize and starting the modern poker boom, the so-called Moneymaker effect.

Finding a good mentor is crucial to learning any new skill—and one of the things the best mentors do well is know when to delegate. It's been decades since Erik opened David Sklansky's *The Theory of Poker*, the book that first propelled him into the poker world when he picked it up on a whim in a used-book shop. And he isn't used to taking on students, let alone those who know nothing about the game. So for the basics, he'd sent me to the person who wrote the textbook—literally. *Harrington on*

Hold'em is a classic. Erik may not have given the basics much thought since Sklansky, but Dan Harrington had distilled them for thousands. And luckily for me, he happened to be in New York.

"I think it went really well," I tell Erik. "I learned how to beat roulette."

DAN AND I MEET at the Midtown hotel where he's staying on his visit from the West Coast. I'm not sure what to expect but am pleased when he greets me wearing a white baseball cap—in all the photos I've seen of him, he has on one hat or another. I've read his books and can't quite believe he's willing to go through the nitty-gritty of poker with me.

We bond immediately as we head to the café for some breakfast. We both grew up without much money, it turns out. I tell him how lucky I am that my parents are supportive of this latest adventure, cheering me on despite the financial risks, but confide that my grandmother has slightly different views.

And he tells me that those views may never change, no matter what I do. He recalls the moment he told his mother he won the World Series of Poker. "Well, what do you think, Mom? I won a million dollars. I'm world champion of poker!" he remembers telling her. And she replies, "Oh, that's great, Danny. You know, we have a cousin, Pádraig Harrington. He's a golfer, and he just won eighty thousand dollars over in the Spanish Open." Dan persists. "Mom, I won a million dollars. I'm world champion." And she has one answer. "Listen, Danny, he's doing well on the European tour."

"So what do you want to know?" he asks me, between sips on a morning coffee.

Everything, I tell him. I want to know everything.

I'm expecting a lesson in beating the odds, in calculations, in the power of position and optimal strategy. And I do get some of that—but what I mostly get instead is a crash session on the importance of failure.

"Look, you've read my books," Dan says. And I have. It was the first step in Erik's lesson plan for me, what he called the foundational element of my journey. Before I did anything else, I went out and bought copies of Dan's books—and read them, pen in hand, cover to cover. Let me tell you, my margin notes would make a literature grad student pale with envy. I've meticulously gone through each section, highlighting, underlining, filling up pages with marginalia. I may not have known how many cards are in a deck until a few weeks ago, but this I was born for.

Erik has never taught anyone before, and his own early experience is not particularly applicable to me—I don't have any current plans to stop everything and start spending all my time at the modern equivalent of the Mayfair Club, butting heads with the best players in the world for days on end. What's more, the world of poker has changed a great deal since he came up. For one thing, there's online poker, which means you can get more experience in less time than ever before. For another, there are powerful computer algorithms that help you work out strategies and run millions of simulations in seconds to answer strategic questions that used to be approached by the brunt of sheer repetition and experience. Dan's books are the closest thing he can think of as a primer to everything—a way of setting up the basis of my journey without overwhelming me from the beginning.

"At least I think they'll be OK for you," he says at first. "Let me know how it's going. If it's too hard, we'll think of something else."

Through the waning days of summer and into the early fall, the margin notes are my life raft. They are the only thing I have that is concrete— and my only sign that I am learning anything at all. Erik has been clear from the beginning: certain markers have to be met before I can move forward in my poker journey. If I'm to work with him, I can't skip steps. First I read and watch—read Harrington, watch streams with real hands being played by the best players. ("Sign up for Run It Once," he tells me early on. I find out it's a coaching site, and when I start looking at the library of available topics, I suddenly feel very, very lost and very, very small and very, very silly. What was I even thinking? What in the world is a merged three-betting range and why does turn bet sizing on three-flush boards merit multiple hours of conversation?) Then we discuss—I ask questions and Erik determines that I have enough of a theoretical basis to get started playing without completely losing my shirt. Then I begin to play for real—online, for tiny stakes, but for real money, to see how I do in putting the lessons into practice. Play money simply won't cut it. Plenty of people who kill at Monopoly would make terrible real estate agents. Only after I start consistently winning money online will I get to do the thing I thought I'd be doing right away: going to Vegas to play in real life—somehow, online doesn't feel like real life even though the money is real enough—in real casinos, at real tables, with real chips. (I've already bought my very own chip set in preparation. I've seen the videos, after all, and everyone knows how to do that thing where you mix two stacks of chips into one with your hand. Riffling, I find out it's called. The first time I try it, the chips fly all over the room in a flurry of red and green. I quickly find a YouTube tutorial and start to practice. "Maybe focus on learning to play first," my husband gently suggests when he happens upon me devoting a little too much attention to my new dexterity challenge.)

Even from Vegas, it's still a long road to the WSOP. The Main Event is a $10,000 buy-in. That's high stakes for an amateur who knows nothing. If I'm not prepared, it will be the rough equivalent of taking the bills and using them as kindling for a really lovely bonfire. A beautiful experience of warmth and color, quickly followed by ash and a slightly unpleasant odor of smoldering wet coals in the air. Erik is nothing if not responsible. And he takes his role as mentor quite seriously. If I want him to be my coach, I have to agree that he will not be letting me anywhere near a $10,000 tournament, book or no book, if he doesn't feel I at least have an outside chance at success. For that to happen, I have to get to the point where I'm consistently cashing in lower-stakes tournaments, working my way up from the smallest to the bigger ones.

It's already September. The Main Event will be in July. That's ten months—a bit under a year. And I'm not even to the point of having played a single hand in an actual game, live or online. So I'm holding on tight to those Harrington books. If I read them closely enough, I'm hoping, they'll provide enough of a boost that the rest will go quickly and smoothly. It doesn't bode well that it's taken me far longer to get through them than I'd planned—it's a new language for me, just as Erik told me it would be—but I remain the endless optimist. At least when I have a book deadline to hit.

And so before I ever met Dan in the flesh, I not only read his books. I reread his books. I dissected his books. Erik and I have spent multiple sessions, over multiple weeks, going through my notes and questions one by one to develop a working base of how to play. These haven't been your traditional lessons. We don't sit and review. There are no lesson plans. There are no specific topics to cover or goals to hit. Instead, we walk. Erik is a big walker. Ever since he got a Fitbit, some years ago, he has been religious in hitting his daily step count, and as I will learn, walking is a big part of his routine, come rain or shine, in New York or Vegas or anywhere else in the world, whether he's in between playing or in the middle of a tournament. It's not just for exercise. It's his way of thinking, his way of reflecting, his way of relating, his way of learning.

We walk, we talk, and we let the pace of the afternoon determine the flow of the conversation. As the majestic Hudson glitters blue on our left and the flowered carpets of Riverside Park open up on the right, I try my best to keep up with his long strides while strategically perching my phone on the side of my bag to record the conversation, alternating between fishing a dog-eared *Harrington* out of said bag to find the pertinent pages and holding a mini notebook to jot down especially important thoughts that I want to make sure to revisit. It doesn't help that I'm not the most coordinated person in the world, and I often find myself performing interpretive dance moves to catch a falling phone or pen while trying to not break stride. I'd like to tell Erik that his step count doesn't care about how quickly those steps were taken, but I don't quite have the breath left to do so. We must look like a very odd duo.

Our earliest walking conversations are, as you'd expect, among the most basic. I've drilled down the super basics—the ground rules, so to speak. You are dealt two cards. You decide whether to play them or to fold. If you do play them, you call or raise. Everyone else follows the same decision process, going in a clockwise direction starting from the player to the left of the big blind, a position called, appropriately enough, under the gun. And then you make that decision again every time new information, in the form of new cards, appears. At the end, if only one person holds cards when the betting is done, she wins the pot. If the hand goes to showdown—that is, the final bet is called—the person holding the best cards will win. In rare cases, the pot can be split if the cards are the same, or if both players are playing the board, or the community cards (that is, when what's on the board beats the individual hands). But what of the slightly less basic basics?

"Harrington is big on different types of players," I report to Erik. "Are you a conservative player, an aggressive player, a super-aggressive player, or this or that?"

"I don't think you need to decide that at this time," Erik says, laughing. "But I'm glad he's laying out all those approaches."

"Well, why would I ever want to be anything other than super aggressive?" I ask. "He basically says that the only players who he can't ever really predict are the super-aggressive ones, because they'll play any hand, so it's impossible to tell what they're holding at any given point. But if that's true, why wouldn't you always want to play like that?"

One of the first things I've been learning is starting hand selection: I know you get two cards and have to decide whether to play them or not, but what cards should you be holding, at what position at the table, to decide that your hand is good enough? Erik has explained that the earlier you open, the stronger your hand needs to be, because more players are still to act. That makes sense. In any decision, information is power. The earlier you act, the less information you have. With multiple people still waiting to make their decision, the landscape may well change. He's talked about the value of various starting possibilities. The pocket pairs—two cards that are the same. The suited connectors—cards of the same suit that are one apart in ranking, like a seven and an eight. The suited one- and two- and even three-gappers—cards of the same suit that are sort of related but not immediately adjacent, like a six and an eight of hearts. The suited wheel aces—an ace with a low second card of the same suit that can make a straight, or a wheel. They all have different strategic value, he's told me. They all need to be part of a well-rounded arsenal. Some are good on their own. Some are good because they give you board coverage—that is, you can make strong hands in a variety of situations. Some are worthwhile for blocker value—key cards that lower the chance your opponent has a strong hand. Some are powerful because they can make monster hands that will get maximum value from weak opponents. And he's explained how you can't play all those cards in the same way all the time, especially given my lack of experience. "Basically, you can't go too wrong in the beginning if you play good cards" is one of the first concrete pieces of information he ever gave me. But what Harrington seems to be saying makes a lot of sense to me, too: If I suddenly start opening hands that aren't expected of me, in super-aggressive style, how will people know how to react?

Erik starts laughing. And the way he begins to say, "Well . . ." sounds an awful lot like the *Well* . . . I give to aspiring writers who've just read Kerouac for the first time and are having a mind-blowing epiphany that I already know is not going to end the way they think it will. "Well, there's definitely an appeal to it. Aggressive people are going to get you. They are going to get you in a lot of spots where you're going to be like, you know, I can't handle the pressure or whatever. They're very good at finding that," he says. "But they also could get themselves in spots where they're giving away a lot. I agree with Dan that they're really challenging to play against and you don't necessarily always want them at your table— but then you'll get a beautiful gift from them. You can forgive them anything then." By beautiful gift, Erik means a lot of chips. Hyper-aggressive play, he tells me, can be a short-term boon. But most of the time, those players go broke. And at the highest levels, they don't last more than a heartbeat.

My enthusiasm for this particular section of Dan's work, he says, reminds him of poker as it was ten or so years ago. "There was a time when these hyper-aggressive guys could do very well. Some of them were stars. And then the overaggressiveness ironed them out. They're on the rail now. You have to find the balance, and some of these guys don't put the brakes on, ever. In the highest buy-in events, in the hundred-Ks, you really have to be able to put the brakes on. There's an entirely different style, winning a two-hundred-dollar online tournament and winning a hundred-K."

So what's the answer? Action Dan and Erik himself actually offer a pretty compelling case study by their success: Be solid, fundamentally. Cultivate the solid image. And then add the hyper-aggression, but at the right place and the right time. Not always, not continuously, but thinkingly.

There's never a default with anything. It's always a matter of deliberation. Even seven-deuce—the worst hand, statistically speaking, that you can be dealt—can be playable in the right circumstances. The thing is, the circumstances are usually not right—and the hyper-aggressive player may run over everyone for a while and forget that at some point, it will all come to a screeching halt. Of course, being too conservative is also a liability. You become predictable. And often times, you lose the ability to press the fold button. You've been waiting so patiently for a good hand that you won't let it go. "If you want to be good in big tournaments," Erik tells me, "like, let's say you're playing a field of four hundred people. You have to be involved in many more hands, because just good cards aren't going to get you there. They're not going to get you there a high enough percentage of the time." And so despite knowing fundamentally sound strategy, you have to be willing to part with it. "It turns out that people who are sort of involved and reckless are more likely to go deep." To go deep means to make it through a large portion of the field. "You just have to be smart about it."

I nod. It's not the answer I wanted, but it's the answer I get. There's one more question from the Harrington books that I want to ask before this particular walk is done. What exactly is "M" and do I care? It's a term I've circled in red, to make sure to review. It seemed awfully important to be designated with a single letter. M, Erik explains, is a way of thinking about your position in a tournament. "You have to be aware of everyone's stack size," he tells me. "When you get to Vegas and start playing, I want you to write down hands for me. And for every hand, you need to tell me how much everyone has behind. You have to always be aware of it." Normally, people think of stack sizes in terms of big blinds. M takes it one step further, by quantifying your risk of going broke. How many orbits around the table can I sit and not play a hand? Your M is, basically, your cushion for putting in the minimum each orbit. The lower your M, the more in danger you are of busting the tournament sooner. And the letter M itself? It comes from the last name of a player named Paul Magriel. "I want you to meet Paul when you're in Vegas," Erik tells me. "You should ask Dan about him. Tell him to tell you how M came about."

But as it turns out, I forget to ask Dan. Mostly because he cuts off any more technical questions with one thought. "We can go over everything you should be paying attention to, but the truth is, until you start playing a lot, it's just information overload."

I nod. I certainly know the dangers of too much information in an experience-free vacuum. And I realize that my piles of margin notes and the barely legible notebook jottings of Seidelian wisdom don't necessarily need any more friends, at least at present.

"But here's what I can tell you. The thing you have to conquer most obviously is yourself," Dan continues. "Mike Tyson said it best. 'Everyone has a plan until you get punched in the mouth.' And he's right. Until you go through a month of everything going wrong, you won't know whether you have what it takes. You will never learn how to play good poker if you get lucky—it's as simple as that. You just won't."

He's not talking about hazing. It's not the attitude of "no pain, no gain." Nor is he giving me "permission to fail." Instead, he's talking about something very different, something so fundamental that we often forget about it whether we're learning something new or just going about our lives: you need a way of testing your thought process. Before I get fancy with strategy, with the curlicues and trappings of expertise, I need to answer something far more basic: Am I thinking correctly? Before I start experimenting with writing free verse, have I learned how to think through a poem's basic structure? Before I start adding those exotic spices to my recipe, have I learned how to make a basic white rice?

And the only way to do that is by failing. By writing bad poetry. Burning your food. Turning in shitty first draft after shitty first draft. "You have to suffer defeat," Dan continues. "As brutal as it sounds, that's the way it is."

The benefit of failure is an objectivity that success simply can't offer. If you win right away—if your first foray into any new area is a runaway success—you'll have absolutely no way to gauge if you're really just that brilliant or it was a total fluke and you got incredibly lucky.

The real reason Erik is still around, Dan tells me—I'll have to see if Erik agrees on this one—is that he can take chances but still retain enough balance to pull back. Action Dan got his nickname because of a conservative image. Erik isn't always known for running wild bluffs. "There are many great players who play with a lot more courage than Erik or I will ever know. The trouble is, that's inherent in their personality and that contains the seeds of their destruction." They go on hot streaks—but they don't know what it takes to lose with grace and keep going. "You'll see a whole bunch of superstars from ten years ago, and you're not going to find any with money today. They were superstars because they were able to bring it to the edge, they had ability, but when things went a little bit wrong they either fell apart or didn't know what to do with the money and spent it all on drugs and sports betting. So were they actually courageous? No."

Nothing is personal. Everything should be treated like a business. My goals need to be pure: to run the best business I can. "Some of these other people had a goal to become famous, or even more, they just wanted action," Dan says. And that's their eventual downfall.

Do I know what I don't know? Am I thinking well? "As a professional gambler, you have to understand: if you don't have an objective evaluation of what's going on, you're a loser," he tells me. "This game will beat you—it's as simple as that. If you don't understand what's going on, the game will say, 'We're taking your money away from you.'"

What's crucial, Dan says, is to develop my critical thinking and self-assessment ability well enough that I can constantly reevaluate, objectively, where I am—and whether where I am is good enough to play as I'm playing. It's not about winning or losing—that's chance. It's about thinking—the process. Dan himself is a living illustration of how true this is: he quit not during a downswing but at the top of his game.

"Nine years ago, I'd just won $1.63 million. I'm walking out of the tournament, and I look around, I say, 'This is it. I can't take this crap anymore. I win $1.63 million and all I do is feel tired and beaten-down. This is just not worth it.' I just right then and there decided I wasn't going to play serious poker anymore. My heart's not in it." Most people won't tell you to quit after the biggest score of your life. But Dan could tell that he was getting weaker, he was getting older, and the field was getting stronger. He'd quit before he had fallen behind.

And thus my first real poker lesson isn't about winning. It's about losing.

"You become a big winner when you lose," Dan says. "Everyone plays well when they're winning. But can you control yourself and play well when you're losing? And not by being too conservative, but trying to still be objective as to what your chances are in the hand. If you can do that, then you've conquered the game."

And it resonates. After all, losing is what brought me to the table in the first place. It makes sense that learning to lose in a game—to lose constructively and productively—would help me lose in life, lose and come back, lose and not see it as a personal failure. It resonates—but it's a tough ask. Dan nods. "It's still tough to do. Even for me, and I have a lifetime of experience, that's not an easy thing."

We say our goodbyes. He missed his morning gym session, but he's off to enjoy his "quiet retirement."

Oh, and I did learn how to beat roulette. Turns out all you need is a Department of Defense supercomputer, a software program developed from the work of Claude Shannon and Edward Thorp in the fifties, and an earpiece. Also casinos that don't know what you're up to. Get too greedy and you're out.

"DAN IS GREAT," ERIK agrees. And, yes, everything he has told me is true: one of the keys to success, Erik says, if not *the* key, is objectivity. And objectivity is a hard thing to come by.

"It's good that you're starting with a rare realistic understanding of what you're up against," he says. "You know that these swings happen, that there's a randomness to the way these swings happen."

It doesn't make me feel much better. I'm a writer, I want to remind him. I don't have much money to lose. It's easy enough for someone with over $30 million in earnings to say.

But actually that's unfair. When Erik was just starting out, he had nothing—and he nearly lost it all. He'd dropped out of college to play backgammon—that's when he first met Dan—but then decided to go back to a more traditional career path. He'd met his future wife, Ruah, and knew he had to get "serious" about life. So he went to Wall Street—just in time for the crash of 1987. He lost his job. And Ruah was now pregnant.

He didn't take the loss personally. Instead, he reevaluated his options and buckled down on his studying. He was, in essence, "scared into playing well." And he started winning. Why did he emerge on the other side while so many others didn't? Obviously, there's the talent factor—Erik is clearly someone who is very good at the component parts of poker—but there's a larger skill at play: his absolute lack of ego. His willingness to be objective about himself and his own level of play.

"When things go wrong, other people see it as unfairness that's always surrounding them," he tells me. They take it personally. They don't *know* how to lose, how to learn from losing. They look for something or someone to blame. They don't step back to analyze their own decisions, their own play, where they may have gone wrong themselves. "It's a really big handicap in life to think that way. All of us can step into that sometimes, but it's important to know the difference. It's like that great Kipling quote: 'If you can meet with Triumph and Disaster, and treat those two impostors just the same . . .'"

I nod. I know the one.

"I love that. This is such a fundamental part of poker. The wins really go to people's heads. And the losses—they can't deal. It's so easy to be delusional in this game," he tells me.

I jot it down. Understand the dark side of variance first: that's the only time you'll actually learn to process your decision making well. Because when you're winning, it's just too easy not to stop and analyze your process. Why bother if things are going well? When it comes to learning, Triumph is the real foe; it's Disaster that's your teacher. It's Disaster that brings objectivity. It's Disaster that's the antidote to that greatest of delusions, overconfidence. And ultimately, both Triumph and Disaster are impostors. They are results that are subject to chance. One of them just happens to be a better teaching tool than the other.

In the classic demonstration of the illusion of control, the Harvard psychologist Ellen Langer had students guess the outcome of a coin toss, heads or tails. They were then told whether they were correct or not in their guesses. In three separate setups, the outcomes were predetermined in a specific order: they could be distributed in an intuitively random pattern, there could be more correct guesses clustered near the beginning, or there could be more correct guesses clustered near the end. In each case, the absolute numbers were the same. The only difference was the order.

But the results couldn't have been more different. After the guesses concluded, Langer asked each participant a series of questions: Did they feel they could improve on this task? Did they feel they were particularly talented at it? Did they need more time to get better? Would they be better with limited distraction? And so on. In each case, the obvious answer is no: to answer otherwise is to classify something that is the outcome of chance (a coin toss) as being in the realm of skill. But the obvious answer is not the answer she got. When students had a random progression or one where the accuracy clustered near the end, they did indeed answer in the negative. But when the correct answers were clustered up front, they developed a sudden myopia. Why yes, they said, they *are* quite good at this, and yes, they *would* improve with time. Success led to an abject failure of objectivity: suddenly, they were in the throes of the illusion of control. They thought that they could actually predict the results of a coin toss.

If we lose early, we have a shot at objectivity. But when we win at the start, that's when we see the illusion of control playing out in full swing. As Langer titled her paper: "Tails, I Win. Heads, It's Chance." Though Langer's work is from the seventies, when I was in graduate school, Walter and I replicated the effect precisely with our new subjects: it remains just as strong. The outcome rightly shouldn't matter. And yet how it does.

"The beauty of poker is generally, delusion is punished," Erik tells me. You may get away with an illusion of control in the short term, but if you persist, no one will know your name in a few years' time. In real life, we can remain deluded indefinitely. If we choose delusion over objectivity in poker, we are eventually doomed.

I admit to being nervous. Objectivity at its purest is a big ask. Can I truly hack it?

Erik certainly can. Somehow, even over smoked fish, he manages to demonstrate just how able he is to learn from feedback and to change his actions accordingly.

"Do you not like the way egg yolks taste?" I ask him as our orders hit the table. I've ordered the lox and bagel platter. He's ordered some salmon, too, but also an egg-white omelet, just as he had at our first ever meeting. To me, that seems like cutting out the part that makes eggs *eggs*, and even though I don't yet know Erik well, I can't help but comment.

"No, I like them," Erik says. "But I read that it's healthier to only eat egg whites."

I'll soon learn that Erik is big on nutrition science—but that he's always willing to listen if someone points out contradictory evidence. Which is precisely what I now do, even pulling out my phone to punctuate my mini lecture with references to newer work. Nutrition is a tricky beast, and nutrition advice offered in a vacuum, even trickier. Many people will bristle and shut down—who are you to tell them what to eat when they've already formed an opinion? Erik listens. He reads. He nods. And the next time we have breakfast, he orders the full egg. I resist asking if it tastes better, but I imagine I see a satisfied look on his face. I take out my phone again, this time with a quote I pulled from one of my favorite Nora Ephron essays. "You can eat all sorts of things that are high in dietary cholesterol (like lobster and avocado and eggs)," she writes, "and they have NO EFFECT WHATSOEVER on your cholesterol count. NONE. WHATSOEVER. DID YOU HEAR ME? I'm sorry to have to resort to capital letters, but what is wrong with you people?" She reserves special pity for the egg-white omelet. "Every time I'm forced to watch [friends] eat egg-white omelets, I feel bad for them. In the first place, egg-white omelets are tasteless. In the second place, the people who eat them think they are doing something virtuous when they are instead merely misinformed." She goes on to say that no amount of haranguing from her tends to change anyone's mind—a common enough effect, especially when it comes to nutritional beliefs. Erik laughs and eats his eggs, yolks and all.

As I RIDE THE subway back to Brooklyn, I realize Erik hasn't given me much in the way of concrete advice. Our conversations remain more theoretical than I would ideally prefer. It strikes me that the experience feels somehow familiar, this dynamic of back-and-forth with no real answers forthcoming to any of my questions—or, rather, the only answer being one of "Well, it depends; why don't we think it through for ourselves?" It's not quite a Socratic dialogue—Erik doesn't keep me hanging to that extent—but it's an interaction that focuses more on process than prescription, on exploration rather than destination.

When I complain that it would be helpful to know at least his opinion on how I should play a hand, he gives me a smile and tells me a story. Earlier that year, he says, he was talking to one of the most successful high-stakes players currently on the circuit. That player was offering a very specific opinion on how a certain hand should be played. Erik listened quietly and then told him one phrase: "Less certainty. More inquiry."

"He didn't take it well," he tells me. "He actually got pretty upset." But Erik wasn't criticizing. He was offering the approach he'd learned over years of experience. Question more. Stay open-minded.

And then I realize what I'm reminded of: Dante and Virgil. Dante, in a strange place, not knowing what anything is or where it might lead. Virgil, his guide through this infernal landscape, who doesn't offer directions but rather stands to the side as Dante forges his own path.

When people find out I'm working with Erik, they immediately want to know what he thinks of certain plays and how he himself plays certain spots. Will the elusive champion finally give up his secrets? For Erik, the answer is simple: there is no answer. It's a constant process of inquiry. A hand can be played any number of ways, as long as the thought process is there. And Erik may himself decide to play the same cards, in the same position, even against the same opponents, in a different fashion from one day to the next. There is no certainty. There is only thought.

And yes, it *is* frustrating. I *do* want answers. I *do* want a guide for what to do with my pocket tens from the small blind following a raise from under the gun and a re-raise from the hijack. Enough philosophy, I want to yell. Give me certainty! Tell me if I'm supposed to call or shove or fold. Tell me if I'm making a big mistake! But the Virgil buddha will not be shaken. And I'm left with that frustrating not-quite-rage that, weeks later, I miraculously find coalesced into knowledge. Poker is all about comfort with uncertainty, after all. Only I didn't quite realize it wasn't just uncertainty about the outcome of the cards. It's uncertainty about the "right" thing to do. The only certain thing is your thinking.

A number of years ago, Erik heard about a seminar led by Mike Caro. Caro is famous for his book on tells—live, in-the-moment reads of others at the table. "He's a pretty eccentric guy," Erik says. "And he's walking around the stage and starts off by saying, 'What is the object of poker?'" I nod in agreement. A question I've been asking myself frequently.

Erik continues, "Somebody says, 'Winning money.' He says, 'No.' Somebody else says, 'Winning a lot of pots.' 'No.' He says, 'The object of poker is making good decisions.' I think that's a really good way to look at poker."

He thinks for a bit. "When you lose because of the run of the cards, that feels fine. It's not a big deal. It's much more painful if you lose because you made a bad decision or a mistake."

He won't tell me how to play a hand not because he's being mean but because that answer comes at the expense of the ability to make a decision. Of the discipline to think through everything for myself, on my own. All he can give me are the tools. The building blocks of thoughts. I'm the one who has to find the way through.

It may make me frustrated in the short term. But at least I won't be in any danger of falling into the egg-white trap in an area I know nothing about. If you're skeptical of any prescriptive advice to begin with, if "less certainty, more inquiry" is your guiding light, not only will you listen; you will adjust. You will grow. And if that's not self-awareness and self-discipline, I don't know what is.

The Mind
of a Strategist

New York, Late Fall 2016

"He will win who knows when to fight and when not to fight.

He will win who knows how to handle both superior and inferior forces.

He will win whose army is animated by the same spirit throughout all its ranks.

He will win who, prepared himself, waits to take the enemy unprepared."

SUN TZU, *THE ART OF WAR*, 5TH CENTURY BC

I soon develop a new morning routine. Several days a week, I make my way to upper Manhattan for a walk with Erik. The rest, I practice a decidedly bizarre sort of reverse commute. A subway from Brooklyn to the Fulton stop in Manhattan. A transfer to the PATH train that will take me under the Hudson River. And a walk from the station to the nearest coffee shop that will have me—sometimes a Starbucks, sometimes something a bit more fancy. Sometimes I'll be in Hoboken. Sometimes Jersey City, if the mood strikes. I order my price of admission for the next few hours, open my laptop, and enter the world of online poker.

I don't put much store in the ten-thousand-hour rule—even if you modify it with the caveat of *Well, maybe not ten thousand precisely, but a very large number that is comparable across individuals and activities.* The evidence simply does not bear up to scrutiny. Some people achieve much larger gains with much less investment than others who study far longer and work much harder; that's the simple truth.

The example that's been cited over and over as the quintessential ten-thousand-hour illustration is the story of the Polgar sisters, a trio of girls whose parents decided to train them to be champion chess players from the moment they could hold a pawn. But if anything, the sisters illustrate the limits of practice. Sure, they all became excellent at chess. But each one had a different trajectory. For the best of the bunch, it took far fewer hours—while the "worst" (I say worst in quotes because she is a highly accomplished player) has never attained the same level despite countless hours of practice. Chess is the perfect test activity, and here, it's played with as close as you can get to ideal environmental control, and still the role of other factors—genes, aptitude, determination, whatever you want to call them—shines through. And chess is an activity that should rightly be the most susceptible to practice: one that is what Robin Hogarth terms a "kind" learning environment, where you receive immediate feedback. What you learn can be applied straight off, and you know right away if you've made the right decision or not.

Most real-world environments are what Hogarth calls "wicked": there's a mismatch between action and feedback because of external noise. Activities with elements of surprise, uncertainty, the unknown: suddenly, you're not sure whether what you've learned is accurate or not, accurately executed or not. There's simply too much going on. And so, in most environments, the problem is far more severe.

But despite all this, one thing is undoubtedly true: while practice is not enough and there's not even close to a magic number for its effectiveness, you also cannot learn if you do not practice. If you're serious about anything—playing chess, writing a book, becoming an astronaut, playing poker—you have to learn the composite skills. No one is so naturally gifted that they can just get up and go. Even Mozart needed some lessons. If you're trying to learn poker, there's simply no equivalent to playing the game, seeing how hands play out, learning the feel of different situations. And the most efficient way to get the kind of practice that used to take people decades of casino sessions to acquire is by playing online. Hands are dealt quickly, action is kept going by timers on every decision, and situation upon situation unfolds in mere minutes, rather than the hours it would take in a live game.

Among everyone I consult, there is a consensus: I have to play online if I want to improve on any sort of manageable timescale. The only problem is that online poker is illegal in New York, my home state. At first the news confuses me. We have lotteries galore. And fantasy sports ads greet me all over the city. Surely poker is more skill-based than all of the above?

Being new to the poker community, I haven't been privy to the drama that now comes flooding at me from every person I ask to explain. This is where I am introduced to the tangled alphabet soup that is poker legislation—a soup that gets at the very heart of why clear decision making is so important, and how often extraneous considerations become mired in what should otherwise be clear-cut.

It all started with a piece of 2006 legislation called UIGEA, or the Unlawful Internet Gambling Enforcement Act: it was no longer legal to process payments for anything gambling-related on the internet. And poker was gambling. Or so it seemed. The definitions were a bit murky. Horse racing was exempt—but dog racing was not. Fantasy sports? Skill, of course. Other sports betting? Gambling, naturally. One definition stated that "a person engages in gambling if he stakes or risks something of value upon the outcome of a contest of chance or a future contingent event not under his control or influence, upon an agreement or understanding that he or someone else will receive something of value in the event of a certain outcome"—but language was quickly added to exempt things like trading and real estate speculation, which would otherwise seem to be included. The psychologist Arthur Reber calls the result "an unconvincing apologia designed to separate what are regarded as socially accepted forms of gambling from those that are not." Or politically convenient forms of gambling from those that have strong lobbies opposed to them—like poker.

For a few years, it seemed like poker might be able to scoot by under the radar. But on April 15, 2011, known as Black Friday in the poker world, UIGEA was put in force for the first time. All three major poker sites that hadn't yet left the US market—Full Tilt, PokerStars, and Absolute Poker—were indicted and their assets frozen. And that looked like the end of online poker in the US.

There was nothing barring individual states from legalizing it, though, so, slowly, some have come on board. Including New Jersey. Which is why I can now play online poker in this Gregory's Coffee and look out across the Hudson at Manhattan—and while I sit here, what I am doing is perfectly legal. But the moment I cross back, I suddenly become a criminal. It's bizarre when you stop to think about it, but then again, politicians have never exactly been known for their logic or evenhandedness. And I'm willing to bet that more than one of them has the equivalent of a Soviet grandmother sitting on their shoulder, whispering, "Evil, evil, evil!"

This, then, is why I find myself here, in a state I've never given so much as a second thought. I fire up a tournament and press Record on my computer.

BACK IN MANHATTAN, ERIK sits next to me as I start the footage.

"I like the puppy. Great touch," Erik tells me when he sees the screen. "We'll have to make you a puppy T-shirt for live play."

I've chosen an image of a tiny blond dachshund puppy for my avatar. I'm curious how people will respond. (I got the idea from a stream with one of the best players in the country, Jason Mercier. His avatar was a puppy, and that had inadvertently influenced my impression of the type of player he'd be—not at all accurate, I'd learn.) My screen name: thepsychchic. One word, all lowercase, chosen after much careful deliberation to embody as many of the traits I want to convey to my opponents as I can. Psych, short for psychology—or psychic, as many of my perhaps not-quite-literate opponents will read it. Or psycho. Will I psych you out, read your mind, go berserk? And, of course, chic: the missing *k* lends both a visual symmetry and an opportunity for the psychic misread, but in the end, chic reads "girl" even to the illiterate. And in the man's world that is poker, people don't play against *girls* the way they play against *real* people. They may think they do, but they simply don't. In one study of online poker, men bluffed 6 percent more often against someone with a female avatar than a male or neutral one—but, when confronted with that possibility, refused to believe it.

In one of the first hands of the game, I raise an off-suit jack-ten from early position and receive multiple callers—that is, many people decide to put in the same amount of money as I already have in order to see how the first three common cards, the flop, will turn out. The flop comes all spades, and I have none in my hand—but it has a king and a queen, giving me what's called an open-ended straight draw. Any ace or nine will give me a straight, five cards in a row. And straights are good hands. They beat almost everything. Except, of course, flushes, which are five cards of the same suit. If anyone has two spades in their hand, they already have me "drawing dead"—even if I make the straight I'm gunning for, I lose. If anyone has even one spade, they cut my "outs," or the cards I need to make my straight, by two. Now, if the ace or the nine is a spade, even though I make my straight, they make their flush and I am, once again, beaten. But it's pretty fair to say that, at this point, none of these considerations are crossing my mind. What I'm thinking instead is roughly this: I don't want to look like exactly what I am—someone who doesn't know what she's doing. I don't want to look weak.

I'm third to act—both the small blind and the big blind are in the hand—and they check to me, a way of passing on any action to see how I might react and what I might do. It's generally accepted to check to the pre-flop aggressor—that is, if you have to act before the person who made the final raising action before the flop, you check and see what happens. There are two more people acting behind me, so whatever I choose to do, I have to be aware that, in total, four people will need to make a decision after I make mine—the two who haven't yet acted, plus the two who have already checked but will have another opportunity to do something different if anyone happens to bet and reopen the action.

I decide it would be an excellent idea to bet my straight draw. I don't yet have a made hand, sure, but I have a wonderful draw and I want to win all those chips. With four callers, there's a lot of so-called dead money in the pot. I decide to put in a half-pot bet (half the number of chips already in the middle). The player next to act folds their hand—hurrah!— but the player after decides to call. And then, horror of horrors, the small blind raises. A big, hefty raise. I don't have much of a choice but to fold, having lost both my initial raise and that half-pot bet.

"OK, we have a lot to talk about," Erik says as the hand plays out without me.

I turn to look at him and try to read his facial expression, but it's the usual calm blank.

"First, why did you raise there?"

"Well, you told me that jack-ten is a good drawing hand, so I thought I should play it. And I've won with it before—no one sees you coming!"

That's my first error. Not only do I mistakenly think that the off-suit variety is just as good as the suited (it isn't), but I have ignored one of the most important elements of pre-flop play: position.

"You can't open that hand until much later," Erik says. "There are just too many people behind you who can raise—and then you'll be in a really bad spot for the rest of the hand."

In any interaction, you want to have as much information as possible. When you're the person acting last, you have the best of it. You already know your opponents' decisions, their plays, their opening bids. In a negotiation, you have the power. In an argument or debate, you have the power. You know more than they do. They have to initiate. You have the benefit of responding. Position is king.

We go on, back and forth, through the entire hand, to determine that I made every single mistake I possibly could. After I was already in, I should have checked rather than bet the flop. And since I did bet, I should have bet a completely different size. The only thing I did correctly was, at last, to fold—after lighting a good chunk of my chips on fire.

But the most crucial mistake I made wasn't necessarily the poor strategy—"You'll get there, that's the easier part," Erik says—but the fact that I don't have good reasons for most of my decisions. I was so preoccupied by everything going on, including the little timer counting down how long I had to act, that I left my thought process behind for some assorted facts that were easily accessible to my memory. "Because you told me that it's a good drawing hand" simply isn't a valid reason to raise. And "because I want to win the chips" isn't a good rationale for betting. (Neither is the reason I don't quite vocalize to Erik, or even admit fully to myself: I didn't want Erik to think I was being too weak and passive by playing too conservatively. After all, he did tell me earlier that the aggressive side of strategy is what tends to win tournaments.) And my bet sizing? Well, I have no idea why I bet the way I did except that a half-pot bet seemed reasonable. Bigger and too many of my precious chips go away, and I'm kind of attached to them; smaller and no one folds, and I want them to fold so I can win.

"We've talked about this," Erik says. "You have to have a clear thought process for every single hand. What do I know? What have I seen? How will that help me make an informed judgment about this hand?"

I know we've talked about it, but it's so much harder to execute when there are all these things going on and the timer clicking down! Why does the timer click down like that? Why are the bet size sliders so hard to get right? That alone takes a good twenty seconds. What kind of sadist designed this interface?

"For every action, you have to go back and think through everything you know and come to the right conclusion. You can't act too quickly."

Even with an evil time clock?

"Even with a clock. We have them in the high rollers. You'll see when you come out to Vegas." In the tournaments Erik plays, even though the action is live, the amount of time you have to come to a decision is limited: there are clocks that generally give you thirty seconds, before you have to use your time bank. Online, you have an actual time bank; live, you have cards that you give to the dealer that serve as an extension of sorts.

This worries me: one of the ways I manipulated stress and hot emotions when I was designing my psychological studies was by introducing time pressure. I saw decision quality degrade in participant after participant as the seconds ticked down. People stressed, panicked, and acted on impulse. And I certainly feel the pressure online. Just the threat of the clock makes me want to act immediately so that I don't incur its wrath. I can feel it watching and judging me, the little bugger.

"You'll get used to it—it's really not a big deal," Erik says. "Even a few seconds of reflection, that's all you need to just go through every action. Stop and take a breath and think through your alternatives. Am I folding? Am I calling? Am I raising? Everything is always a possibility. You have to be careful you're not acting too fast. It's a major hole for a lot of people. Even I'm sometimes guilty of it."

It's solid advice. It's the difference between mindful activity and mindless activity. The good thing is, as a novice I don't yet have any muscle memory, good or bad—actions I take because "you always bet here" or "you always check here." There's no "always" in my arsenal. I have to actively search through alternatives—and so, I can develop more thoughtful habits.

"The fact that you're a beginner is good. You still question everything," Erik says. "Especially at the beginning, you start with the fundamentals. But then slowly, you can start getting into the habit of thinking through every option in a different light. Thinking through the possibilities and seeing what else is available."

When I was in college, I studied military theory and history in addition to psychology. I wasn't just interested in decision making; I wanted to know about some of the most strategically important decision making in the world. And so, I read about campaigns and wars and conflicts. And, of course, the classics. Carl von Clausewitz's *On War*. Sun Tzu's *The Art of War*. In the midst of trying to get all the strategic pieces of one fairly simple poker decision into my head, what Erik is saying prompts an epiphany of sorts. This is like a campaign where I am the commander—except there are no other forces besides me and my actions.

I've never really thought about a single situation in my own life in this light, but now it actually makes sense. Before any campaign, or, indeed, even minor military action, you need to evaluate the situation, the territory, the nature of the enemy. You can't just plow ahead with one strategy because it worked in the past or you've seen someone else employ it successfully. Each time you act, you have to reassess based on what is now known versus what was known before. You need to have a process, a system, a plan—one that evolves with feedback. If you don't, how will you know whether the outcome of your battle—a bad one in my case, but successful ones, too—is the result of skill or luck? If you've just lost your chips, was it because you chanced upon an unlucky situation—or because you planned a poor campaign?

My jack-ten: it's a weapon whose value changes depending on when and how it's deployed. If I have superior position on my opponents—the benefit of being last to act, the benefit of being able to observe all the enemy forces' actions before I have to decide on my own, the perspective of higher ground from which I can assess the situation in its entirety—it goes up in value dramatically. I have maneuverability. And I have the last word. No one can surprise me. I close the action. But if I have to deploy it first or second, with hostile forces that could still sneak up behind? Suddenly, it withers. Now I may find myself squeezed in multiway action, not knowing what actions still remain. My vision blurs and the uncertainty increases. Suddenly, the proportion of known and unknown information shifts. These aren't the all-terrain, all-purpose pocket aces that I should feel comfortable launching at any point. This hand is very context dependent. (And even those aces would far prefer having the proverbial higher ground.) Position is information, and the more information you have about your enemies, the stronger you are. Position doesn't ensure I won't be ambushed, of course, but it makes the scenario just a bit more controllable.

What's more, the action here is multiway. Multiple enemies. And everyone knows how much harder it is to fight a two-front war, let alone four-front, than a one-on-one battle. "When you're multiway," Erik tells me, "you tend to have to be more straightforward." There are simply too many variables to juggle. Like a general working out a multistage plan, I have to think multiple streets ahead. Will I be in a good position to react if the hand continues? I bet because I want them to fold, but what if they don't? What do I do next? What if they raise? How do I respond then? Every good strategist has to think through all the possible permutations. The more players there are, the harder it is. And yet, if I'm to be reflective rather than reflexive in my actions, I have to learn to do it, and to do it in the time allotted.

It certainly doesn't help that this is one of the first hands of the tournament: my timing is off for any major moves. I don't yet know anything about any of the players. I haven't had a chance to form any reads. I don't know my enemy. What are the weak points? The strong points? When do I defend? When do I attack? How do they behave when they're strong? When they're weak? Do they bluff too often? Not enough? Just right? It's a headache thinking about it for one player, let alone four of them.

Online poker may not be as good for reading people as live games, but that doesn't mean you can't study patterns of behavior. How players bet, when they bet, how much they bet. If you play with someone enough, you begin to sense what kind of player they are. Some are aggressive and loose: they play too many hands and bet their life when they do. Some are aggressive and tight: they bet insanely, yes, but they only play very strong hands. Some are passive and weak: they love to play as many hands as possible but will fold the moment someone raises the stakes on them. In an online environment, you have the ability to not only play against the same people repeatedly, but then to take notes on their profile and color-code them. That way, the next time you meet them, you see right away where they fit into your rating scheme.

Had I observed more hands, I would have realized at least one important thing: at this particular table, in this particular battle arena, people really like to fight. They've put on their military gear, and by god, they are going to go into battle. They didn't come here to sit on the sidelines and watch while others do the fighting. They want to be in it themselves. Here, people really like to see flops and turns. They don't often fold to bets; they want to see it all through to the river. That knowledge would have told me that the action was very likely to be multiway on most any hand. And that, in turn, would have informed my choice of weapons and tactics—stronger weapons, stronger positions, more select lines, but more aggressive ones once selected. Lines that can stand up to multiple attacks over multiple steps. For such a campaign, I would need hands with more robust equity—that is, hands that have the possibility of constant improvement—instead of my meek little weakling of a draw.

The terrain here is also not conducive to my particular strategy. "You have to learn to pay attention to board texture," Erik tells me. Is it a dry board, one where the cards don't have much relation to one another— different suits, values spread far apart, making it unlikely that someone has a strong draw? Is it a wet board, one where the cards are closely connected—two or three of a suit, cards that could form a part of a straight, a landscape that means players who don't yet have a strong hand can suddenly find themselves with a monster if a draw completes? Is it a static board—no new cards are likely to change the situation that much? Is it a dynamic board—many draws, like straights and flushes, are available, and any new addition is likely to change the advantage and can significantly change the value of your hand? The texture is the changing battleground. Different textures require different strategies. You're not going to launch the same campaign in the mountains as you will in the plains as you will in an ocean battle. Dynamic boards need you to tread lightly and think ahead more carefully; static boards allow you to be more shortsighted without suffering the consequences too greatly. That single-suit board might be great for bluffing if I were heads up, playing against a single opponent—but multiway, it becomes a swamp for me. At this stage in my journey, the point isn't to master the precise approach I need to take on every single possible type of terrain. It's to realize that terrain is something I have to learn to pay attention to, take into account, and adjust to. I'll master the precise movements of the adjustment as I go. But it's surprising how many people never even pause to think and blunder on, prior strategy in hand, no matter that their original map may have been gravely mistaken. I did that here, and Erik's job is to make sure I don't do it again.

I've been unthinking in far more ways than that. My half-pot bet? Why did I do that? Bet sizing and what it accomplishes is an incredibly useful analogue for most any decision. How much are you risking to accomplish what, exactly? What are the situations where you want to bet frequently and small? Where do you want to bet less often, but big? When do you over-bet? When do you want to appear pot-committed, like Thomas Schelling and his rogue driver playing a game of chicken, ripping the steering wheel from the car in a display of ultimate commitment to not swerving? And how does it all change depending on your opponent? Every tactic you use, you have to ask what it accomplishes and whether the same thing could have been accomplished more cheaply. Do you need to send in the whole battalion where a handful of soldiers would do? Is this the job for a scout—a tiny probe bet? Do you need to pull out the big guns and show up with your whole army?

Had I actually made it to the river, I would've needed to really make sure I'd properly sized up my opponents. "If there's a possible straight or flush on board, it's more likely someone is bluffing on the end. And it can also be a good spot for bluffing yourself," Erik says. But how do I know that? I haven't seen a single showdown to know anyone's real tactics here, and I certainly am not at the point where I can pick out good opportunities for the old feint or two.

Which brings us to the most important point of all: I'm not a very good commander yet. I don't know enough. I don't see the full battlefield. I'm not even sure if I'm picking up the right weapon. In this case, for instance, I decided my hand was a great drawing hand because Erik had demonstrated something similar with the same hand—except of the suited variety. I didn't think much of it. After all, I'd read that suitedness adds only 2 percent of equity to your hand, and boy, didn't I feel good in that knowledge. Two percent is not a lot. It's basically the same thing.

Except it really isn't. Any tactician or strategist would tell you immediately that any edge is huge, and 2 percent is a big deal. What's more, suitedness makes something a far stronger weapon: it's easier to play. You have an added psychological edge because now you can navigate many situations much more clearly. But I don't yet know this. I don't feel it. I don't understand it. My edge is precisely zero at this point. And the thing

I'm worried about? Not whether I'm thinking through this correctly, but whether or not I look weak. A good commander never cares what others are thinking. Perception matters only insofar as you're using it strategically to shape your image for future actions.

Unless, of course, it's your superior who is doing the looking. And now that Erik has spoken, I do admit it. "I thought I'd look weak if I just checked, that you'd tell me I need to be more aggressive. You told me not to play scared."

"First of all, you can't think like that," Erik tells me. "I mean, you actually are very weak here and you shouldn't even be in this hand, but that's not the point. The point is, you can't play based on how it will look. Not playing scared is not the same thing as being aggressive. It means not making decisions because you're afraid. It's not about being passive or aggro. You can be way too aggro and still scared. And being passive can be strong."

I nod and take a big bite of the almond croissant I brought over in a big pastry assortment. Criticism, especially warranted criticism, always goes down better with something sweet.

Erik continues, "You know, this is actually really important. A lot of players actually start playing worse when they're on livestream"—when a poker table is televised so that people can see the cards—"because they're so worried about how they look."

In the early days of televised poker, Erik was famous, or infamous if you ask some, for refusing to show his cards to the camera or card reader. It wasn't because he was afraid of looking stupid. It was because he didn't want to reveal his strategy. These days, it's no longer viable to avoid showing your cards, and it never really hurt him to begin with: he's one of the best players I've seen at being able to adjust his play.

What do you picture when you think of the most successful hunter in the animal kingdom? Likely a lion, or a cheetah, with its majestic run, or perhaps a wolf stalking its prey. They are all striking beasts. They are all powerful. They are all deadly. And none of them is even close to being the most successful. The cheetah comes in highest, killing approximately 58 percent of the animals it hunts. The lion is next, at less than half that— one quarter of its intended kills hit the mark. And the wolf captures only 14 percent of what it stalks. The true deadly killer is one that hardly anyone would think of: the dragonfly. According to a 2012 study from researchers at Harvard University, the dragonfly manages to capture an astounding 95 percent of its targeted prey. It may not look as glamorous or be the subject of fan adulation—it's unlikely anyone sees the tiny flying alien look-alike as a kindred spirit—but it's a far more effective predator. Its eyes have developed to spot the tiniest deviations in motion. Its wings allow it to swerve and swoop in unimaginably quick configurations. And its brain has evolved to not only see possible targets but predict their future movements with startling accuracy. The dragonfly is so good not only because it sees what its prey is doing, but because it can also predict what it will do and plan its response accordingly.

In the world of poker, Erik is the dragonfly. He doesn't strut or preen. He doesn't announce his presence with a roar. He just watches quietly— and then changes his hunting approach based on what he's observed in his prey. He doesn't just know what his opponents are doing. He can predict what they'll do and how they will look doing it, and he will craft his own future movements accordingly. It's fitting that, while an insect rather than a bird, the dragonfly is a creature that flies. There's a distinctly avian quality to Erik's watchfulness.

The first time I see Erik's dragonfly stealth mode in action is in a hand that I don't actually watch in person, but on a stream, a few years after it happens. I've heard its legend and have tracked it down to review in advance of my own foray into live poker. It's May 2015, and Erik finds himself heads up for the title of EPT Grand Final Super High Roller champion—a €100,000 buy-in event where the winner will get over €2 million. His opponent is a young newcomer from Poland, Dzmitry Urbanovich. Over the past several months, Urbanovich has been ripping up the European poker scene. In March, he won the EPT high roller event in Malta, for over half a million, followed closely by three wins and one second-place finish in side events at the same festival. He's in the running for the Global Poker Index Player of the Year. He's on an absolute tear. "It was classic young gun versus dinosaur stuff," Erik tells me later. I haven't mentioned my dragonfly theory to him, and even if I had, he'd likely still argue for dinosaur status. Even though he keeps making final tables, he still sees himself as a lumbering beast of the past, constantly waiting for that fatal asteroid.

The match begins with Urbanovich in a commanding three-to-one chip lead. But over the last several hours, Erik has clawed his way back and has taken the leading position. At the start of the dragonfly hand, he has forty-one big blinds' worth of chips to Urbanovich's seventeen. Erik is in the big blind, with jack-four of diamonds. It's not a stellar hand, but heads up, any suited hand, especially one with a high card, soars in value. His opponent limps into the pot, calling the amount of the big blind, and Erik checks. The flop comes ace-ace-six, with two spades and one diamond. Not much there for Erik to hang on to, other than the possibility of running diamonds. Erik checks. Urbanovich checks as well. So far, no extra money at all has gone in the middle. The turn: the king of diamonds, giving Erik the flush draw. He checks again. Now Urbanovich bets three hundred thousand, or about half the pot. With his flush draw, Erik calls. The river is a five of hearts—a complete blank. Both the spade and the diamond flush have missed. The straight draws have missed. And Erik has nothing but jack-high—not where you want to find yourself with lots of money at stake. He checks. And Urbanovich bets just under half the pot. At this stage, many a player would instantly fold. What is there to think about when you hold a hand that has missed completely and is beat even by other high-card hands? But Erik is not many a player. He's been watching, he's been flexing his wings, and he has predicted that this specific scenario may unfold.

He shakes his head. For the first time, he breaks his signature table pose, left elbow resting on the table rail, arm extended across his chest with his hand resting on his right shoulder. He scratches his chin. He leans back and lets out a sigh. He bites his lip. He shrugs to himself. He stares at Urbanovich and at the board. Three minutes have gone by and he still has not folded. After one final look at Urbanovich, he throws some chips in the middle: he has made the call. Urbanovich flips over four-deuce of spades, for a missed flush draw, and Erik's jack-high is good. Urbanovich raises his eyebrows with a slight smile, as if he can't quite believe it. After a battle that lasts over five hours, Erik goes on to win the title and what is, at that point, the largest ever cash of his career. In winning, he is his usual humble self. "I would have been thrilled with second," he tells Joe Stapleton, the commentator interviewing him at the trophy presentation. "I'm obviously much happier with first."

How do you make such a huge call with basically nothing, I wonder? I doubt that I'd ever have the courage to do that—especially on television, where I risk the whole world (or whatever tiny slice of it might choose to watch, which feels very whole-world-like when you're in the bright lights) seeing me set my money on fire. That ability, the one I sorely lack, comes from the dragonfly effect. You observe the slightest motion. Your muscles are primed to respond. And you use your experience to anticipate what your opponent will do and act accordingly. The observation, in Erik's case, is on several levels. There's the knowledge he's accumulated over decades of this general type of situation. "It feels like an ace raises pre-flop. Even likely a king does, too," he says. He's played enough heads up matches to know that the typical aggressive opponent—and Urbanovich is as aggressive as they come—won't be looking to limp in with one of the best cards in the deck in his hand. He will apply pressure right away. "And he's not betting a queen," Erik continues. The queen actually has showdown value: it beats any other missed draw that Erik might hold. "So the bluff is just way more likely than it appears."

But that's just general observation of the past. What really sets Erik apart is his ability to parse the specifics of every opponent. He's come a long way from letting himself fall into Johnny Chan's trap. How has Urbanovich been playing up until now? The answer is, extremely aggressively. Earlier, it was the typical aggression of the strong player. But when they got heads up, that level ratcheted up a notch. As they played hand after hand, Erik observed certain patterns that didn't appear before. "He wasn't too crazy until we got heads up," Erik says. And then he went wild. "His betting did factor in. If he had a hand, is that the way he would bet it? It didn't feel like the story added up."

Typically, Erik acts rather quickly. Here, he takes almost five minutes. "I was trying to go through how he bet the other hands when he had it," he tells me. "With all of the other factors, it was a complex hand." In the past, Urbanovich had bet his big hands for big value—because, as a good player, he realized that he couldn't just bet big with his big bluffs. And he even bet his middling hands with confidence, for what's called thin value: you don't have the best hand you could, but you recognize that you're still getting value from worse hands, and so where many players elect to just check with a marginal hand, so that they don't risk getting raised or called by better hands, you are happy to bet and get paid that extra bit. "He was crushing the tour at the time," Erik tells me. Someone who is running hot is more likely to make moves—and more likely to be betting early with anything decent. "When you're on that kind of streak, it feels like it's yours," Erik says. It doesn't feel like you're running a bluff. It's not difficult. It's yours to take. You are invincible. Certain things that Urbanovich did as he told his usual story weren't present here, Erik decided. This was not the line a player on a streak would take with a value hand.

What's more, Erik is very much aware of how he himself appears. As an old-school pro, he has an old-school image. ("Do you ever bluff?" Urbanovich asks him during one hand a bit earlier in the heads up match. The answer, of course, is yes, but not in that particular spot, where Erik holds the second nut flush, or the second best possible hand on that board. Urbanovich can't find the fold and ends up losing a chunk of his chips.) And the young gun, lacking Erik's experience, may fail to realize that the older opponent isn't just capable of bluffing. He's capable of calling with jack-high. That, too, factors into his aggression. If you think you can get someone to fold with enough pressure, you do it. Only you better do it in the same way each time—otherwise, the observant dragonfly will spot the deviation in motion and act accordingly.

It's all an incredibly complex process, and one that, at this point, I can't fully grasp. Which is what I now tell Erik. And then he laughs. He's ready to tell me his real secret. "The key was, Ike [Haxton] gave me a coffee pill, so I wasn't falling over. It was critical because I was tired." He'd never done something like that in the past, he says, and he hasn't since. "But it was a relevant factor to my energy." Erik was at his limit. He knew he needed energy—pure physical energy. And he asked for what he needed. (*Research caffeine pills*, I jot down.)

In the animal kingdom, he's the killer dragonfly. If we're talking military strategy, he'd be the head of the guerilla infiltration team. Watch from the shadows, don't announce yourself with any flashy movements, blend perfectly into your surroundings, and observe the local forces to see how, exactly, they should be approached. No one-size-fits-all weapon. No predetermined strategy. Just an eminently flexible, and ultimately deadly, system rooted in deep patience and observation before anything else—and then a willingness to do whatever it takes, given the circumstances, to emerge victorious.

"The best players don't really care how they look," Erik says. "The artistry of the top players is fun to watch. And sometimes it can go horribly wrong, because you're so far out on the edge. In no limit hold'em especially, you can look like the biggest imbecile in the world. Like, what in the world was this guy thinking? And you have to be OK with that."

In fact, he continues, he doesn't care how many seeming mistakes I make as long as my thinking is solid. "Sometimes you can even play really bad hands, as long as you have good reasons for why it will work." It's not always the worst thing to play my off-suit jack-ten—if I know exactly why I'm doing it and what I'm hoping to accomplish. If I have a solid battle plan based on good intel, onward.

I tell him about my war epiphany—not in detail, but something really eloquent along the lines of "So, really, poker is like war. And I need a good strategy."

He thinks for a second. "I look at it like you're part of a jazz band." Not what I was expecting, but then again, things with Erik rarely are. "You're trying to play connected and in sync with the rest of the players.

It has nothing to do with you, really. That's not the jazz part. It's all about what are these guys doing, and how do I respond to it?" He continues, "I think there have been players that are successful because they have a style. But to the best extent that you can, you have to be a free thinker. You don't want to have one style, you know?"

It's a very New York analogy. And I do love jazz. It's a softer, more fluid way of looking at it. My vision is a zero-sum one, where his leaves room for a more positive-sum interaction. Mine assumes casualties. His implies that you will be playing together for quite some time, and that you will evolve together as well. Respond to each other, grow over time. It explains his success—if a new player comes in or you switch from big band to cool jazz to free jazz, you have to learn the new language to survive. And he always has.

I admit to feeling a bit deflated. We're only one hand in and I feel like I have to work on basically everything. There's just so much to remember.

"You'll be OK," he assures me. "It doesn't so much rely on memory as it will on experience." I'm playing poorly, but I'm playing. "I'm anxious for you to get more hands in. Your job right now is just to get used to what a good hand is, and how hands play out, and what plays are possible, and what plays are crazy. There's nothing like getting in there and making a bunch of mistakes."

I'm certainly well on my way in that respect.

BUT IT TURNS OUT, despite the dispiriting start, I may be on my way in other respects as well. The jazz analogy was poetic and inspiring. But it's the war mentality that gets me to my first victory—and it can't come soon enough. Playing online is just the first step in my schedule, after all. I've yet to play my first live game—and I won't be allowed to until I can manage better than that ill-fated jack-ten—and the online training is taking longer than I thought it would. I can't make it to New Jersey quite often enough. I can't force myself to sit in random cafés quite long enough to play all the events I want to—I'm developing quite the unhealthy caffeine habit. And I certainly can't multi-table—the term for having multiple tables open at the same time and playing many games at once, either cash, tournament, or both, which is what basically every online pro does. The multi-tabling hand record is held by Randy Lew, or nanonoko, the screen name by which everyone knows him. Back in 2012, Randy set a Guinness world record by playing between twenty-five and forty tables at a time, for a record 23,493 hands in eight hours. The only requirement was that he end with a profit, to discourage him from simply opening tables and folding all his hands. The end result: a profit of $7.65. A far cry from his usual performance, but a demonstration of just how much information a seasoned online professional is capable of taking in at any given moment. (The record for most tables played in an hour is held by the French pro Bertrand Grospellier, popularly known as ElkY. He played sixty-two Sit 'n' Go tables at once. And he, too, ended in the black.) Me, I've yet to master a consistent profit on one. The days are getting shorter. The weather's getting colder. The Main Event is getting closer. And my goal seems sadly out of reach.

"Can't I just skip this and go straight to playing live?" I groan. "No" is all Erik says. "No, you can't." I want to be the little kid who whines, *But you never played online when you were starting out!* But I hold back. I know better. Had he had the opportunity to practice at that rate, he would've set records of his own. He's never been one to forgo a way of making himself better.

It's nine o'clock in the evening, and I'm exhausted. I've been playing in a sixteen-dollar buy-in online tournament since five p.m. I've got plenty of coffee; the owner of the store walked over awhile back to ask if he could play a few hands. I'd been worried he was going to kick me out for sitting too long without ordering more food—I ate lunch here but lunch has come and gone. Turned out he was a poker fan himself. I explained that I couldn't let him play: not only is it not allowed to have anyone else play on your account, but I was recording this for my coach. He shrugged and wished me luck.

There were over two hundred players to start. We are down to just over sixty. The top twenty will get paid. I find myself seated at a new virtual table, and who happens to be to my left but someone whose name is framed in red—the site allows you to color-code any player, and red is my color of choice for the most aggressive opponents I face. I don't remember this screen name, but it seems I've previously labeled this particular guy an AIA, or "Aggressive Idiot Asshole," as much for his betting patterns as for the fact that he referred to me variously as "cunt" and "stupid bitch" the last time we played, according to my notes. (The games have an open chat function, and the players are not afraid to use it. When it comes to me, most comments tend to be of the less-than-pleasant variety, though one player did inject some humor when I beat him in a close hand: "Bad dog." There's no actual conversation or dialogue, though, as my policy is to never respond when someone addresses me.)

On this particular hand, I happen to flop an ace-high flush, one of the best hands you can have. I'm holding a suited ace-three of hearts, and the three cards on the board are all hearts. There are two people in the hand against me: Aggressive Idiot Asshole, and someone I've never played before. The first person to act decides to check. I'm up next, and I can either check or bet. I know I have the best hand. I want to make as much money as I can from it, not just win it. Checking runs the risk of nobody betting, keeping the pot small. Betting runs the risk of everyone folding, which means I don't win anything extra. Here is where my behavioral assessment background comes in handy: I have no doubt that Aggressive Idiot Asshole is going to bet because he always bets when he plays against me, and always bets big. So I check. And he bets. A very large amount. The first player folds. Even here, I don't raise—I simply call the bet. The next card that comes is an ace. Aggressive Idiot goes all in: clearly, I'm a weak, passive girl who will be frightened by the big scary card and fold. I call. AIA shows his hand, which is, quite simply, air: an unsuited king and queen that have completely missed the board. I have the best possible hand, or the nuts, as poker players would call it: an ace-high flush. I win. I double my chips, to nearly thirteen thousand, making me one of the chip leaders at a point where the average number of chips is hovering around eight thousand. (I will exercise the good taste to not transcribe in full the stream of invectives that was subsequently hurled in my direction. Though it's tempting. AIA, if you're out there reading this, know that, with sheer force of will, I'm protecting your good name.) With that lead, I will go on to win my largest ever tournament: just after eleven p.m., I finish in first place. Thank you, Aggressive Idiot Asshole. Please come again. ("Can you break your no chat rule and tell these guys that there is some *great* poker at Aria?" Erik asks me after he reviews my play. "We need some of these fish out here in Vegas. Tell them they can really win big.")

Almost every time I play, I hear Erik telling me: "Pick your spots." Any idiot can win any given hand with the best cards. That's not the point of poker. You get dealt the best cards only every so often, and if you wait for them every time, your chips will run out. What's more, you won't win any money once you finally have those aces in hand, because even the least attentive player will have noticed that you only play with the best hand and will stay as far away as possible. So even when you win, you will lose.

The point is winning over the long term—and winning as much

money as you possibly can with your best hands, all the while losing as little as possible with your worst. And in order to do that, you need to learn to pick your spots: know when to be aggressive, and how to be aggressive. The passive player doesn't win. And the scared player, who always thinks someone can beat him, doesn't win. But the openly aggressive player doesn't win, either; he follows the fate of Aggressive Idiot Asshole. You have to be a strategist. Not playing scared doesn't mean barreling your way over everything and everyone. It means being aggressive, yes, but strategically so: against the right people, in the right circumstances.

My jack-ten fiasco hurt. But it has brought me here. I waited. I assessed my enemy. I crafted a play with him, specifically, in mind. And, sure, I held the most powerful weapon of all—the absolute best hand. There was no need for strategic deception. But I could easily have bet big, betrayed my position, and instead of winning a huge pot won a tiny one. Even aggressive idiots are capable of folding from time to time. This time, I waited. I paused. I adapted. And when he fell, I didn't gloat—I pressed my advantage. This was but one skirmish, and I now had more forces, but the end of the battle was hours away. Still, I played to win, and I acted to win—not because I didn't want to look weak. Aggressive Idiot gave me his chips, but I didn't then go on to lose them. And that, at least, is something.

I feel good. And victorious. And the feeling lasts. A few weeks after my first poker win, I'm approached by a magazine to write an article. I look back through my old emails. I've played with this opponent before: she's asked me to write in the past, multiple times. It was always a little too small a sum for the effort required, so I'd never actually written anything. Every time I mentioned money, she walked away. Part of me just wants to accept this assignment: it's interesting, I've done a lot of work on the background already, and the money isn't all that bad. I've been offered worse. It would actually be a nice and needed boost at this precise moment.

But on some level, part of me must remember: you can't play scared. You can't be afraid of how you look. You can't be afraid someone will walk away because of what you do or don't do. You have to play smart. And so I decide to check back: I'm not really doing much freelance work these days, I respond. I'm working on my next book. Not a refusal, but something that leaves the action open. Turn the decision momentum so that the power of position is on my side. Do nothing without first gauging my opponent's reaction. Reveal nothing about the strength of my hand until I have to. A day later, I receive another email: What if we paid you more than we've offered in the past? This is an opening, and old me would have jumped at it. New me decides I don't actually have to jump at anything; the smarter strategy might lie in another direction. I'm not sure that would be enough, I counter, since I really need to be paid more than I am at my home magazine to make it worth my while given the constraints on my time. In effect, I'm calling the bet, but I don't raise. I simply stay in the hand to see what will happen. Three dollars a word, comes the next email. Done. I've won the hand and extracted more value than I ever thought I could from it. Thank you, Aggressive Idiot Asshole; you have taught me well.

I still don't feel ready to hit the actual felt, but the virtual felt is feeling decidedly less foreign. Maybe I'll make my WSOP deadline after all. I'm suddenly eager to get to Vegas and try my hand at *real* poker—which online poker somehow still doesn't quite seem to me to be.

A Man's World

New York, Winter 2016

"Playing poker is also a masculine ritual, and, most times, los-
ers feel either sufficiently chagrined or sufficiently reflective to
retire, if not with grace, at least with alacrity."

DAVID MAMET, "ABOUT MEN," 1986

The crowd quiets down. Evening gown décolletés, T-shirts that hail from the nineties—I spot not only a Nirvana acid wash but a Metallica homage that may or may not be a concert original—tuxes and baseball caps: everyone looks expectantly at the raised podium.

We are in the grand circular dome of a gilded hall, split among some thirty tables. Some of us are celebrities. Actors. Directors. Athletes. A Knicks star I'm supposed to recognize. Some are celebrities of the poker world. World Series of Poker champions, World Poker Tour champions. Record holders. Stars past and present. Some just love poker and have the cash to buy a seat or table, in support of a worthy charity—or are lucky enough to work for bosses who do. Some, like me, are nobodies—no cash, no fame—sneaking in under the radar. But we are all here to do the same thing: play some poker.

"Now, I know you've been listening to a lot of speeches and just want to get to the game"—appreciative stirrings—"but if you just bear with me for another five minutes . . ." The crowd begins to turn back to side conversations. There may as well be a collective groan. "Just kidding. Dealers, shuffle up and deal." The magic words. Laughter fills the room. It's just past seven o'clock, and the night finally begins.

This is my first live poker tournament. And it's not at all how I imagined or planned it. I have a lengthy trip to Vegas on the calendar in just a few weeks—Erik and I have been working on the itinerary. What in the world is this? Until a few minutes ago, I didn't even know to be nervous. I'd thought I'd be attending my first tournament as an observer, to watch Erik play before hitting the felt myself some weeks down the line. When I was handed an innocuous-looking white card at the check-in table— two lines, one indicating the charity of the night and the other, a table number (five)—I assumed it was for dinner seating. Erik, the one who got me in here in the first place, has other ideas. He gives me a friendly wave. I glare at him.

He greets me with his usual slightly lopsided, goofy smile. "I thought this would be more fun," he tells me. "Enough with the online robots. Time you played your first live hands."

"But I can't play live yet," I protest. Suddenly, Vegas seems very far away. What was I thinking? One online tournament win does not a poker player make. I feel like I've barely just figured out the bet slider on the computer screen. "I haven't prepared. I don't know how to do anything in an actual game."

"It's exciting!" he replies. "You'll be great. Beginner's luck."

"Come on. You know you don't believe in that."

"Hey, it'll be fun. Jamie is playing, too. You can meet her." Jamie is Erik's daughter. Poker runs in the family, it seems—she won her last tournament, Erik tells me with obvious pride. It was another charity event, and she outlasted a few hundred players.

Any other players in the family, I ask?

"Actually, my mother used to play." And win. Erik tells me how she once took everyone down on his dad's movie set—he was directing a documentary film, and the crew got together for a friendly game. His mom emerged a few hundred dollars richer.

"I'm afraid I'm no Jamie," I say. "I don't think I'll be winning anything."

Erik looks over at Jamie with a huge smile. "I really am curious how far I could take her as a poker player. But I don't know. I don't even know that I want to encourage it," he adds after a pause. "Because it's a particularly harsh environment for women. It's almost impossible to be a female poker player and not get online harassment or comments or whatever it is."

That's not the first time he's mentioned it, and this time, something seems to stick in my head. I can't quite figure out what, but my brain starts churning.

The women who do play seriously, though, Erik continues, tend to be in a class of their own. "You know, what's interesting is that the women who play poker are, I would say, much smarter than the men. If you talk to Vanessa Selbst or Liv Boeree, these girls are really brilliant. I mean there are obviously plenty of very bright men as well. But somehow we have a really impressive crop of female players."

I'm not surprised, given what he's said about the environment. It's like finding high achievers with dyslexia. They didn't succeed because of it but in spite of it, and that makes them all the more talented. As a woman, you have such an uphill battle that you have to be doubly exceptional to survive.

I ask if he at least has any last-minute tips. Anything that can help me move from the online world to this foreign landscape? Nah, he says, just play. At this point, tips would just make my brain explode.

"Oh, there is one thing. Charity tournaments are shove fests."

Shove fests?

"They're basically turbos. The blinds go up really quickly. You're going to have to be aggressive. Really ramp it up."

I can only imagine I look a bit shell-shocked. The super-aggro style, I've been learning, isn't exactly my natural habitat. Whenever I try, I wade into jack-ten off-suit territory—wrong place, wrong time, wrong approach.

"Have you downloaded SnapShove?" he asks.

Snap what now?

"It's an app. I mean, it's brilliant. I use it. It was written by this guy, Max Silver, who actually got deep in the Main this year."

"Oh yeah?"

"Yeah. When you're short, you encounter these mathematical situations. SnapShove is basically all you need."

"OK, I'll get it now." I start searching through the app store.

"Have you heard the expression snap fold? A snap fold, you do it immediately. You're thrilled to let it go. So, snap fold. This lets you shove with basically the same enthusiasm. It tells you which hands to go with when you have different amounts of big blinds."

I start looking through the unfamiliar lists of hands and percentages. If online poker feels like foreign territory, this is altogether Martian. I'm thinking of snap folding out of here, back to the safety of Brooklyn. Erik must see something in my expression, because he adds an incentive.

"Actually now that I think about it, this is going to be great practice for Vegas. We do need to work on your aggression. Nowhere better than a turbo."

As I said, that proposition doesn't exactly fill me with glee. Over and over, we've discovered that, despite my promising win against the aggressive idiot, my own aggression needs some major life support. It doesn't come naturally or feel natural—and my consistent inability to rev my inner engine and mow down my opponents is weighing on me more than I realized. Even in my tiny online victory, the strategy that ultimately won was to find the aggressive idiots who would be aggro in my stead, so that I could passively take what was on offer. I didn't exactly pull off any momentous attacks or run any bluffs to be proud of.

Whenever he watches me forgo the aggressive line in favor of the more passive approach—calling instead of raising, folding to a bet on instinct when I should really consider re-raising as a bluff instead, three-betting (or raising a raise) with only the best hands instead of a more aggressively considered selection—he tells me I'm missing important opportunities. "You're getting the fundamentals, but I really think I would rather you start off practicing being a more aggressive player," he tells me. "There's more variance, but you learn more that way. You're involved in a lot of hands." It's OK that the aggression doesn't always succeed. More hands mean more learning, easy as that. And I already know how he and Dan feel about failure.

What's more, he thinks, the fact that I'm female may work in my direction—though that's not certain. "It's a really interesting question: What's the better reputation to have? A maniac reputation, where some people will end up calling you when you have a hand? Or a more conservative reputation, where now you can get away with things more? I really don't know the answer." But before I get a reputation for anything, he says, my anonymity as a female may make it easier to get away with the types of aggressive lines that I'm just not taking.

There's the troublesome suited queen-eight, which I seem to misplay each time I get my hands on it. I recount one hand where I called from the small blind after a raise, only to see Erik start shaking his head before the hand history is even halfway out of my mouth. I stop myself midsentence. "Calling here is a mistake, unless you have a very good read," he tells me. The hand is simply not strong enough to play multiway out of position. I nod, sadly. It's so pretty. I'd hate to fold it. "Actually, you should seriously consider raising it instead," Erik says. It's not strong enough to call but I should raise? "Raise big. Maybe 6x," which means six times the prior raise size. That seems an awful lot for a hand that's not very strong. Erik explains. "Use your image. Coming from you, that's super strong. And even if you get called, you're not in terrible shape. But just calling is lighting chips on fire."

I seem to be lighting a lot of fires. Like when I call the same queen-eight from the big blind—"That's fine; you're getting a good price"—and then fold on a flop where I miss making any pairs after someone bets and someone else calls. "You should consider check-raising here," Erik says. "Coming from you, the check-raise here screams strength." If a player is good, he'll fold most of his hands at that point, so crazy would I have to be to attempt to bluff into three players.

There's a whole lot of "coming from you" that gets thrown in, and I start to see his point. Not only am I an unknown quantity, but I'm female—even online. And even when players can't see my face—"That image will be even more valuable when you play live"—they are met with Puppy. Yes, people will bluff me more. But they may also fold more when I make crazy moves, just because they don't think I'm capable of making them. I can use that to my advantage to play hands more aggressively, accumulating chips in a way I otherwise wouldn't. I've simply taken the passive line by default. Calling, checking, folding. Instead, Erik is telling me, I should challenge myself to be active. To raise. To check-raise. To three-bet.

There's a false sense of security in passivity. You think that you can't get into too much trouble—but really, every passive decision leads to a slow but steady loss of chips. And chances are, if I'm choosing those lines at the table, there are deeper issues at play. Who knows how many prover-bial chips a default passivity has cost me throughout my life. How many times I've walked away from situations because of someone else's show of strength, when I really shouldn't have. How many times I've passively stayed in a situation, eventually letting it get the better of me, instead of actively taking control and turning things around. Hanging back only seems like an easy solution. In truth, it can be the seed of far bigger problems.

When I look around the room now and think back over Erik's throw-away comment about the poker environment, I realize part of what's bothering me. The crowd is full of women—but the people sitting down to play at the tables are mostly men. Sure, there's a woman or two at every table (far more, I'll soon realize, than I'll ever see again, save at a so-called Ladies Event; in any given tournament field, the percentage of women participants consistently hovers around three), but for the most part, it's the bros in suits who are here to play. The evening gowns and décolletés are here to watch and socialize.

It comes to me then, the thing that's been nagging at me, and I don't at all like the realization: a lot of my failure to up the aggression factor is due to my social conditioning. Over the years, I've learned that it doesn't pay to be aggressive while female. It's unattractive to those in power—namely men, but also some of those women who have managed to make it to the top and now don't want to jeopardize their position.

It's not just perception. It's reality. I remember reporting a story a number of years ago about a woman who'd been offered that rare thing in academia, an assistant professorship in the philosophy department of a small liberal arts college. When she emailed the college in question to ask about parts of the offer, the professorship was summarily rescinded. Ap-parently, she was no longer a good fit.

Hannah Riley Bowles, a senior lecturer at Harvard's Kennedy School of Government who specializes in negotiating while female, has an explanation: in her research, she has found that women, but not men, are penalized for asking for more money in a negotiation. They're penalized by men—and they're penalized by other women. Perceived aggression in women is not only not valued; it's seen in a negative light. In men, on the other hand, it's viewed as evidence of great potential. If a woman has managed to make it to a leadership position, she will be seen far more negatively than her male counterparts if she acts in a way that's viewed as authoritative or assertive. If a woman is hired into a workplace, she's far more likely to be judged on her social skills than her competence; men, meanwhile, continue to be valued for the qualifications that actually got them hired in the first place.

When women act in a more feminine, less confrontational way, we aren't being shy or stupid. We are being smart. We are reacting to the realities of the world, knowing that to fail to do so is to incur potentially life-changing penalties. We are socialized into our passivity. After all, don't we want to be liked . . . so that we will be hired and make money and make a living?

I know all this, but I had somehow thought that my training in psychology, my knowledge of these biases, the fact that I've achieved some form of professional success in my life, meant that I had overcome my socialization. That I was standing up for myself. That I wasn't letting what the higher-ups found attractive or not dictate how I behaved. But what poker is showing me, now that I take a moment to really look, is how far that is from the truth. Here I am, learning an entirely new skill, in an entirely new world. I'm studying with the best of the best. I have no bad habits, no prior poor thought patterns, just a blank slate for listening, learning, and absorbing the best approach. I should have, by all accounts, learned correctly. Except of course, that isn't the whole story. A truly blank slate would have listened to her coach and executed—because why not? If Erik tells me to try out a strategy, I should try it out. And I simply haven't been able to. Whenever I do, it feels off and I fail. It isn't that I'm incapable of learning an aggressive approach or understanding its merits. It's that I *have* learned and understood, and want to make it work—but can't because of the emotional baggage that has accumulated, without my awareness, throughout my entire professional life. I'm not a blank slate after all. It isn't a pleasant realization, but it is an important one. Now that I see it, perhaps I can start working through it.

If I don't, I'm not long for the poker world. Part of the reason that there are so few women in the game is that, in an environment that's 97 percent male, the biases we've had to negotiate all our lives are put on a massive scale. There's a lot to overcome, internally, if we're to make it with the best.

Erik may have spotted what I'm only now realizing before I did. He's far from being a maniacal, aggressive player himself—and the fact that he is not so subtly pushing me in the aggro direction makes me think that he's seen that it's a part of me that needs work.

I shake my head in disbelief. That's not me. That's other women. Isn't it?

Erik misunderstands my discomfort as more nerves. "Don't worry. Here, grab a glass of wine. And if you lose quickly, the food here's pretty good," he adds.

"I thought you told me never to drink when I'm playing."

"This is for charity. Doesn't apply. And it may help with the nerves. Make you a little more willing to gamble."

I guess it can't hurt. I'm certainly shaken enough. I take a glass and sit down at the table, scanning the faces. Luckily, I don't spot anyone familiar—the pros have been placed elsewhere. The woman to my left—the only other one at the table—is surreptitiously looking up hand rankings on her cell phone. Does a straight beat a flush? A flush a straight? I feel slightly better. At least I've got those two down.

I TRY TO CATCH Erik's eye for some reassurance, but he's seated on the other side of the room, next to his daughter. They're laughing at something—not at me, I hope. I try to take deep breaths, the calming, meditative approach I preach so frequently in my writing and talks. Mindfulness to help channel calm and circumspection. Surely, if I tell others to do it, I can do it myself. And for a second there, it almost works.

And then the first cards hit the table. This is nothing like playing online. I feel like I'm not getting enough air, a drowning victim who thought she knew how to swim after practicing in the kiddie pool but is slowly realizing that the ocean is not nearly the same thing. (I'll come to think of charity events as the kiddie pool—but that comes much later.) Everything I thought I learned flies out the window. It's like my first time playing online, only infinitely worse because everyone can see my struggle. In the virtual world, they didn't know I couldn't figure out the bet slider and kept misclicking my bets out of a mix of nerves and incompetence. They didn't see me cringe after badly misplaying, or how excited I got when my cards were happy ones—or that I call cards happy or unhappy in my head, and sometimes out loud, depending on how much I like them. Here, I'm out in the open. So many lights and sounds and smells and people to keep an eye on. How does Erik do it?

I'm overwhelmed. I can't keep track of what's going on. I'm certain everyone can tell my hands are shaking. I almost fold pocket aces before the flop. Playing the game live, it turns out, is nothing like reading about it, watching it, or even playing it from the comfort of my computer screen.

But somehow, slowly, I start to doggy-paddle. I don't fold the aces. I may not get as much value from them as I could—once I realize what I have, I excitedly over-bet, effectively shutting down further action—but I do take the pot. Somehow, I luck into winning a few good-sized hands. I'm not bluffing much; I'm too scared. I get a few decent pairs. I'd love to tell you what, exactly, they are, but my brain was so busy trying to re-member and take in everything else that I've forgotten them. Yet despite the memory lapses, something of my initial training has seeped in. I re-member to pause before every decision. I'm still playing the most straight-forward game imaginable—how do people ever bluff under the bright lights?—but at least I'm considering the possibilities and acknowledging my limitations. Sometimes, I even know what I'm supposed to do—I don't usually do it, but at least I understand it. There's a moment when I bet just the right amount and am rewarded with a big stack of chips and a "Well played" from my hedge fund opponent. The hedge fund guy plays it cooler. I can't help smiling. I feel like I'm five years old and just got a star from Mrs. Scott, my kindergarten teacher, for saying a full sentence of English correctly. (I didn't speak a word of the language when I started school. We'd just moved from the Soviet Union.)

The brief triumph is quickly forgotten as the fear returns that soon everyone will spot me for the fake I am. Around me, players are getting eliminated, and I can't help feeling that I should have been one of them already. The room seems to get smaller—the peripheral tables have emp-tied and we move closer to the middle. I'm shuffled from table to table. I don't have a chance to get to know my opponents: just as I get into the swing of a particular table, it's time to move on. I can't judge them. I can't read them. All I can do is try to play as well as I can. But at least I'm still playing. That means I'm either not quite the fishiest of the fish—a "fish," I've learned, is the nickname awarded to bad players with money to lose; "whales" are the ones with a *lot* of money to lose; "sharks" are the pros who pick them off one by one—or a very lucky fishy this particular evening.

"That one's a live one," Erik tells me, more than once, during the tournaments I watch him play. Bait. The players who will reward you with endless cash if you're patient. Live ones are good. And a live one is what I feel I am, at the moment. Despite still sitting at the table, I can't shake the feeling I don't belong here. I can imagine the businessmen at the tables looking at me and saying it in their heads. *The live one has landed.*

A few hours in, I'm surprised to find myself starting to experience a new kind of feeling. This is fun. I'm not half-bad. Of course, the psychologist part of my brain is screaming a single word: overconfidence. I know that the term "novice" doesn't even begin to describe me and that my current success is due mostly to luck—but part of me is certainly thinking that maybe, just maybe, I have a knack for this.

The biases I know all about in theory, it turns out, are much tougher to fight in practice. Online, I was working so hard on grasping the fundamentals of basic strategy that I didn't have the chance to notice. Now that I have some of the more basic concepts down, the shortcomings of my reasoning hit me in the face. After an incredibly lucky straight draw on a hand I had no business playing—the dealer helpfully tells me as much with a "You've got to be kidding me" as I turn over my hand and win the pot—I find myself thinking maybe there's something to the hot hand, the notion that a player is "hot," or on a roll. Originally, it was taken from professional basketball, from the popular perception that a player with a hot hand, who'd made a few shots, would continue to play better and make more baskets. But does it actually exist—and does *be-lieving* it exists, even if it doesn't, somehow make it more real? In basketball, the psychologists Thomas Gilovich, Amos Tversky, and Robert Vallone argued it was a fallacy of reasoning—when they looked at the Boston Celtics and the Philadelphia 76ers, they found no evidence that the hot hand was anything but illusion. But in other contexts, mightn't it play out differently? I've had the conventional thinking drilled into me, yet now I think I'm on a roll. I should bet big. Definitely bet big.

That idea suffers a debilitating blow after a loss with a pair of jacks—a hand that's actually halfway decent. After a flop that has an ace and a queen on it—both cards that could potentially make any of my multiple opponents a pair higher than mine—I refuse to back down. I've had bad cards for the last half an hour. I deserve to win here! I lose over half my chips by refusing to fold—hello, sunk cost fallacy! We'll be seeing you again, many times. And then, instead of reevaluating, I start to chase the loss: Doesn't this mean I'm due for a break? I can't possibly keep losing. It simply isn't fair. Gambler's fallacy—the faulty idea that probability has a memory. If you are on a bad streak, you are "due" for a win. And so I continue to bet when I should sit a few hands out.

It's fascinating how that works, isn't it? Runs make the human mind uncomfortable. In our heads, probabilities should be normally distributed, that is, play out as described. If a coin is tossed ten times, about five of those should be heads. Of course, that's not how probability actually works—and even though a hundred heads in a row should rightly make us wonder if we're playing with a fair coin or stuck in a Stoppardian alternate reality, a run of ten or twenty may well happen. Our discomfort stems from the law of small numbers: we think small samples should mirror large ones, but they don't, really. The funny thing isn't our discomfort. That's understandable. It's the different flavors that discomfort takes when the runs are in our favor versus not. The hot hand and the gambler's fallacy are actually opposite sides of the exact same coin: positive recency and negative recency. We overreact to chance events, but the exact nature of the event affects our perception in a way it rightly shouldn't.

We have a mental image of the silly gamblers who think they're due to hit the magic score, and it's comforting to think that won't be us, that we'll recognize runs for what they are, statistical probabilities. But when it starts happening in reality, we get a bit jittery. "All these squalls to which we have been subjected are signs the weather will soon improve and things will go well for us," Don Quixote tells his squire, Sancho Panza, in Miguel de Cervantes's 1605 novel, "because it is not possible for the bad or the good to endure forever, from which it follows that since the bad has lasted so long a time, the good is close at hand." We humans have wanted chance to be equitable for quite some time. Indeed, when we play a game in which chance doesn't look like our intuitive view of it, we balk. Frank Lantz has spent over twenty years designing games. When we meet at his office at NYU, where he currently runs the Game Center, he lets me in on an idiosyncrasy of game design. "In video games where there are random events—things like dice rolls—they often skew the randomness so that it corresponds more closely to people's incorrect intuition," he says. "If you flip heads twice in a row, you're less likely to flip heads the third time. We know this isn't actually true, but it feels like it should be true, because we have this weird intuition about large numbers and how randomness works." The resulting games actually accommodate that wrongness, so that people don't feel like the setup is "rigged" or "unfair." "So they actually make it so that you're less likely to flip heads the third time," he says. "They jigger the probabilities."

For a long time, Lantz was a serious poker player. And one of the reasons he loves the game is that the probabilities are what they are: they don't accommodate. Instead, they force you to confront the wrongness of your intuitions if you are to succeed. "Part of what I get out of a game is being confronted with reality in a way that is not accommodating to my incorrect preconceptions," he says. The best games are the ones that challenge our misperceptions, rather than pandering to them in order to hook players.

Poker pushes you out of your illusions, beyond your incorrect comfort zone—if, that is, you want to win. "Poker wasn't designed by a game designer in the modern sense," Lantz points out. "And it's actually bad game design according to modern-day conceptions of how video games are designed. But I think it's *better* game design, because it doesn't pander." If you want to be a good player, you must acknowledge that you're not "due"—for good cards, good karma, good health, money, love, or whatever else it is. Probability has amnesia: each future outcome is completely independent of the past. But we persist in thinking that its memory is not only there but personal to us. We'll be rewarded, eventually, if we're only patient. It's only fair.

But here's the all-too-human element: we're just fine with runs when they are in our favor. Hence the hot hand. When we're winning, we don't think we're due for a change in the least. If the run is on our side, we're thrilled to let it continue indefinitely. We think the bad streaks are overdue to end yesterday, but no one wants the good to end.

Why do smart people persist in these sorts of patterns? As with so many biases, it turns out that there may be a positive element to these illusions—an element that's closely tied to the very thing I'm most interested in, our conceptions about luck. There's an idea in psychology, first introduced by Julian Rotter in 1966, called the locus of control. When something happens in the external environment, is it due to our own actions (skill) or some outside factor (chance)? People who have an internal locus of control tend to think that they affect outcomes, often more than they actually do, whereas people who have an external locus of control think that what they do doesn't matter too much; events will be what they will be. Typically, an internal locus will lead to greater success: people who think they control events are mentally healthier and tend to take more control over their fate, so to speak. Meanwhile, people with an external locus are more prone to depression and, when it comes to work, a more lackadaisical attitude.

Sometimes, though, as in the case of probabilities, an external locus is the correct response: nothing you do matters to the deck. The cards will fall how they may. But if we're used to our internal locus, which has served us well to get us to the table to begin with, we may mistakenly think that our actions will influence the outcomes, and that probability *does* care about us, personally. That we're due to be in a certain part of the distribution, because our aces have already been cracked twice today. They can't possibly fall yet again. We'll forget what historian Edward Gibbon warned about as far back as 1794, that "the laws of probability, so true in general, [are] so fallacious in particular"—a lesson history teaches particularly well. And while probabilities do even out in the long term, in the short term, who the hell knows. Anything is possible. I may even final table this charity thing.

One thing is for sure: unless I cure my distaste for bad runs and the sense of exuberance that envelops me during the good ones, I am going to lose a lot of money. And maybe if I lose it for long enough, I'll eventually stop thinking that the cards owe me anything at all—whether that's continued success or an end to a streak of bad runouts. Or that's the hope. Otherwise I'll be one broke poker player.

Despite my bumbling inadequacy, I manage to hang in at the charity event for just over three hours. At half past ten, I bust out on a hand I knew better than to play to the end—king-jack, unsuited. Didn't we just go over this? I chide myself. What was I thinking? Actually, I know exactly what I was—or wasn't, as the case may be—thinking: I was goaded into putting my money in the middle.

I raise. An aggressive hedge fund guy who is running over the table re-raises me. I make my first mistake by not folding. I can't help but think I'm being pushed around and decide to hold my ground. And that may well be true, but I'm not picking the best spot or way to do it. Part of me knows that holding my ground with such a marginal hand is a mistake—and that if I play at all, I should be raising instead, upping the aggression and running the bluff, Erik's "coming from you . . ." echoing through my head—but the other part lacks the nerve to raise and is too stubborn to fold. And so I call, leaving myself precious few chips. And then I whiff the flop completely. The board in no way matches my cards. I have almost no prospects of actually making the best hand. It's either bluff or get out. The hedge fund guy, though, is first to act, and he puts in a massive bet—enough to force me to go all in if I want to call. I don't really have many options. I can't bluff anymore, because if I call, I'm depending on the rest of the board to run out in my favor, with no real shot at winning, since even his bluffs likely beat my current hand. But just as I'm miserably about to fold my cards, a gentleman to my left intervenes.

"What? Are you going to let him get away with that?"

I laugh nervously.

"Come on, you have to call. He's bluffing, can't you see?"

The table all chimes in, confirming my duty to call, and I, putting aside everything I've learned, do so. The hedge fund guy turns over aces, and my first live poker tournament is at an end.

I wander away, hating myself. I knew better than to do that. That wasn't my knowledge playing. That was the worst possible combination of traits: insecurity and gutlessness, leading to half measures that will never win. I've let them get to me. I didn't want to be pushed around—but I wasn't comfortable doing the pushing around, either. And the result is this mess of a hand. I'm hopeless at this game. And apparently, I'm hopeless at life. A gutless female who wants to be liked more than she wants to win. Maybe I don't want to go to Vegas, after all. Maybe the WSOP is better off without me.

I wander over to watch Erik, who is, of course, still in the game.

"You're out?" he asks.

"Yup."

"What was the hand?" He leans back in his chair, shoving his cards lightly into the middle of the table—he's folding this one.

I tell him about the ill-fated king-jack, omitting all the details that I'm still too angry about to share.

"Yeah. You shouldn't have played that," he says matter-of-factly, never shy in pointing out mistakes. "I probably play king-jack less than most players. It's just not a good hand."

I nod, a bit miserably.

"But hey, you lasted awhile. So that's good. Pull up a chair."

As Erik lets me steal glances at his hole cards—this is called "sweating," I later learn—I ponder my failure to emerge onto the live poker scene with flying colors. The truth is, I haven't been a novice at something in a long time. I can't recall the last time I tried to learn an entirely new skill. I feel out of place. How did I fail so badly? Why couldn't I remember any of the skills and strategies I'd been studying and practicing so carefully? I thought I knew what I was doing. I'd even shown I knew it—at least some of it—when I was sitting comfortably ensconced behind a computer screen. Why did it all disappear when I needed it most, during this, my first live test? I did stay in for a few hours, true, but given my plays, I can't rightly attribute my temporary success to any real show of skill.

The simple truth is that I was overwhelmed. We've been primed to believe that memory is reliable, and that emotion makes memories more intense. Back in 1890, William James described emotional memories as "so exciting emotionally as almost to leave a scar upon the cerebral tissues." High emotion, high impact, high recall. According to that logic, all of my knowledge should have come out with flying colors in the intensity of the moment. I should have risen to the occasion, recalled what I'd been learning, and performed. But we now know that's not exactly true. Not only do memories change over time, but the more emotional the landscape, the less we're able to engage them with any specificity. Put us in a situation where emotions are running high—a beginner in a poker tournament, say—and no matter how certain we may be that we're in full command of everything, specific details will evade us. We'll be able to access the gist of the thing, but not the intricacies of the thing itself.

In other words, I'm not necessarily a poor student, as I brand myself that night—especially after I bow out early to go to bed, even though I should rightly stay and watch Erik play. (He ends up finishing second. "You'll need to up your late-night endurance," he tells me before I leave. "Poker's a marathon.") I'm just a novice, overwhelmed by emotion, who can't think clearly.

But here's what happens over time. Some events—a death, a tragic attack, a fatal accident—are emotional for everyone, always, by sheer virtue of what they are. But a poker tournament is emotional only if you're in a position similar to mine—a scared beginner. After you've been at it for a while, you forget what the big deal ever was. It becomes second nature.

At that level of knowledge, you no longer consciously process all the complicated actions required to play. There are, however, opportunities for learning at both stages. In the novice stage, everything is difficult and you have to work hard just to keep it straight. But you also *realize* how difficult it is—and are attuned to how much of your success is dependent on other people and on chance. Doing well at poker isn't just about playing well; it's also about playing well relative to everyone else—and even with the best players, you can still lose because chance can be a bitch. (The winner over Erik in that tournament? An absolute amateur.)

Once you gain proficiency, you also lose perspective. You go on autopilot—I've got this covered; I can even check my phone while behind the wheel, I'm that good. You forget that what you're doing is actually exceptionally difficult, and how much chance is involved. That, of course, is when you're most susceptible to bad luck. Car crashes happen most frequently near your home for two reasons: the first is simple base rates—you drive more frequently in your home area—but the second is comfort—if you're going on autopilot and texting anywhere, it's in the places that are most familiar.

The trick is to get past the plateau. The relationship between our awareness of chance and our skill is a U-curve. No skill: chance looms high. Relatively high skill: chance recedes. Expert level: you once again see your shortcomings and realize that no matter your skill level, chance has a strong role to play. In poker and in life, the learning pattern is identical.

I may be a scared and nervous novice, but at least I have the perspective to acknowledge it. And I'm starting to learn where many of my shortcomings are stemming from. That's no minor feat—and it's taken poker to bring it out.

That's the good part. The bad part is—well, my work is cut out for me. And my shortcomings are substantial. Here I am, eight months from the biggest tournament of the poker world, and I'm letting myself be goaded into a hopeless call with a hopeless hand. Theoretically, I've learned quite a bit. Practically, I'm a borderline lost cause. How can I ever aspire to play a $10,000 buy-in with professionals when I can't even hack a charity event with people who've never played before? How can I hope to compete in Vegas when I'm seemingly incapable of acting on any of the knowledge I've crammed into my head in the past few months even here, where the stakes are so low?

That night, I wake my husband up from a deep sleep to confide that I don't think I'll be able to make a go of it. The king-jack has got me down. The realization that I've internalized more gender stereotypes than I care to admit has got me down. The immensity of the whole undertaking has got me down. Somehow, sitting in front of a screen, I never felt the scope of the thing in the way one single night with actual players and cards and chips and all of it has made me appreciate. I don't even want to take the PATH to Jersey anymore, let alone a plane to Vegas. Maybe poker and I are not meant to be.

Part of my brain knows it's silly to jump to any conclusions from one night, but the rest of me just feels tired, dispirited, and disillusioned. I mean, come on, I couldn't even muster the stamina to stay a few hours more at the charity event to gain valuable experience, instead crawling off to go to bed like a little kid. How dare I think I can last in a multiday endeavor, twelve, thirteen, fourteen, hours a day, into the early hours of the morning?

"Go to sleep" comes a barely awake voice. "You always tell me everything looks better in the morning. Take your own advice."

He turns over, signaling the end of the conversation.

And so I go to sleep. And he's right. The next morning does bring clarity. I take my laptop bag, and I make my way to the subway. I may not be ready yet, but I'll be damned if I'm going to admit defeat. Wouldn't that be compounding stereotype on top of stereotype? I'll show them, I think as I board the PATH to Grove Street, a Starbucks firmly in my sights. I'll show them all.

No Bad Beats

Las Vegas, Winter 2017

"You never can tell whether bad luck may not after all turn out to be good luck. . . . One must never forget when misfortunes come that it is quite possible they are saving one from something much worse; or that when you make some great mistake, it may very easily serve you better than the best-advised decision."

WINSTON CHURCHILL, "MY EARLY LIFE," 1930

The one thing that tells you everything you need to know about Las Vegas is that it shouldn't exist. The incongruity hits you from the moment you first glimpse it from the airplane. First the mountains, capped with snow. The snow vanishes, and it's just mountains with patches of desert. Then simply desert with nothing to interrupt it. Soon after, neat squares of identical houses that look as if they were plucked straight from Monopoly. And suddenly, green, lush oases in the midst of it all: golf courses. The stark contrast the vibrant green forms with the yellows and browns that meet the eye wherever else you look is the most prominent visual cue that you are entering a zone that was not intended by nature.

Indeed, Vegas was dreamt up out of almost nothing. Before Hoover Dam gave it steady water and power, it was a struggling town most notable as a stopover for those who wanted to get to the *real* city, Los

Angeles. And it was hardly even that after its only railroad declared bankruptcy in the 1920s. A "little desert town, main-line rail base camp for the construction camps" is how *Time* magazine described it back in 1931. A base camp rises out of necessity and, more often than not, all but disappears once that necessity is over.

When the construction of Hoover Dam began, Vegas was anything but ready. "People are streaming in from everywhere. There is no room in hotels. The town needs 1,000 more homes and 150 more stores. There isn't a gas plant in town," recalled one visitor, Blair Coan. "Milk has to be shipped in. So does ice cream. All post office boxes have been rented and the general delivery line is a block long all day. Six big gambling casinos are operating. About the only thing Las Vegas doesn't need is restaurants. We've got 57 now. There are seven drug stores and 50 groceries. But the town has only six policemen and none in uniform."

The "big gambling casinos" weren't exactly that. It wasn't until Bugsy Siegel brought in the mob and built the Flamingo that Vegas started acquiring something of a more permanent sheen, as a place that wasn't just on the way to Hollywood but somewhere Hollywood fantasies could come to life. And then Hollywood itself came to Vegas. In 1966, Howard Hughes, the reclusive millionaire mogul, moved into the Desert Inn—and bought the whole hotel rather than leave. He soon owned much of the town. And by the time Steve Wynn decided to build the Mirage, the first of the truly modern Vegas resorts, in 1989, the mob was all but replaced by Hollywood glitter. Vegas should have disappeared into desert. Instead, it became a living, walking fantasy.

The moment you're off the airplane, the lines between fiction and reality blur. This is not a typical airport. From the gate, it is straight to the slot machines. If Vegas on a grand scale is the dream of developers and visionaries, on the individual scale it is the dream that has captivated the

American mind from the first westward expansion: striking it rich. It's the gold rush that never dies. Much more than Los Angeles ever was, it is the city of dreams. Vegas is the true America. The city of hope. With help from lady luck or the strength of your own pluck, anyone can make it.

Once you exit the twilight zone between transit and part-casino, it becomes even harder to tell whether reality still exists or has receded completely. The Strip, that central part of Vegas that holds its myriad casinos and resorts, is engineered so that you never have to see sunlight. There's Venice under a clear blue sky, with its canals and its piazzas all under one roof. There's Rome under the stars as you get hopelessly lost among the vast colonnades of Caesars Palace. If flying is an exercise in perspective, seeing the tiny earth from above and realizing just how tiny you yourself are as part of it, the Vegas casino is the opposite. It's designed to capture your attention and make itself look like the world in its entirety. That's the true vision of its developers: this is all of life, and you need never leave.

Casinos are conceived in a way that depletes your decision-making abilities and emotional reserves. Some of it is on purpose. The slot machines, the free alcohol, the amenities crafted so that you never need to look outside the casino walls. But some are side effects. I don't know if Sheldon Adelson studied the psychology of creativity or emotional well-being, but had he done so, he'd know that by building a world where you never have to go outside, he was building a world designed to curtail them.

Fresh air, sky, water, trees: these are the elements of clearheadedness. Our minds reset in the presence of greenery. We feel more relaxed after nature walks. We're less angry, more alive, more thoughtful. Even urban greenery—that is, environments like parks as opposed to actual woodland—can have a similar effect, lowering the stress hormone cortisol, heightening our sense of pleasure, improving our ability to solve difficult problems. ("So casinos aren't designed for great decision making?" Erik asks me when I share my reservations. "Who would've thought.")

Casinos in general—and poker tables in particular—are germ incubators. They are probably worse even than a preschool, since there the surfaces at least get disinfected when the cleaning crew comes through. I've touched chips that seem to have been in use since the 1970s without so much as a rinse. Once, I had to tell a player not to touch me after he wanted to demonstrate that he'd washed his hands in the bathroom—by placing a wet hand on top of my arm.

I hate Vegas, I think to myself as I wheel my suitcase away from the slot machines, toward the exit. The cold air hits me in a burst of disbelief. It's full-on Vegas winter. No one ever told me that Vegas can get cold, and that in addition to all the other unpleasantness, I'd also be shivering. Goes to show what I know about desert climates.

"I think I hate Vegas," I tell Erik as I hoist the suitcase into the back of his car. For my first foray out West, he's decided to pick me up at the airport.

"I know the feeling," he says. "It's no New York. But we've got some good things planned." We have a full schedule of poker ahead—I have a lot to do if I hope to have a shot in hell of competing in the WSOP, just six months away. I may have gotten over the initial jolt of my charity debacle, but other than that one foray into "real-life" poker, I've confined myself to the online arena. This is going to be my first real experience playing on a daily basis—"You'll never get good unless you put in the hours," Erik says. "And you learn best when you're playing every day." I need to make the most of it. I've trained for many things in my life, and I know that six months is pushing it. There's no time to spare. Except, perhaps, for a small break here and there to fit in a full schedule of eating.

I've been promised some of the best sushi ("really exceptional and underpriced") and Thai food ("one of the best Thai restaurant cities in the world; very underrated part of Vegas") of my life. Thai, I can get behind. Sushi in Vegas? I'm skeptical, but I've learned to trust Erik. If he says it, it must be true.

For now, though, we aren't going to play, study, or eat. We're going to observe Vegas in action.

"You know Penn?" he asks me.

Like Penn and Teller?

"That's the one."

If by "know" he means "have seen on TV," then sure, I know Penn.

"We're going to stop by his old house. It's about to be destroyed by a tank."

What?

Apparently, Penn Jillette has built up a colorful monster of a house, lovingly nicknamed the Slammer—it does have an original prison toilet—that he's recently sold to a developer. Rather than have a momentous property go to waste, he's decided to memorialize it by including its destruction in a movie he's making, *The Grounds*. So, as one does, he has rented a Russian T-90 to drive through the thing and bring it down. We're going to watch.

As we stand on the catwalk—the house has a catwalk; I somehow can't get over that fact—and listen to instructions to avoid the downstairs area because of structural integrity concerns, the tank rumbles forward and through. A wall crumbles and dust rises. Actors dressed as zombies (at least, that's what it looks like to me) scatter in formation as the tank rolls through the courtyard and the next wall comes crumbling down. None of the onlookers bat an eye. And I realize that in Vegas, games and life, fantasy and fact, have become so fused, so seamlessly connected, that it's no longer quite possible to tell one from the other. This is an adult playground on a lifelike scale.

Maybe I've come to the right place to find that missing inner gambler. After all, anyone can be anyone here.

I WRITE OUT A poker schedule in my notebook: Caesars or Planet Hollywood at ten a.m., Monte Carlo or Mirage or MGM Grand at eleven. I'm looking through the daily tournaments and seeing what I can fit in so that I still have time to watch Erik play the high rollers. There are dozens to choose from. Ooh, here's one at the Aria! That's where Erik plays. It's a beautiful poker room, and I'm excited they host something that's closer to my budget than his $25,000 and $50,000 buy-ins. I eagerly write it down with a star next to it.

"No." Erik's response to my starred decision is quite definitive. "You can't play that one." But why? It's so convenient and exciting. "You're not ready for Aria."

Why not? I've been playing online almost daily. And I've even made almost $2,000 doing it! How does he want me to play a $10,000 buy-in down the line if I can't even play this?

"First of all, the players here are too good. You need to start at a lower level."

Hmph.

"And second of all, one hundred forty dollars is way too expensive. You need to build a bigger bankroll before you can play that high." I feel a blow to my ego. He doesn't think I can pull off a baby tournament. Also, what's a bankroll?

Turns out, even though I've gotten quite a bit further on the strategy end since that charity tournament, I have some other basic holes to fill. Bankroll, I learn, is exactly what it sounds like: the amount of money you have to devote to poker. Most people drastically under-budget, especially in tournament poker, where the swings are much larger than in cash. Until I start winning the $40 tournaments, I can't play in the $140 ones. I get a quick crash course in poker economics. Some players have backing. The specifics vary deal to deal, but broadly, it means that someone fronts you the cash for all your poker playing and you split the winnings. If you keep losing, though, you go into something called makeup, where you need to make up your losses before you pocket any wins. Then there's staking. People can buy a percentage of your action for the same percentage of your winnings—say, 10 percent for 10 percent. If you've had good results, you can sell at markup: someone pays a bit more for the chance to have a sweat, or piece, of the event. Or there's swapping. If you respect another player's game, you can ask to swap a certain percent. So you get, say, 5 percent of anything they win, and vice versa. All of these are ways to manage risk. The best professionals know when to lower the gamble, not just when to ratchet it up.

The reality is that more poker players than not go broke—even the pros. It's simply not sexy to be too conscious of your bankroll. "They should know better, but they spend way too much," Erik tells me. "One of the most difficult things is seeing gifted players that don't have a mental understanding of real variance, so that they might have an eighteen-month streak or a two-year streak when they make two million, five million, whatever. And they feel like the cards can't go against them, so they spend it, are reckless with it, gambling, casinos." And then the inevitable happens: "They go through a down streak and they have nothing left to show for one of the most incredible runs of the last ten years. It just happens over and over."

Throughout our lives, we're taught to budget, of course—or at least, we hear that word bandied about plenty. Have enough saved for emergencies. Don't spend too much. But it's easy to come up with excuses: I'm not making enough to put anything into savings; my rent is too expensive; I live in New York City—how can you expect me to save? And oftentimes, we successfully avoid being punished for poor financial decisions. We don't get sick. We don't lose our jobs. Our lack of cushion doesn't catch up with us in a real sense. We're more or less OK.

Poker is far less forgiving. If you play too high, risk too much, go too big, you will inevitably find yourself confronted with going broke. Many pros pride themselves on just how often they've gone broke and come back—but to Erik, that's not a point of pride. Because you can never rely on being able to get that loan, get that backing, and have the chance to rebound. At some point, if you go broke, it will be for good.

Indeed, one of the secrets to Erik's success is his ability to stay calm even in the downturns. "One area where I seem to be good," he tells me in an uncharacteristic moment of saying something positive about himself, "is that the financial swings have always been manageable for me. I get through them. I'm not subject to a lot of the emotional swings that other players are subject to. And I think that's been highly valuable. You have to take these things seriously."

When you put it that way, in the prosaic business-ese of bankroll management, it becomes clear just how crucial it is to respect the power of luck, the role of variance, if I'm ever going to learn to understand it. Yes, in the long run, the Eriks of the world will be ascendant, their skill triumphant. But you will never see the long run if, in the short term, you don't buffer yourself against the vicissitudes of chance. It's not an ego thing. It's practical survival. True skill is knowing your own limits—and the power of variance in the immediate future. Because who knows how long "immediate future" might last? After all, probability distributions don't care about the past. Skill is not being an idiot who signs up for $140 tournaments when I don't even have a designated bank account for poker playing and am taking all the tournament cash out of my monthly life budget. Without a safety net, your skill couldn't matter less. You can be the most talented player in whatever your chosen profession, but if you're not buttressed against the immediate impact of the worst case scenario, you may never get a chance to recover. I grimly assent to lower my target.

"I think we need to take you off-Strip," Erik says after looking over the rest of my list. "I want you to see the real Vegas. Where the real characters are."

He decides on a casino I've never even heard of: the Golden Nugget. "This is old-school Vegas," Erik says. "This will give you a real feel for what the place was like." And with that, we're on our way downtown. There's Binion's, where the first ever WSOP was held, in a room too small to hold even the side events in the modern era. I see its famous horseshoe and make a mental note to return to the place where so much history has been made.

"The WSOP has really changed since I started playing," Erik reflects as we drive past. Because it's bigger, I ask? "Bigger, but also the variety of events is just amazing. You have buy-ins at the highest level. Like the One Drop." That's a million-dollar event, if you're counting. "And then there are a lot of things that I think you're going to end up wanting to play that I don't think you even know about."

We are pulling up to the Nugget, and it looks very . . . yellow. Not gold. More like a sooty dull mustard. Is this really where I'm going to start my Vegas poker-playing career?

"If you start doing well at these consistently"—Erik nods toward the entrance—"I think you'll have a real edge at some of the bigger ones. You could even think about the Ladies Event at the WSOP."

The Ladies Event? What? That's the first moment I realize that there's actually a chance, not just a nighttime jitters nightmare scenario, that I won't be ready to play in the event I want to play. That this whole conversation hasn't been about building me up to the big leagues, but rather letting me down easy, to show me that maybe the little leagues are my eventual destiny.

"I don't want to be misunderstood," Erik immediately follows. He clearly sees some dismay in my eyes. "Obviously, you're shooting at a much higher barrier. I know that, and I'm with you. I want to make sure you know that what I meant by that is it's the first place you could have a real edge at a real buy-in."

I nod silently. I do understand. But my enthusiasm for the Ladies Event is limited. If it's not clear from the name, it's an event for female players only. It used to be a $1,000 entry, but then men started entering for laughs (and because of the impression that a female field would be particularly soft, that is, with weaker players), so the buy-in was raised to $10,000, just like the Main Event—with a $9,000 discount for women. (To avoid butting up against anti-discrimination laws, the event technically has to be open to men.) And, yes, rightly or not, it is considered the softest event in the whole WSOP.

"I think timing-wise, it would be pretty optimistic to feel like we could get to those higher buy-ins quickly enough. But we can find these smaller games in Vegas, where you can just start getting in time and saying, 'Oh, this is not so bad after all.' It would be so valuable."

I know that Erik is just trying to be realistic. He's all about expectation setting, and all about practicality. Only playing within your bankroll.

No unnecessary risks. Only playing higher if you have an edge. But it can be dispiriting to hear it. I make my face into a mask of firm resolution. If I can help it, my future will hold the Main, not the Ladies. I can't fully articulate it yet, but the mere idea of the Ladies Event is leaving a sour taste in my mouth. I understand the intention—to bring women into a game that is 97 percent male, to give them a shot at a bracelet when the reality of open events (those not limited to female players) is that, since the start of the WSOP, only twenty-three have ever been won by women, out of just over fifteen hundred (1,503 at the end of 2019). That's 1.5 percent of bracelets held by women, even lower than the overall percentage of female participants would have you expect. Not a rosy picture. Yes, I completely understand the intention, but somehow, segregating women into a separate player pool, as if admitting that they can't compete in an open player pool, feels equal parts degrading and demoralizing. I don't yet know what kind of a poker player I'll end up being, more aggressive or more conservative, more creative or more traditional, more steady or more zig and zaggy. I don't yet know what my reputation will be, how my game will progress, how my instincts will develop, what style will come to feel most *mine*. But before walking through my first set of casino doors, into the Golden Nugget and a fifty-dollar shot at glory, I make myself two promises. First, I am going to stick with this. I will master this game, even if it takes more than a year. I will be a winning player. I will be someone to contend with—or give my all trying. And second: if I'm known as anything in this game, I want to be known as a good poker player, not a good female poker player. No modifiers need apply.

THE MAN'S FACE IS what I notice first. It's vulpine, the eyes darting around the room, searching for some opening. If Erik wanted me to see characters, here's one for sure. He looks like he's here for the kill, a throw-back to a Wild West I'm not sure ever existed but that certainly exists in my imagination, complete with guns and knives and fists. He should rightly be wearing a Stetson to match his bolo tie and boots.

I'm standing in line at the registration desk—I've finally found the poker room after wandering down some half-glassed hallways, past the slot machines and tables and misplaced escalators. Even though they are muted with age and use, the colors here are dizzying in their clashing in-congruity. The floor is a series of black, gold, and red Tetris pieces. The walls glitter with gold diamonds. The neon from the slot machines bounces off every surface. There seems to be a fine layer of dust over it all—not actual dust, but the residue of years of passing humanity. Smoke, perfume, min-gling bodies. It's unmistakably lived-in, and unmistakably alive.

The Fox, as I'm calling him in my head, is lurking nearby, not quite looking at the registration line to see how many people might enter this afternoon tournament. I hand over my cash.

"You have a player's card?"

I shake my head. I didn't know I needed a card. No one told me about cards. Why didn't Erik warn me? I must look like a lost lamb; the weath-ered face of the woman behind the desk softens for a second.

"Don't worry. You can get one over there. It's quick." She waves vaguely to her left. "Next."

Ten minutes later, I'm back, newly minted card in hand. The man is still there, still lurking, still stalking. The tournament is about to start, but I've just about made it in time. I'm nervous about being late. I can't be late to my first tournament. I try handing over my cash again, and now, it's accepted. Time to play at my first ever Vegas poker table.

I find my way to one of the worn brown chairs. I hand over my little seat card, and a stack of chips is pushed in my direction. I glance around. Everyone looks comfortable. Their stacks are laid out neatly. A few players are riffling chips. I still haven't mastered the art. Any time I've tried with more than three in each stack, I've been met with exploding chip fireworks. I make a mental note to practice harder. A few chairs at my table are still empty.

We start to play. Ten or so minutes later, the Fox comes over to the table and sits at one of the empty seats. My seat is right in the middle, seat five, and he is over to my right, seat two. (As I learn, poker seats are numbered in a clockwise direction, with the one seat directly to the dealer's left. I get lucky with my draw this time. It's right in the middle, whichever way you count. I'm unable to make a rookie mistake.)

"Howdy!" he tells the table. "This looks like a friendly bunch."

We smile and greet him.

"Good thing," he continues. "Because I've never really played before. I'll need a lot of help."

My antennae go on high alert. I've read about people like this—hell, I've studied people like this. The old strong-means-weak and weak-means-strong gambit, the innocent newbie act. It's one of the oldest tricks in the book. I'm the real novice here, and I'd rather die than tell anyone it's my first time in a casino poker room. I may be wrong, of course, but somehow I doubt Mr. Fox is new to this.

"Aw, damn. I don't know if I'm supposed to call or fold or what!" The Fox is making a big show of confusion at the end of a hand. He exaggerates his vowels, as if to say, I'm not from here—I'm just a harmless geezer. "Aw, I guess I'll just call and see what happens."

His opponent turns over two pair. He turns over a straight. "Is that good? Do I beat him? Or does he get my money?"

"Well done, sir!" says his helpful neighbor, who seems to have taken it upon himself to be Fox's mentor throughout this tournament. Am I the only one who notices that something seems off?

Fox continues in similar guise until the first break—and somehow, the majority of the chips at our table seem to have accumulated in front of him. As we get up to stretch our legs, his neighbor shakes his head in wonder. "Well, must be beginner's luck. An hour ago he didn't know what a full house was, and now look at all of those chips!" There are affirmative murmurs all around. I stay quiet.

Soon after the break, Fox is in a pot with another player, facing a big bet on the river. He hems and haws as he plays with his chips, and at last, he flips a chip into the middle. His opponent tables the nuts—the best possible hand on the board.

"Wait, wait! Don't show me your cards! I haven't decided if I'm going to call yet," Fox protests.

"You threw in a chip," says his opponent. In a live game, throwing a single chip into the middle signals a call.

"Aw, shucks, nah, I didn't!" Fox is sadly shaking his head. "I'm just clumsy with these. Being so new and all. It slipped!"

"Let it go," says the protective neighbor. "He's a newbie."

I don't know enough to speak up—I'm a newbie myself—but I don't like this one bit.

"I fold, I fold!" Fox makes a show of mucking his cards.

And that's how I meet my first angle shooter—someone who likes to use the old angle, or underhanded tactic, to take advantage of his opponents. Old Vegas, indeed.

I bust soon after—no luck in this first foray—but I've learned quite a bit more than I ever could have if I'd stayed ensconced in the online world, and more than I think I would have in a slicker poker room. Not because angle shooters don't exist there, but because they are more likely to flock to lower stakes with newer players.

I can see, too, where the old shark and fish analogy comes from. Fox is certainly circling the minnows. He's the predator, and we are his prey. It strikes me then just how stark and zero-sum this landscape can be. Appearances deceive. There aren't many winners in poker.

How often do I find myself in a landscape like this, I wonder, only I'm not tuned in, not paying attention as closely as I should, not able to separate the signal from the noise—and so, not able to realize that I've got a shark biting at my heels as I swim merrily along and think he's on my side? How often have I been that friendly, helpful neighbor? Certainly, I've been here more than once, in noisier environments. Moments where I thought someone was on my side only to be stabbed in the back. Promising starts to a friendship only to realize someone was looking for an angle, and once they had what they wanted, they (and their friendship) evaporated. It feels nice to feel useful and appreciated—until you realize you've been used. Here, at least, it's out in the open if you know where to look.

My next few tournaments don't go particularly well, either. After the Nugget, I try my luck at Excalibur, at Harrah's (Erik laughs when I tell him where I'm going—not because of the location but because I've pronounced it "hurrah"), at the Mirage. Each venue offers a slightly different experience, and with each hand, I start seeing more and more of the patterns I've been learning about play out in real life. It's not all the aggressive shark tactics of the Nugget. There are the passive players, the conservative players, the active players, the loose players. There are the ones who like to drink. There are the ones who like to play and never fold. There are the ones who are vacationing and here to have fun, the ones who take it seriously and are here to win, the ones who are here to take advantage of others, and the ones who simply want to make a few friends at the table. There are the talkers, the stalkers, the bullies, the friendlies. With each game, each bust-out, each hand, I take it all in and write it all down. How do I adjust? How do I make myself known? How do I present myself so that I can finally go from losing to winning?

I enter a sixty-dollar daily tournament at Bally's, which I only now discover isn't pronounced "ball-ees," the way I've been saying it in my head. It's small, only two tables' worth of players, but I feel a certain pride in watching the numbers dwindle to a single table, then eight, seven, six. . . . I'm in the final four. And it's hard for me to contain my excitement when I find myself with a flopped set of nines. There's a bet before me, and I joyously shove all my chips into the middle. This is it. All my learning is paying off. I will finally have my first tournament cash. I get called by a flush draw, the flush hits, and I'm out. I'm devastated.

I WALK BACK TO the Aria, where Erik is playing a slightly higher buy-in event, at $25,000 a pop. He's on a break and I start recounting my unfortunate demise.

"Stop," he says, when I'm not even done with the part about having my shove called after flopping the nines. I stop, a bit confused. We haven't even gotten to the good (or, rather, bad) bit. And it's very unlike Erik to cut me off. He's one of the best listeners I know. I look at him expectantly.

"Do you have a question about how you played the hand?"

"Well, not really," I answer. "I mean, I had a set. . . ."

"Then I don't want to hear it."

I'm taken aback.

"Look, every player is going to want to tell you about the time their aces got cracked. Don't be that player," he continues. "Bad beats are a really bad mental habit. You don't want to ever dwell on them. It doesn't help you become a better player. It's like dumping your garbage on some-one else's lawn. It just stinks."

Well, that certainly gets the point across. But aren't I allowed to vent just a bit?

As it turns out, no, no I'm not.

"Focus on the process, not the luck. Did I play correctly? Everything else is just BS in our heads," Erik tells me. "Thinking that way won't get you anywhere. You *know* about the randomness of it but it doesn't help to think about it. You want to make sure you're not the person in the poker room saying, 'Can you believe what happened?' That's the other people."

I haven't quite thought of it that way, but as always, the man has a point. How we frame something affects not just our thinking but our emotional state. It may seem a small deal, but the words we select—the ones we filter out and the ones we eventually choose to put forward—are a mirror to our thinking. Clarity of language is clarity of thought—and the expression of a certain sentiment, no matter how innocuous it seems, can change your learning, your thinking, your mindset, your mood, your whole outlook. As W. H. Auden told an interviewer, Webster Schott, in a 1970 conversation, "Language is the mother, not the handmaiden of thought; words will tell you things you never thought or felt before." The language we use becomes our mental habits—and our mental habits de-termine how we learn, how we grow, what we become. It's not just a question of semantics: telling bad beat stories matters. Our thinking about luck has real consequences in terms of our emotional well-being, our decisions, and the way we implicitly view the world and our role in it.

There is no such thing as objective reality. Every time we experience something, we interpret it for ourselves. How we phrase sentences—are we the one doing the acting or being acted upon?—can determine whether we have an internal or external locus of control, whether we're masters of our fates or peons of forces beyond us. Do we see ourselves as victims or victors? A victim: The cards went against me. Things are being done to me, things are happening around me, and I am neither to blame nor in control. A victor: I made the correct decision. Sure, the outcome didn't go my way, but I thought correctly under pressure. And that's the skill I can control.

The repercussions of that frame shift are worth considering. In poker, if you're one of the bad beat dwellers, you can still just hop into the next tournament and regale the table with talk of the unfairness of the poker gods (you'll be a sought-after companion, no doubt). If you suffer a bad beat in life, it may set you back considerably more—and last a lot longer. All of a sudden, your framing matters significantly more. A victim of the cruel cards? This may serve as something I think of as a luck dampener effect: because you're wallowing in your misfortune, you fail to see the things you could be doing to overcome it. Potential opportunities pass you by; people get tired of hearing you complain, so your social network of support and opportunities also dwindles; you don't even attempt certain activities because you think, *I'll lose anyway, why try?*; your mental health suffers; and the spiral continues.

If you think of yourself instead as an almost-victor who thought correctly and did everything possible but was foiled by crap variance? No matter: you will have other opportunities, and if you keep thinking correctly, eventually it will even out. These are the seeds of resilience, of being able to overcome the bad beats that you can't avoid and mentally position yourself to be prepared for the next time. People share things with you: if you've lost your job, your social network thinks of you when new jobs come up; if you're recently divorced or separated or bereaved, and someone single who may be a good match pops up, you're top of mind. That attitude is what I think of as a luck amplifier. Sure, you can't actually change the cards, and the variance will be what it will be—but you will feel a whole lot happier and better adjusted while you take life's blows, and your ready mindset will prepare you for the change in variance that will come at some point, even if that point is far in the future.

Indeed, it's easy to see how the bad beat seeps into everything. It's not just complaining about the runout. It's complaining in general. Once you do that, you slide into dangerous mental waters. I have a bad table draw— why are all the good players at my table while I see so many easier tables around? I'm card dead—why are other people getting all the big pairs, and I'm getting unplayable crap? (Later, Erik will pull me aside in a big tournament and tell me he's worried about my thinking. I'm describing things as happening *to* me rather than taking responsibility for my actions. If I don't stop, I'm not long for this event.) The bad beat frame determines how we look at others.

The great players don't play that way. It's too draining, and it makes you too much the victim. And the victim doesn't win. Bad table draw? It's a challenging table that will force you to play well. You can't change tables, so you may as well call on all your inner powers to play the best version of your game. See it as an opportunity to learn. Card dead? No one knows that. If your face reads *card dead*, everyone will walk all over you as you meekly fold. If you decide to take the opportunity to cultivate a conservative image and then make a well-timed move, suddenly you have the upper hand. The best players don't need pocket aces to win. Everything is in how you perceive it.

It's the old glass half-full versus half-empty, except we live it all the time without realizing it. Bad beats drag you down. They focus your mind on something you can't control—the cards—rather than something you can, the decision. They ignore the fact that the most we can do is make the best decision possible with the information we have; the outcome doesn't matter. If you choose wisely, you should make that same choice over and over. Focusing on the unlucky runout is just toxic—and even if you're not putting the garbage in someone's yard, it's already poisoning your mind and making you less able to execute clearheaded decisions in the future.

"Let's make a deal," Erik says. "I don't care about the result of the hand. I don't care if you won or lost. When you're telling me hands, don't even say how it ended. I want you to do your best to forget how it ended yourself. That won't help you."

I nod. He mistakes my silence for chagrin at being reprimanded. But really, it's me going through my past to count the times I've let bad beats weigh on me, long before I'd ever heard the term. And thinking how much emotional energy I could have saved and invested productively had I just followed that simple piece of advice: no bad beats. Forget they ever happened.

"Break's over. Come on, you can watch us play." And we make our way back to the poker room.

Texting Your Way
out of Millions

Las Vegas, Winter 2017

"If a man look sharply, and attentively, he shall see Fortune: for though she be blind, yet she is not invisible."

FRANCIS BACON, "OF FORTUNE," 1625

The concentration of some of the world's best players in this little gathering is palpable. These past weeks wandering the casinos, I've gotten used to the chatter, the drinks, the beers and cocktails that everyone seems to consume at a steady pace just because they're free. I've gotten used to the endless table talk, everyone fancying themselves an expert reader of humanity and gunning to get an edge with the old "Are you really doing that with top pair?" and then looking pointedly for a reaction. This is a different world.

I recognize some faces. There's Doug Polk, in a tank top that says #BAZAM. I've been watching some of his strategy videos. There's Cary Katz, wearing a black jacket, blue shirt, and baseball cap with "PokerGO" across the front. Erik introduced him to me earlier as the founder of Poker Central, a multimedia poker company. There's Daniel Negreanu, a.k.a. Kid Poker, who seems to be the only one happily chattering away. There's a player who looks exactly like Harry Potter, a mess of dark hair swept to the side, dark-rimmed glasses, everything there but the scar (Ike Haxton, I'll later learn). There's one who looks like he's arrived straight from Burning Man, with a shock of spiked neon pink hair (Justin Bonomo). Another who looks like he should be finishing an Ironman triathlon, not sitting playing cards (Jason Koon). One who looks like a very friendly cartoon character—every time I glance in his direction he is smiling and bopping his head to some inner music (Dan Smith). And a whole host of players who look like they just dropped in from a grad seminar on aerodynamics. Many bespectacled, some be-scarfed, one be-fedoraed.

It's a motley bunch. But I don't yet realize quite how motley. What I'll come to learn over the next months is something I can only guess at now. Vegas is the true America in another way, too. More so than anywhere else, what you find at the poker table is as close as it gets to the fiction that is the American dream. Sure, there are the players who come from money. The ones who come from educated, solid families. One has a philosophy degree from Brown. One used to teach economics at Harvard. They wouldn't be out of place in any boardroom.

But then there are the others. One of the players comes from rural West Virginia, where the poverty rate is over 20 percent. He was raised by a single mother, and his abusive, alcoholic father was often in jail; he experienced bouts of homelessness, and a whole lot of people told him he was "never going to amount to anything." And here he is, worth millions and considered one of the best players in the world. One was raised by his grandparents after his drug-addicted mother was arrested yet again. One comes from a tiny village in Belarus and made his way out by hustling the local bookie starting in his early teens. Many didn't finish high school, let alone college. And they're all sitting here, the same as their more traditionally pedigreed counterparts. The Ivy Leaguers next to the business moguls next to the kids who started with a five-dollar bankroll that was most of what they had to their name.

Everyone is allowed. No one will turn you away because you didn't come from the right school or have the right connections or diplomas. If you can afford the buy-in, you can play, simple as that. There's no interview process where a hiring manager can decide you rub them the wrong way. You're not penalized for bad social skills or annoying habits. Unlike other sports, there's no need to be genetically endowed with the right height or musculature. If you're blind, deaf, or any other way physically impaired, you can still play—indeed, many a player started from a hospital bed when no other activities were possible. I've met more than one who has called poker a literal lifesaver. There's no unspoken wall of what you are or aren't supposed to do, say, or be. All you have to do is play poker well. If your skill is good enough that you've earned the right to play, welcome. It's what America hopes to be, but never, not in any other profession, actually is.

Of course, it's not perfect. There's no such thing as actual meritocracy. As with all things, it helps if you have the freedom to learn. As Ike Haxton—he of the Brown philosophy degree and multiple professors in the family—tells me later when I make this point, "Whether or not it's actually having a bankroll, being from a socioeconomic situation where you don't have to be working full-time doing something sufficiently lucrative to feed and house yourself when you're a young adult—I think that helps a lot." In everything, stability and support are important components in success. In their absence, there's that much more to overcome, that many more obstacles that need to be moved before you're on the same path as the next guy who was more fortunate. And, of course, there are all the other lotteries of birth: your genes, your gender, your situation. And the lottery of outside life events as you grow up—do you even have the chance to learn what poker is and try to play in the first place? And the lottery of variance when you just start out in the game. Do you get lucky early in your career or not? There's a German player, Fedor Holz, who went on a historic run a few years ago—a series of tournament results so good that someone programmed a probability distribution chart to see how likely it was to repeat. Fedor's run, it turns out, was on the far right side of the distribution, an outlier that, while statistically possible, had a less than 1 percent chance of actually happening. He was an excellent player, but luck was also on his side. Somewhere out there, I know, are the anti-Fedors: the people on the other end of that distribution who got such bad luck at the start of their foray into the world of poker that they never even realized they had the skill to continue. There's never really such a thing as a meritocracy, ever, but this world is as close as I've seen. Sure, some people don't choose to enter it—that 3 percent female figure is never far from my mind—but if they do, they have the chance to prove their worth.

I slide unobtrusively into a chair behind Erik, ready with a notebook and pen in hand. I'm here to gain some brilliant poker insights from brilliant poker minds. I need to be ready to record anything at a moment's notice. After all, how can I hope to reach the next level unless I'm prepared to devote the time and energy to studying and analyzing the play of the best in the world?

"So when's the last time you did E?" one player says, continuing an interrupted conversation. E? A poker term I haven't yet discovered?

"Oh man, not since EDC. Are you going this year?"

A frantic Google reveals EDC to be Electric Daisy Carnival—a festival that makes it clear that the E in question is not in fact a poker term. It seems there is much I have yet to learn about the world of high rollers.

I try to follow the action. After every hand, Erik gives me a peek at his cards before discarding them, so that I can see how he played but can't give away anything while the hand is still going on. "You don't want them to have two faces to look at," he explains. While his opponents may not be able to get a read on him, they very well might on someone who is as inexperienced as I. I know enough not to take offense at the suggestion that my poker face may leave something to be desired.

Even with the delay in seeing his cards, I can appreciate the jazz musician in action. It strikes me then that out of all the members in the group, Erik is the bassist. The one holding everything together, adjusting imperceptibly to balance out all the other instruments. If you're not listening, you might not ever hear he's there at all. But a great bassist can make or break a group. He's not the soloist—the sax, the trumpet, the cornet that blasts its way front and center, announcing its presence to the world. He's not the drummer whose aggressive beat propels everything forward. He is just there, under the radar, but shifting his play in ever-so-subtle rhythms as the music changes around him. Quieter now, now more aggressive, now a strut, now a steady beat. I can almost hear the music of the cards.

The conversation turns to daily fantasy sports. The Super Bowl is coming up, and apparently everyone has more than a passing interest in the fates of the Falcons and the Patriots. I'm asked for my opinion only to realize that I've been mistaken for Erik's daughter Jamie, who plays in a daily fantasy sports league.

Erik takes down a huge pot against Cary Katz. Cary turns to me. "He's the silent assassin," he says. "He quietly kills people."

The silent assassin. That sounds about right. The other nickname I've heard is Seiborg. The robot-like creation that can never be defeated, never be made to bleed, never show emotion. Of course, soon they'll all be calling him the Dragonfly, if I have anything to do with it. Better a stealth insect than a heartless automaton.

We enter another break. "How are you doing?" Erik asks.

"It's a bit overwhelming," I confess. "There's a lot going on."

What I'm thinking is, how will I ever possibly play even remotely close to this? I can't even begin to fathom the thought process that goes into every hand. It's like when I read Mikhail Bulgakov for the first time, in junior high—and vowed never to be a writer. I'd wanted to write my whole short life, but faced with the perfection of *The Master and Margarita*, I gave up. I could never achieve anything close to that. Why even bother? That's how watching the high rollers at work makes me feel. Poker had started seeming doable enough, with rules that were fairly straightforward and strategies that weren't that tough. And now this. It's an entirely different stratum of competition.

Erik nods. "When you're at the table, the amount of focus that you can generate is really rewarded," he tells me, urging me to try to take in as much as I possibly can. "Pay close attention. You're more likely to pick up patterns in betting, tells and things like that. There's so much happening."

I nod. Pay attention: what he's always told me. But there's only so much attention I have, and so many directions in which it's being pulled. Luckily, it seems I'm not the only one who finds focus difficult.

He continues. "This is the funny thing about modern poker: even top players are sitting there, on their phones, and they're missing all the information that's on the table. It's really kind of insane."

I smile. Both because it's funny to me to think of these incredible players missing anything at all, and because I suddenly realize that what he's saying echoes closely the quote I chose to open my first ever book. It's from my favorite poet, W. H. Auden: "Choice of attention—to pay attention to this and ignore that—is to the inner life what choice of action is to the outer. In both cases man is responsible for his choice and must accept the consequences."

Pay attention, or accept the consequences of your failure.

"I want you to watch Chewy closely," Erik says. "When it comes to focus, he's one of the best there is."

How did I not notice him earlier? Erik has mentioned him many times to me, but he didn't tell me what to expect. And Chewy certainly stands out. Disheveled hair flowing below his shoulders. A full beard that covers his lower face and neck. A maroon hoodie pulled over his head. He looks like he just stepped off the Appalachian Trail. His online name is LuckyChewy—Chewy for short—and he is one of the elite poker players of the world. Real name: Andrew Lichtenberger.

I'm probably not alone in thinking, at first glance, that "Chewy" refers to his resemblance to Chewbacca. It's a touchy question, but I decide to risk asking—I'm a journalist, after all, and can play the reporting accuracy card. I learn, to my disappointment, that Star Wars is not to blame. At the beginning of his career, Chewy always had a stack of chewy bars— some Chewy brand, some just chewy—on the table next to him, and he snacked on them throughout the game. And, chewies in hand, he would reach the final table of event after event. Hence, LuckyChewy.

Today, there are no bars in evidence. This is the first time I am seeing him in person, and what I notice right away isn't the beard or the hair or the washed-out sweats. It's the poise with which he carries himself at the table. His posture is perfect. Both hands rest lightly on the felt, long fingers perfectly quiet, resisting the rustle of chips or flip of cards. His gaze is even and intense, absorbing the whole of the room. He's the embodiment of focus. When I glance at him two hours later, the only thing that has changed is the size of the stack of chips in front of him. It has tripled.

If we were on a yoga retreat, Chewy would hardly stand out. (Indeed, he wrote a short poker book—fifty-five pages—called *Yoga of Poker*.)

But despite my initial bemusement, now that I'm focusing on observing everyone's, well, focus, I see that Erik is right: Chewy is a rare exception in the world of professional poker—indeed, in any professional world I've ever encountered, even at the elite levels. Most of the players around him are fiddling with their cell phones, texting away, scrolling through the sports scores and asking if a nearby TV can be switched to a different channel, making bets, and following a hand only when they, personally, are involved. Chewy, like Erik, is always present and watchful. He talks to no one. His phone is nowhere to be seen. His eyes constantly follow each player, and it seems to me that he must surely be picking up on subtle behavioral patterns that elude me. I keep waiting for him to pounce—but he plays quietly and, it seems, more passively than many of the others. He is biding his time.

Finally, he's in a hand. He raises and is called by a top player from Germany—let's call him Edward—and an older amateur, a businessman who often plays for high stakes—we'll call him Bob. Card after card, Edward keeps betting relentlessly. Two thirds of the pot after the flop. A full pot on the turn. Bob, on the other hand, keeps calling. On the final card, the river, Edward shoves all his chips into the middle. Bob calls. Bob has the hand of all hands: a straight flush. There goes Edward and his naked ace-high.

Bad luck, right? Actually, not entirely. Chewy had been involved in the hand to begin with, but after the first call from Bob, he folded his cards and sat out. I ask him later what he was thinking. Here's what he noticed about Bob that evening: Bob hadn't been playing all that many hands—and of the hands he started, he didn't simply call any bet. Sometimes he folded. Sometimes he raised. Sometimes, when his bet was re-raised, he'd fold, and sometimes he'd call—and in the moments he called, chances were he had by far the best hand. His call signaled real strength.

He waited for the action to come to him. If he seemed calm, Chewy knew his cards must have been truly exceptional. This was a moment to fold, no matter how good your hand may have seemed to begin with. And so, without a second thought, Chewy threw his top pair into the muck.

But Edward had spent most of the game looking at his Twitter feed, following only the plays he was involved with personally. He picked up on none of this—and he hadn't played with Bob much in the past. And so, when it came time for the hand in question to unfold, Edward followed the strategy he had set up from the onset, based on a precisely calculated algorithm that showed how to act with his cards, in his seat, given the number of chips he held in front of him versus the number of chips in Bob's possession.

Edward studies hard—no one can accuse him of being a dabbler in any respect—and is an excellent, highly regarded player with millions in earnings to his name. But his approach is dictated in very large part by solvers—computer programs that run thousands of simulations of hands to tell you what the "game theory optimal," or GTO, way to play any given hand would be. Once he sees his cards before the flop is dealt, he already knows how often he'll be raising this hand, how often he'll be three-betting it or calling if someone else raises, how often he will fold. When the flop comes out, he likewise already sees all the frequency permutations in his head. In this particular case, he holds a key card, the ace of diamonds—a blocker to the nut flush. With two diamonds on the board, he knows that no one else can be drawing to the nuts, because he has the card that would make the best possible hand. Now, if another diamond comes, he can credibly represent having the nuts, even though he has only a single diamond. If I have a blocker, I block you from having the hand I'm representing.

Blockers are all the rage, I've learned. They inform many of your most successful bluffs—and many of your most successful folds. If you're hold-ing blockers to your opponents' value hands, bluff away. At the same time, you want to "unblock" their bluffs—that is, not hold any cards that interact with the hands they may fold. It gets complex quickly, but the main point is this: my holding a card means you can't be holding that card. And if the card is a valuable one, I now have an important piece of information in determining my play.

But here's the thing about blockers: blocking a value combination doesn't mean your opponent can't have a value hand. If you hold an ace, sure, there's less of a chance your opponent has pocket aces—but he's still allowed to have them. Blockers improve your probabilities, but they are still far from certain. And what solvers and highly algorithmic and math-ematical approaches sometimes end up doing is giving you a false sense of certainty: because the math tells me this, I'm more confident (correctly so), but perhaps a bit too confident given the extra data. And so I may fail to take in new data—the behavior of a player at the table, say—as I make my decision because I have a slightly misplaced sense of security. *He can't possibly call me here*, goes the thinking.

The extra information should rightly give you more confidence—but nothing close to certitude. The relationship between information and confidence is a highly asymmetric one. In one demonstration of the effect, a group of doctors was asked to form a professional opinion on a patient's diagnosis based on a patient file. They also had to state how sure they were in their conclusions. Then they were given more information and asked once again for both their diagnosis and their level of certainty. What the researchers determined was that the accuracy of the diagnosis didn't actually improve—but the certainty in that diagnosis became much greater. And that disconnect, the overconfidence in your opinion that comes from thinking you know more than you do simply because you have more information available to you, can be a dangerous thing.

In this particular case, Edward does block the nut flush, it's true. But there is also a straight flush possibility out there, one that becomes a reality on the river. By that point, though, Edward is so invested in his game plan that he fails to adjust. Lack of presence has brought down many a player. ("What was he thinking?" Erik tells me on the next break, when we discuss the hand that Edward and Bob played. "Bob would have never played a weak hand that way. If you'd been paying attention to what he was signaling, you knew he had a flush, at the very least." And Erik seems to not be alone in his opinion. Ike, who's been following our conversation and heard Edward's short rant at his departure, chimes in with his signature half laugh: "The good thing about poker is there's enough luck that you never have to admit it's your fault you lost.") Attention is a powerful mitigator to overconfidence: it forces you to constantly reevaluate your knowledge and your game plan, lest you become too tied to a certain course of action. And if you lose? Well, it allows you to admit when it's actually your fault and not a bad beat.

The connection to bad beats runs even deeper. The more focus you can bring to something, the more attention you pay, the more you maximize your skill edge before the bad beat can even happen—and so you minimize the times when you leave your fate in the cards. You fold before that runout that you will then foist as garbage on whatever neighbor happens to be near. You can't avoid bad beats altogether. But paying attention is one of the best ways I can see of minimizing the window for negative variance to peek through. In an age of constant distraction and never-ending connectivity, we may be so busy that we miss the signals that tell us to swerve before we're in the bad beat's path.

One of the most often-cited quotes about luck comes from Louis Pasteur: chance favors the prepared mind. What people often forget, though, is that the full statement is quite different: "Where observation is concerned, chance favors only the prepared mind." We tend to focus on that last part, the prepared mind. Work hard, prepare yourself, so that when chance appears, you will notice it. But that first part is equally crucial: if you're not observing well, observing closely to begin with, no amount of preparation is enough. The one is largely useless without the other.

Richard Wiseman, a psychologist at the University of Hertfordshire, once ran a study where he asked people who considered themselves lucky or unlucky to look through a newspaper and count the number of photographs. The self-described unlucky took about two minutes, whereas the self-described lucky took a few seconds. The task was identical, but the self-identified lucky people were much more likely to notice something the others missed: on page two, in huge letters, were the words "Stop counting—There are 43 photographs in this newspaper." Prepared mind or not, in the absence of observation it matters little.

You're not lucky because more good things are actually happening; you're lucky because you're alert to them when they do. "Although we cannot deliberately evoke that will-o'-the-wisp, chance, we can be on the alert for it, prepare ourselves to recognize it and profit by it when it comes," William Beveridge writes in *The Art of Scientific Investigation*. If we want to be successful, "we need to train our powers of observation, to cultivate that attitude of mind of being constantly on the look-out for the unexpected and make a habit of examining every clue that chance presents." We can't control the variance. We can't control what happens. But we can control our attention and how we choose to deploy it.

Edward had a prepared mind—that much is certain. But his observation was off. His choice of attention betrayed his knowledge and skill.

And so Edward is eliminated from the tournament. Erik goes on to fourth place, Ike to fifth. (Chewy is eliminated just before the money. In my mind, he had come in second—but memory and fact-checking don't always mix. It's telling that I'd given him a proverbial podium finish, so impressed was I by his aura of presence.) It didn't need to go that way, of course. In the scope of one tournament, variance can get anyone. You can be the most focused and present player out there, make the best decisions possible, and still bust. But it does offer me immediate reinforcement on the lessons of the day.

The image of Chewy sitting, Zen-like, amid the clinking chips and flashing phones and constant call of "Drinks, beverages!" from the cocktail waitresses walking around the tables doesn't leave me. I ask him if we could meet and talk about his approach to poker. I'm hoping some of that unruffled poise may transfer by osmosis. He agrees, and I soon find myself in a nondescript Starbucks, doing my best to get to the heart of his aura. Is that intensity of focus a conscious decision or a sort of by-product of his personality? Is it natural or learned, cultivated or coming easily?

I'm not surprised to hear that there's nothing easy about Chewy's ability to summon what seems like infinite focus. Yoga is just the beginning of his practice—and, he says, it's not quite enough. He is also a kung fu and tai chi practitioner. "The element of flow that yoga does, typically through vinyasa, is different in kung fu. It's more approached in kind of a tai chi qigong series. I'm not sure if you're familiar with that." I have no idea what tai chi qigong is, but it seems natural that military discipline would hold part of the answer.

"It's really simple," he explains. "Tai chi just means energy movement, and qigong means energy pulsation. It's just mostly standing form, just movements. The idea is, you're letting your body freely flow in such a way that each movement is determined by the previous movement. So it can be an endless flow, continuous movements where the functionalities maintain."

Each movement determined by the prior: there is no preset plan; just a way of constantly reacting to the moment. Of course, that approach necessitates focused attention. An Edward follows the plan. A Chewy follows the flow.

And flow is how he sees the entirety of the game. "There is a flow to poker, to the way that the events unfold," he says. "I sort of look at it in a macro sense similar to tai chi. It's all about the movement of energy. Take even simple boxing. If I jab, jab, jab, jab, jab, jab and do no blocking, I'm going to get taken out. Someone's going to kick me or something. You have to be tactful in your movements, strike when it's right to strike, block when it's right to block, move when it's right to move." And to do that, it's not enough to just watch your own energy. You have to keep track of the entire table. The energy flows between players. "Everything in poker is always some sort of flow of energy, where whoever can apply the right amount of pressure and allow the right amount of retreat will win. If you find that balance, it's really nice. That's what will allow for success," Chewy says.

The idea seems solid, to be sure. But how to attain it in practice? Chewy, it turns out, also has an incredibly Zen attitude toward losing. Like Dan Harrington, he firmly believes that losing is essential to learning how to win—but the attitude toward loss is a very different one. Where Dan views it as a way of teaching yourself strategic lessons and analyzing your game, finding your mistakes and plugging your leaks, Chewy sees it in more cosmic terms. When he loses, he sees the loss as part of a larger pattern. "Maybe in the big picture of life, beyond what we can see immediately in this moment, we weren't meant to win that hand because some other stream of events had to transpire for us to be successful," he says. It's the same idea of flow, of one event causing another in a seamless succession of ripples whose pattern you have no way of predicting in advance.

Philosophically, it's a powerful way of viewing life. ("Poker is exactly like life, but with instant karma," Chewy remarks.) Practically, though, it implies a degree of nonattachment that seems oddly out of place in a profession built around maximizing expected value, in the financial rather than spiritual sense. But Chewy means what he says on every level—and has taken it to the extreme, in order to see where it brings him. For one, he sold his house and committed to a minimalist lifestyle. "You could probably put all my belongings into a regular compact car," he tells me. "You'd still probably have enough room for a few passengers." For another, he temporarily gave up the major incentive of his profession: money. I ask him about a rumor I'd heard that the prior year, he'd swapped out 100 percent of himself in the Main Event. That is, he'd traded so many pieces with players that were he to win, he himself would have nothing. (As it happens, he came in 499th, for $22,648, none of which he saw.)

He laughs. "I probably wouldn't do that again. It was a fun experiment and I'm glad I did it, but it is a little bit silly because—I don't know, to me I see a spiritually minded approach to life as a mentality that kind of embraces abundance. To swap out all of yourself in the Main Event isn't very abundant. It's abundant for your friends, but it's not very abundant for myself. But yeah, it was fun." "Fun" is an interesting adjective for giving up what could be millions of dollars as a lesson in nonattachment. But it seems to work for him.

In the end, he's just grateful that he gets to do something he loves for a living. In the grand scheme of life, there simply isn't a place for negative emotions. "Some people just become overly emotionally invested in their sadness and their misfortune," he says. "They forget to be grateful to be in the tournament, and then they lose their remaining chips." That's a bad attitude. Not only do you feel bad, but your decision making suffers. "Everybody has a great opportunity to succeed and prosper at whatever they do, and everyone has some kind of unique gift. And I see that oftentimes, the most difficulty we cause ourselves is kind of fighting against the grain of what is healthy for us."

Before we part ways, he tells me that I'm in good hands with my training. Erik, he says, is remarkably in the flow. Even though he doesn't meditate in the formal sense, he is more meditative than not in his attentiveness and the synergy that emerges between his focus and the table. And then Chewy adds yet one more metaphor to the Seidelian list. "I think Erik's like a mountain. You know what I mean? He's very confident and sturdy. And I may be more like an obsidian blade. It's a little crazy, it can go wrong, but if you hit the target, it's going to be really effective." He pauses for a moment. "I guess I should say he's more like a volcano because volcanoes can attack. Mountains don't really attack." A volcano does seem apt. A dragonfly-dinosaur-volcano. It's becoming clear that Erik is one hell of a mixed metaphor.

After that coffee, Chewy and I lose touch for a while. For most of 2017 and 2018, he disappears from the poker circuit; there are some bad runs, some tiredness, some personal changes, a need to step away. I run into him again almost two years later, during the summer camp that is the WSOP, where players old and new all converge on the Rio from around the world. I hardly recognize him. The beard is gone. The hair is in a tidy cut. The faded maroon hoodie has been replaced by a neat gray T-shirt. He gives me a big hug and we quickly catch up—we're on a break between events and need to get back to the tables. He still does yoga. He still does martial arts. And his recent third-place finish at the World Poker Tour's marquee event at Bellagio, for almost a million dollars, was a welcome reentry into a world whose competition he felt he needed to put aside for a bit—just so he could enter it once more, fully fueled and ready. One thing has changed, though. "My hair was a lot longer when you last saw me," he says, smiling.

But that's two years away. Tonight, the hair is still long, the variance is still on his side, and the energy flow is as it ought to be. Chewy is an island of stillness in a flow of treacherous white waters that threaten to pull me under. His words are one thing that makes sense when so much else in this land of poker still seems entirely foreign. I leave the high rollers with my head bursting with terms I hadn't known existed. Blockers. Capped ranges. (CAPPED RANGE, Jason Koon has written in my notebook in neat capitals during a break: *When there is a limit to an opponent's hand strength due to the way a hand has been played. Ex. If we know a player will 3-bet AA preflop he is "capped" at middle set on AQ3.*) Fold equity. It's overwhelming. I feel like I will never make sense of it all. I tell Erik as much.

"It will all make sense, eventually," he tells me. "Don't sweat it too much."

I nod.

"What's the plan for tomorrow?" he asks. "More tournaments?"

"Yup, exactly. Oh, and I'm finally meeting Phil Galfond."

"Oh, that's great. I'm glad you're making that happen. Phil is one of the best. He knows all these highfalutin terms. He's much more math-y than I am. He'll sort you out."

I nod again. I certainly hope so.

A Storytelling
Business

Las Vegas, March 2017

"Lie to me by the moonlight. Do a fabulous story."
F. SCOTT FITZGERALD, "THE OFFSHORE PIRATE," 1920

The only thing I know about Phil Galfond is that he once bought two loft-like apartments in the East Village, one floor apart, and had them connected with a slide. A stainless steel, curvy, custom-designed contraption that was apparently just a tad too fast for steady comfort. (When it came to getting from one floor to the other, Phil grew to prefer the more traditional stairs.) When he left New York for Las Vegas, the slide stayed behind. It was eventually sold for $15,000.

I'm expecting a swashbuckling bro, probably with a tattoo or several, dressed to the nines, and I've braced myself for what will, to this early bird, likely turn into a too-late evening with shots of something so cool and cutting-edge that I've never heard of its existence. But Erik has told me that Phil is one of the best players and likely the single best poker teacher in the world, and that I should do everything I can to work with him. After multiple weeks in Vegas with nothing to show for it except a dwindling bank account and some close calls—"almost cashed" doesn't quite cut it, I'm learning—I'm eager to meet with anyone who might help me improve. I know I can't take a magic pill or find the magic words that will replace practice and study, but I'm optimistic that maybe Phil will offer some ineffable *something* that will give me a good push in the right direction. At the very least, I think as I walk down from my hotel room and start trying to thread my way through the casino maze to find our meeting spot, I should learn some interesting slide techniques for my next visit to the water park.

What greets me instead is one of the most affable, mildest-mannered human beings I've ever encountered. No tattoos that I can see, only a neat beard, a gray T-shirt and jeans, and a huge smile—someone who looks like he'd be far more comfortable at a tech startup than a Manhattan nightclub. *You don't look like someone who wanted a custom slide*, I want to tell him. *Thankfully.*

"It's so nice to finally meet you." Phil gives me a big hug. "I've heard great things." His voice sounds ready-made for narrating soothing nature documentaries. I breathe a sigh of relief.

Over dinner, I learn that not only is Phil one of the best players in the world and the owner of that training site Erik had me sign up for, Run It Once, but he's in the process of making RIO into a far bigger business— his own poker website, for one, and a number of other "secret plans" that are the reason for us meeting in a more out-of-the-way restaurant. ("I want to dodge the poker players at Aria!" he texted me earlier.) He's about to leave for several months in Malta to help with the business—a few of his partners join in for dinner—but in between it all, yes, of course, he'd be happy to help me with my poker journey. What a great use of his time.

I feel bashful for even asking, but he seems completely sincere when he offers his help. He and Erik, it seems, have more than a few things in common. They both truly love poker and are excited at any opportunity to grow it. "It's such a great game," Phil tells me. "I'm really excited for you to be excited." The selfless passion is the absolute opposite of what I'd thought to expect from poker players—isn't this game all about selfishness?—but something I'm coming to realize is not as rare as you might think.

When I tell Erik later about my shock at the incongruity between what Phil actually is and what my mental image of him had been, he laughs. "Ru"—that's Ruah, his wife—"and I were always against our daughters dating any poker players," he tells me. "But we decided that if it came down to it, we'd make an exception for Phil." (As it happens, Phil is married to Farah Galfond, an actress turned poker pro, whom I meet later that night.)

If my homework on Phil has yielded a badass apartment slide—the first residential slide in all of New York City, he tells me!—his homework on me is a bit more thorough. He's read some of my writing. He knows I studied psychology. He has digested it all and figured out an approach to the whole of the live poker scene that seems personalized to my mind and the way that I understand things best.

"What you need to know first and most important of all is that poker is storytelling," he says. It's a narrative puzzle. Your job is to put together the pieces.

"I know that you've already gotten a good start—and Erik is an amazing teacher. But"—and here he foreshadows a realization that it will take me another four or five months to reach myself—"I really hope that you don't end up choosing the easier way to learn because of time pressure. This is a beautiful game, and I think you have the mind to appreciate it. But you're not going to be able to take a shortcut."

I'm not one for taking shortcuts, I tell him. He understands—but, he cautions, an artificial timeline may make for a less than ideal learning process. The Main Event is now only four months away. And while I may have won a tiny online tournament and have access to great poker minds, and could, he tells me, have a real shot at making the money come June if I spend those four months living and breathing poker, he hopes my ambitions will go deeper.

There are a few ways to learn poker, Phil tells me. One is to go the way of rote and memory. "It works well, without a large risk of failure, if you memorize and implement everything properly," he says. You can study technical play, look at push-fold charts for late-stage tournaments (the SnapShove app Erik had me download earlier), memorize fairly tight opening ranges for earlier in the game to "stay out of trouble," and get down a competent strategy for how hands should play out later. "This," he says, "is the quickest way to get to competency."

I nod in agreement. He's right. We know that in most any environment, the best way to not screw up, so to speak, is to follow a specific protocol. Checklists, step-by-step modules: these lead to high proficiency in minimal time. If, that is, everything goes according to plan—or fails in anticipated ways. The rote learning method is excellent for high volume and high immediate output, but when it comes to swerving off the lesson plan or reacting to unforeseen events, it leaves you less able to deal. You reach competency quickly, but mastery will prove elusive. It's like the tests you cram for in school only to realize a few months later that you can't remember a single thing—or, when you reach the next class, that you aren't sure how to apply anything that you do remember correctly. You may know a concept, but you're less able to think through decisions for yourself.

Knowing the mechanics of three-betting or the specifics of blockers is all well and good, but these are things I can memorize, at the end of the day. I can develop a protocol for reacting to certain behaviors in certain ways with certain cards—and I'll be more or less OK. But this is the equivalent to cramming ideas and memorizing concepts rather than developing the tools of critical thinking that will allow you to deduce and apply them on your own, even if you don't know their names.

For short-term profitability, a rote-based approach is key. For long-term growth, I need to revert to my inner Sherlock Holmes.

"In the game of poker, you're a detective *and* a storyteller," he tells me. "You must figure out what your opponent's actions mean, and sometimes more importantly, what they *don't* mean." What exactly does he mean by that, I wonder? Is it like the dog that didn't bark in "Silver Blaze"—the absence of information that conveys crucial evidence? In that particular story, the fact that a dog didn't bark meant that the intruder was someone the dog knew; had it been a stranger, there would have been noise. In a phenomenon known as omission neglect, we often pay attention to the barks but not to the moments when they are absent: we ignore what is omitted.

That's not quite Phil's point. Instead, he's looking at the overall narrative fabric. "You have to poke holes in the story he's trying to tell, and from that, deduce what he's trying to hide."

But you have to be aware that you, too, are subject to the exact same process. Everything you can think about someone else can also be applied to your own actions—something we forget all too often, at the table and off.

"You're constructing your own story at the same time, doing everything you can to make sure it will add up." In other words, before you do anything, think ahead to how that action fits into your narrative arc. If it doesn't, well, perhaps it won't work out the way you'd like it to. You need to be aware enough of your own narrative that it coheres, comes together, makes sense. "The times I have my largest advantages over an opponent are when they think the story they're telling makes sense—and I know that it doesn't," he tells me. "I know how they'd play certain hands better than they do."

As a writer, you always need to know what motivates your characters. Why are they doing what they're doing? If you haven't thought through the motivation, the behavior will be off. They'll suddenly do things that make no sense. Their stories will veer into the unbelievable. In poker, it's much the same thing. You need to find the motivation to find the narrative cohesiveness. What is this person's story—and does what they are doing make sense given what you know? Identifying motivation is key if I'm ever to become anything other than a merely competent player. Always ask *why*: Why is someone acting this way? Why am I acting this way? Find the why and you find the key to winning.

"That's my challenge to you," Phil says. Never do anything, no matter how small it may seem, without asking why, precisely, you're doing it. And never judge anything others do without asking the same question. "Every action your opponent takes has a reason behind it, whether conscious or unconscious," he says. One of the most common things he hears from people who are starting out—and sometimes even veterans of the game—is how hard it is to play with bad players. They are impossible to read, the argument goes, because "they could have anything." Not true, Phil argues. "Even terrible players make the plays they make for a reason, and it's your job to figure it out," he tells me. "When a hand is shown down, try to walk back through your opponent's decision and come up with reasons they might have had for taking the actions they did." Don't judge them. Don't berate them, even in your head, by thinking what an awful play they've made—a bad bet, a crazy call, an insane raise. Just try to figure out the why behind it.

It's powerful advice. How often do we go off on someone for making a decision that we, personally, wouldn't have made, calling them an idiot, fuming, getting angry? How much time and emotional energy we'd save if we simply learned to ask ourselves why they acted as they did, rather than judge, make presumptions, and react. And how much money we'd save on bills for our shrink if we paused to ask the same about our own actions and motivations.

Don't forget the why, I write down and repeat silently to myself. I don't even want to think about the number of times I've done things *just because*. I know in theory that I should know the reason I make any choice, but how often I've simply acted, in the hurry of acting, without stopping to reflect.

I look over my notes. Phil is offering me a full-on mental reframing that seems to be sitting quite well. I'm not an army commander. I'm not a jazz musician. I'm a detective. I'm a storyteller. I'm what I always have been—except more so.

Before we say good night, Phil has one more piece of advice: I need to get out there and put this all into effect. It's good that I'm observing and learning and seeking advice from so many different people, but there is such a thing as too much. "Too much studying without playing makes it hard to fully absorb knowledge," he tells me. It will leave me with a head full of statistics and facts—and a mess when it comes time to execute.

Ah, the old description-experience gap. Phil may not know the term, but he understands the concept—exactly what he's been trying to tell me this whole time about poker terms. You don't have to have studied the description-experience gap to understand, if you're truly expert at something, that you need experience to balance out the descriptions. Otherwise, you're left with the illusion of knowledge—knowledge without substance. You're an armchair philosopher who thinks that just because she read an article about something she is a sudden expert. (David Dunning, a psychologist at the University of Michigan most famous for being one half of the Dunning-Kruger effect—the more incompetent you are, the less you're aware of your incompetence—has found that people go quickly from being circumspect beginners, who are perfectly aware of their limitations, to "unconscious incompetents," people who no longer realize how much they don't know and instead fancy themselves quite proficient.)

I SPEND THE NEXT week playing day after day after day, taking conscientious notes, talking them through with Erik, and putting in diligent hours. I'm a detective, a storyteller, an explorer—not a lost minnow about to be eaten by the sharks. It's a mantra I repeat over and over, hoping that it will eventually stick.

Tuesday morning, I wake up early to make my next tournament: a ten a.m. start at Planet Hollywood. I'm surprised that any actual poker players are awake this early, but somehow they are—though maybe, like me, they're not *actual* actual poker players. I make my way across the walkway over the Strip that connects CityCenter and the Miracle Mile Shops, promptly get lost in a two-story Walgreens that I had thought was the entrance to the casino, and eventually emerge into the actual Planet Hollywood. The poker room is in the middle of all the action, center of the casino floor. I head to the desk, player card at the ready—I know the drill now, I'm an old hand—and ask to register for the daily.

It's a good turnout today. Over the weeks, I've learned that sometimes these morning events get only a table or two of players and we have three already. I'm geared up to go.

The structure is a turbo one. Every twenty minutes, the blinds increase. It's a structure built for aggression and quick resolution. If you sit around too long, you'll find yourself without any chips at all, so you have to act quickly—but act *too* quickly and you'll find yourself out. I've slowly been getting myself more acclimated to the fast pace of the daily tournaments and trying to follow my lessons as best I can with the time constraints. Today, it finally feels like it's coming together. I focus. I pay attention to the players. I try not to panic with the rising blinds. As each hand is dealt, I imagine myself explaining the *why* of any action before I act. Some players start busting. I'm still in.

We are down to just one table and I look down at pocket queens, an excellent hand. I raise. I get called. And another player decides to shove. Past me might have just folded, assuming one of the two players had me beat and not wanting to risk my entire tournament. But today's me knows enough to call. I've been bluffed all week. And I've faced misplaced confidence all week. I know that they may well think they have me beat without it being the case. Looking confident and being strong are not one and the same.

The player after me folds, and we flip over our cards. My opponent has ace-king. It's about as good a situation as I could hope for, short of him having a worse pocket pair. Sure, he can hit an ace or a king, and sure, I'm not exactly thrilled. I'd much rather he have ace-queen or ace-jack, reducing his chances of beating me. But at least as of now, I'm a little bit ahead. It's what's known as a classic race, a coin flip: Does the pocket pair hold, or does the ace-king outdraw it to win? The variance this time around is on my side. I hold and more than double my stack of chips. And suddenly, I'm the table chip leader.

There are five of us left, and I seem to catch some looks going on between the four who aren't me. All of them, of course, are men. "So you want to talk about a chop?" the player to my right asks me. A chop is when the remaining players in a tournament agree to divide up the money rather than continue playing. Sometimes, it's done in a way known as a chip chop—you get the amount of the prize pool proportional to your portion of the chips. Other times, it's done according to a principle known as ICM, or the Independent Chip Model, in which each chip is not created equal: your payout also takes into account the existing payout structure (the percentage of the prize pool designated to each place) and your likelihood of finishing in your current position. Either way, you divide the money and call it a day.

As the chip leader, I'm the one to persuade to chop. I look around at the other players. I have more than twice the next stack. I shake my head. "No, thank you. I'd like to play."

Another player busts. "Come on, let's chop," says my neighbor.

"Yeah. Let's just chop," says my other neighbor.

"It's in your best interest to just chop," says the third remaining player. "You're in a position of power now. You'll get more money. But you know you're gonna lose all those chips just as quick as you won them. Just you wait."

That does it. That's one push too far. The phrasing so upsets my sense of self that I adamantly shake my head no, not trusting myself to make a coherent verbal argument. I don't yet know the word "tilt," but that's what that sentence, dripping with condescension, does to me—injects emotion into my decision process. You don't need to know the word to feel the feeling.

When you defend your dissertation in grad school, at least at Columbia, you have the option of having your defense be private, with just the committee members, or public, open to anyone who wants to attend. When it came time for me to plan mine, I decided on the public option. I was nervous to be presenting to some of the best psychologists in the world—but also had to make sure that what I said would be accessible to everyone in the room, even those with no knowledge of my topic. There was one section in particular I fretted about: how to explain the sense of overconfidence that smart people so often exhibit without making anyone feel personally under attack. I'd settled on one particular illustration, but until the moment I actually used it in my talk, I didn't know if I'd have the nerve to pull it off.

That's because the illustration involved calling people "big swinging dicks." I'd borrowed the image from Michael Lewis's description of the old Salomon Brothers trading floor in *Liar's Poker*. The people who'd made the most money and were allowed to have certain privileges as a result were referred to on the floor as big swinging dicks, and Lewis's aspiration was to one day be a big swinging dick himself. The image had stuck with me, and I decided that, when illustrating the failure of the best minds to adjust to reality and their persistence in being irrationally proud of their strategy and performance and, well, balls, I'd bring up the big swinging dicks. And I did. And to my immense relief, the great Walter Mischel and company burst out laughing. It was, after all, the perfect image for the kind of misplaced, single-minded aggression that we'd observed over and over in people who failed to account for the outsize role of chance in shaping events around them.

That's what I think about now, at this, my first ever final table. It's all about big swinging dicks, isn't it. To them goes the money, the support, the adulation. The most irrationally exuberant have the most entrusted to them. They're used to pushing others out of the way with the force of their swagger. They're used to the mes of the world agreeing to a chop and letting them have more money than they'd get otherwise because I'm cowed by their confidence and think, *Yeah, you're right, I will lose all my chips just as quickly as I won them*. Part of me understands, of course, that they may well be right. But the other part is ready to swing a bit herself.

Down to three—chop, chop? no—then two, and then, miracle of

miracles, only one. I have won my first ever live tournament, along with some $900. I am over the moon.

"Will this be reported to the Hendon Mob?" I ask the man who's counting out my payout. The Hendon Mob is the website that tracks all poker players' tournament winnings, and I'm excited at the thought that I will be Hendon-official. It's a certain badge of honor, in my mind. It means I've actually progressed.

He looks at me with something like pity. "Sorry, honey. We don't report our dailies to Hendon."

I'm momentarily saddened by the news—but the feeling of more than $900 in my hands and the knowledge that I have my first ever victory is enough to get me to forget the slight. I've now paid for my whole trip with one win. I have a bankroll! I am a player! Somehow, this is far more exciting than winning online.

I emerge into the sunlight and send two text messages—to Erik and to my husband. The texts are identical: "I won my first tournament!!!!"

To Erik, I send a follow-up: "Can I play the Aria tourney now?"

"You've earned it."

That evening, I'm sitting at Aria—not watching, sitting!—at last. I feel exuberant. I've earned it. Erik himself said so. I bust quickly enough; there hasn't been some sort of miracle switch from losing to winning. But the next day, I play again. And the day after that. And then I finally have it: my first ever Hendon cash. I place second, and this time, it's far more than $900. I have $2,215 newly added to my name, and I am on fire.

It's not just the money—though that, of course, is amazing. Over $3,000 for poker! That's a real start to a bankroll, not to mention essential if I'm to play in the WSOP. I can now contemplate taking a trip to one of the bigger poker stops on the tour, to pave the way for the summer. Before, those were out of my pay grade. Now it's something to consider. "It would be good for you to start playing a few higher buy-ins and see how those feel," Erik tells me. It's not a reasonable trajectory to go from $50 or even $150 buy-in tournaments straight to a $10,000 one. There are countless levels in between, and each has its own players, its own challenges. Even I'm not naïve enough to think that the game I'm playing at my level is the same one played as buy-ins increase. The skill level goes up, the complexity goes up, the challenge goes up. These small successes in the Vegas dailies aren't enough to guarantee success elsewhere, nor are they enough to sustainably fund any sort of move up in stakes. But they are a start, and for my purposes, that is good enough. I realize now how grateful I should be that Erik limited me to sub-$100 buy-ins to start. I've been in Vegas, on and off, for almost two months—and that's how long it's taken to get here. That's a whole lot of fifty-dollar tournaments, which quickly add up to a lot more than fifty dollars. It's dispiriting, playing event after event after event with nothing to show for it. It saps my motivation. It makes me feel like everything is for nothing, that I can't improve no matter what I do.

And so beyond the cash, this win, this first Hendon score: these are crucial for my confidence. It's the knowledge that, at last, all the studying, the hours, the effort, are showing some signs of paying off. It's the boost I need. Who knows. Had there been no results at all, I might have given up. Shaken my head, dismissed the experiment as failed. True, I still don't know if I have what it takes to compete at a higher level. But at least I now have the beginnings of a new faith in myself, in my ability to learn, in my ability to not be cowed in this world where I'm a total stranger. And if I take a moment to think about it, two months isn't actually that long. That's how long it took between my sitting down at my first tournament and my winning my first tournament. Sure, a baby tournament. But a win is a win.

Maybe the training has all come together. Maybe Erik's guidance, on a bed of Dan's foundation strategy, peppered with technical insights from the high rollers, sprinkled with meditative wisdom from Chewy, have all finally been stirred into a whole with Phil's storytelling imperative. With the quick final tables at Planet Hollywood and Aria, it certainly feels that way. And maybe, of course, I've just gotten lucky. It's far too early to tell. But I've suddenly regained my desire to find out.

Before I leave Vegas, Erik and I sit down and devise a plan for the next few months. In April, just a month and a half away, the European Poker Tour will be holding its annual event in Monte Carlo. "It may not be a bad idea for you to go," Erik says. That's about as close of an endorsement as he'll ever give to any specific course of action, lest he seem too prescriptive. "Not a bad idea," "might make sense": I've come to see these tags as occasions to write multiple exclamation points in my planner. They mean "Do this." Erik never wants to seem pushy, like he's forcing me into one course of action or another. After all, there is no certainty in poker. But when he frames an idea in the "It may be useful" light, that tends to mean that the idea is one you should definitely pursue. He never gives me directions. But he does, if I listen closely, give me his thoughts on what might work to raise my game to the next level. "They usually have a lot of smaller side events you could play, and the players are much stronger. It will be a good test before the WSOP, and the timing is good." Already, he says, I've been making a lot of progress. It's not just my cashes. It's the way I've been describing hands. I'm no longer leaving out important information. I'm noting things naturally that I failed to notice completely before: Stack sizes? I've got ya! VPIP? You bet (nothing to do with VIPs, as I'd first thought; it's simply the percentage of times that a player voluntarily puts money in pre-flop, a rough gauge of someone's aggression). Deviation from usual bet sizing? Noted. It turns out that I'd been picking up things all along. It just didn't feel like it when I didn't have any results to back it up.

Monte Carlo will be an important test. But even though it's right around the corner, a month and a half is too long to stay away from the tables, he cautions. So we map out some smaller stops in the meantime. A few tournaments close to New York, at Foxwoods and the newly opened Maryland Live! Casino, should do the trick, Erik decides (I'll cash in one and whiff the other, as it will turn out—but at least I'll be playing every few weeks, results aside, getting in hands and going through every single one to see if I'm playing correctly), to be mixed with online practice and some strategy lessons on Run It Once. We'll check in every week to see how I'm doing, and if everything is feeling good—that is, if I'm thinking through things the right way, making the right decisions, playing hands well, not if I'm winning—April will see me crossing the ocean to play at a major poker stop. And if that goes well? Well, it's just a month from the end of the EPT to the first event of the WSOP—and just two months to the big one, the Main. If I can successfully clear every hurdle—that's a bit too far into the future, but either way, I'm eager to keep going.

WHEN I GET BACK from Vegas, a change, it seems, has already taken place. A few weeks later, I find my husband quietly observing me after I get off the phone with my speaking agency. I've just turned down an engagement—the first time I've ever done so in my entire speaking career—and told them that I was worth more than what they were offering.

"Is everything OK?" I ask him.

"You know, you take much less shit from people than you used to," he says thoughtfully, with something I take for admiration. "That's really good."

I smile. I may be a big swinging dick yet.

The Gambler
and the Nerd

Monte Carlo, April 2017

"I must pay tribute to that powerful but capricious lady, Chance, who chose to bestow her beneficence on my personal life even though I spent much of my mathematical life trying to prove that she does not really exist."

MARK KAC, *ENIGMAS OF CHANCE*, 1985

I'm James fucking Bond. Cruising in a helicopter from Nice to Monte Carlo. Konnikova. Maria Konnikova. It doesn't have quite the same ring, but I'll take it. Also, James Bond wouldn't be terrified. I, on the other hand, am planning out my obituary. After all, helicopters crash at alarming rates: 3.19 accidents per every hundred thousand flight hours, the FAA website informs me several weeks before my trip, when I Google the phrase every normal person clearly searches before traveling, "helicopter crash rates." Is that a lot? A little? I don't know, but I'm not keen on finding out. It's 3.19 too many for my liking. What kind of sadist invented helicopters in the first place? All those sharp blades, twirling around rapidly enough to decapitate you in a millisecond.

I spent the last hour of my red-eye from New York trying to achieve a suitable state of Zen. This will be my grand entrance, after all. My bursting out onto the *real* poker scene, so to speak. Or so I tell myself. Monte Carlo is the big leagues. Everything up until now has been batting practice. The Vegas dailies, the Foxwoods and Maryland Live! excursions: small-time local. Monte Carlo: international baller. It won't do to have me looking this side of terrified. Alas, that hour of cultivating my inner calm has just been negated by the seeming eternity I've been stuck in the Nice airport since landing. Once I found the helicopter connection desk, I was told that flying conditions out of Nice are currently too risky and all Monacair flights are temporarily grounded. I've suggested that I may just as well take a car, but no, no, they insist, the helicopter is worth the wait.

Good news! An attendant jogging quickly in my direction tells me that there has been a "*bref éclaircissement des nuages*" and would I come this way, "*vite, vite, sîl vous plaît*," and board lest we miss it. Miss the clearing in the clouds, that is. I run behind her, bags in tow, terror in hand. What if I haven't been *vite* enough and we did, in fact, miss it? I'm not ready to go down in James Bond glory, especially as my hand-eye coordination is decidedly less developed than his.

The terror soon turns to awe as the clouds clear and I see the perfect blue of the Mediterranean, surrounded by hills with blinding colors. Patches of ochre, brilliant yellow, deep green. Jagged stone disappearing into waves. It's beyond beautiful and I temporarily forget my imminent demise. I imagine myself as I must look, perfectly windswept hair, calm gaze, poised for greatness. I smile with satisfaction. James fucking Bond. (When I later look at a photo, the jet-lagged reality is more Austin Powers.) We touch down. I have survived, and Monte Carlo is mine for the taking.

That first night, I make my way up the hill to the famed casino. I'm not yet playing—the tournament I'm here for, the EPT, takes place in a different venue, right on the water, and anyway, Erik has warned me against ever playing straight off an airplane; jet lag and clear thought are not bosom companions. But I want to see where it all happened, where my story, in one sense, was born. After some stairs and turns, I find myself under rich lights, surrounded by jewels, gowns, white tails, dark tans, money. I inhale. The smell of effortless wealth. Of the heart of a country where the lowest allowable balance to open a bank account hovers at €1 million. In other venues, when you win a high roller you're the local hero. Here, the locals consider you with an amused sort of almost-pity. *Oh, you're excited about your million or two. How quaint!* I'm in the Casino de Monte-Carlo. And as I walk over the gilded carpet, I can almost picture it as it must have happened. There, over on the left. Roulette, 1936.

THE ODD MAN IS seated at the roulette table. It isn't his physical appearance as such that is striking—slicked dark hair, beginning to recede at the temples, concentrated face, thick knitted eyebrows not unlike those of the hopeful gamblers that surround him. It is, rather, the large sheets of paper he has placed in front of him, covered in neat rows of indecipherable figures and numbers—a compendium of seeming order amid the gambling chaos. To Klari, it exerts a certain undeniable pull. She has always had a mind for the mathematical. She decides to take a closer look. And so, as her husband, Francis, makes his way to a table of his own, she approaches the gentleman with the small pile of chips and the imposing stack of papers.

John appears delighted by the interruption; he's always thrived on crowds and conversation. It certainly doesn't hurt that Klari is young and beautiful—thick brown curls, petite, a radiant smile that seems to animate her entire body (he's also always thrived on female attention)—and that she is interested in his theories. He introduces himself as John—Johnny, she'll come to call him—and explains that he has devised a statistical system, a sophisticated calculation of probabilities, that will enable him to overpower such a seemingly chance-based endeavor as the roulette table. It even has a parameter to account for the possibility that the house is crooked, the game imperceptibly rigged. It still has some kinks and is not yet "foolproof," Johnny explains, but that evening, he is "determined to test it thoroughly." He has high hopes. Klari smiles, laughs, and wanders the casino in haphazard circles before settling at the bar for a cocktail. Mathematics she loves. Gambling, even of a systematic sort, is not for her.

Some cocktails later she notices Johnny approach. "I shall never forget the meek and apologetic way he sidled up to my table and asked if he might join me," she will later write. She nods assent. "Of course, pull up a chair. I hate to be a lonely drinker."

"A drink—what a splendid idea—I would love to have one with you, but are you sure you can afford it?" comes John's reply. You see, he explains, my system didn't work quite as planned. He is now flat broke.

The place is Monte Carlo, and while John von Neumann's system does indeed have some kinks to work out, it will eventually give birth to some of the most powerful applied mathematics of the time. And Klari—she will divorce that decidedly more conventional husband and become John's wife. (She will also become one of the first and best female computer programmers in the world.)

It's a funny thing, luck. A man goes broke one minute. He meets his wife the next. He tries to reverse engineer chance. He realizes he cannot, for now—but finds that the secret to gambling is the secret to the most complex of probability distributions, the most involved and weighty calculus of the twentieth century. Maybe he cannot do it yet, but one day, his invention, that calculator of all calculators that will be known as the computer, just might. And the heart of modernity is conceived not in a laboratory but in a casino.

And here I am, at the seat of von Neumann's insight—the place where the man whose work sparked my own interest in poker played the hands that would create his master theory. It feels right that this is where my first real test will be held. My first real foray into the global, professional poker scene. No longer local daily tournaments; a major international event for which people gather from all over the world. Poker may not be the Cuban Missile Crisis, but to me, right now, it's serious stuff. Maybe here, at the epicenter of von Neumann's eureka moment, I'll come closer to cracking its code once and for all.

It's thus with grand aspirations that I make my way to the Salle des Étoiles, the Room of Stars, where the European Poker Tour is being held. It's considered one of the most beautiful poker rooms in the world, and I can understand why. I've certainly never seen its equal, before or since. The main tournament area forms a circle. The roof of that circle retracts, revealing the sky and letting players, for a brief moment, feel a bit less disconnected from the rest of the world. The walls of the room are glass, opening on a sea vista wherever you look. If only every poker game could be played under the stars. It seems appropriate. Chance, fate, celestial powers.

I arrive a bit early for my first event, the €1,100 National Championship. I want to see how Erik is doing—he flew in a few days ago, to play the high rollers—and get my bearings. There's nothing I hate more than feeling rushed. It throws me off and starts me off on the completely wrong foot, whatever I happen to be doing. This is doubly true when the tournament in question is more expensive by a factor of five than any I've ever played before and the caliber of player will likely be vastly superior to anything I've ever encountered. This is a different playing field in every sense, and I'll be damned if I'm even a second late. I want to take my time, get a feel for the place, get acclimated and centered, in the moment for when the big moment arrives.

That's why it throws me a bit off-kilter when the first thing that catches my eye is a certain commotion in the left corner of the room. It's where Erik is playing—the section reserved for the $100,000 buy-in tournament (shorthand: the $100K; tournaments at the $1,000 mark and above are referred to in pokerdom by the amount of money you pay to enter, not by any event name), otherwise known as the *Who are you kidding, you'll never, ever play here, not in a million years* section. I've never seen a super high roller in action before, but I expect it will be comparably more serious, say, a hundred times more so than the lowly $1K. This is where the Real Players play.

What greets me instead as I make my way over to find Erik is a somewhat strange sight. In between two poker tables is a prone figure in a bathrobe. Towering over him, stopwatch in hand, is none other than Kevin Hart, the comedian whose face graces the movie poster at my local Brooklyn subway station. "Time's a ticking," he hollers. "No way you're winning this one." The prone figure shows signs of life and begins to rise into a plank pose, which is when I recognize Dan Colman (lifetime tournament earnings: over $28 million, more than fifteen of those courtesy of a win in the $1,000,000 Big One for One Drop).

"One, two . . ." The scene gains additional clarity. Kevin Hart is counting push-ups. A small crowd has gathered, cheering along. Some players are standing at their seats to look over. Dan finishes another push-up and runs back to his table to look at his cards—it seems he is also playing. He discards them and rushes back to the floor.

What I'm witnessing is a prop bet in action. Prop bets are bets on a specific proposition—say, that you can complete 105 push-ups in under twenty-two minutes in the middle of your $100K. I've read about them. I've never seen one acted out.

"Come on, boy, ten, eleven, you're pushing it!" Kevin Hart is screaming. "Two more! Push it, push it, go! Twelve, thirteen . . . oh, you're buckling! This is gonna fuckin' hurt!"

Dan doesn't buckle—that would invalidate the bet—and gets up to break for a few precious seconds.

"Shake it off, shake it off!" coaxes Igor Kurganov, a pro player who appears to have taken Dan's side of the bet. "Let's go!"

Dan is back on the floor.

"This is it right here!" screams Hart.

"One, two, three . . ." They're counting off the next set.

"Yeah, yeah, yeah, motherfucker!" Kevin Hart is loving this, even though it's looking like he might lose. Seven. Eight. "Yeah, motherfucker! You get there." Nine, ten. "Damn it, son of a bitch is strong. You fucking buckle. You buckle. You buckle right now, in the name of—!" Again, Dan doesn't buckle. He makes it to 105, the timer reads 21:52, and the bet is won.

"Great job!" Igor yells.

"Motherfucker," offers Kevin Hart with a handshake.

Ah, the decorum of the super high rollers.

This may be the first prop bet I've seen, but the bets themselves are ubiquitous in the poker world—and far older than hold'em itself. Usually, they are a bit more of a sure thing than Dan Colman's stand against

Kevin Hart. As the fictional gambler Sky Masterson relates the advice his daddy once gave him in *Guys and Dolls*, "One of these days in your travels, a guy is going to show you a brand-new deck of cards on which the seal is not yet broken. Then this guy is going to offer to bet you that he can make the jack of spades jump out of this brand-new deck of cards and squirt cider in your ear. But, son, do not accept this bet, because as sure as you stand there, you're going to wind up with an ear full of cider."

Titanic Thompson—real name Alvin Clarence Thomas, the likely inspiration for Masterson, nicknamed Titanic because he sank everything in his way—is considered to be among the earliest of a long line of players whose interest in bets of any sort echoed and sometimes outweighed their interest in poker. Titanic scammed more than one round of golf and famously won a bet against Al Capone, when he wagered that he could throw a lemon onto a building across the street (he'd weighed the lemon down with lead beforehand). The stunt that earned him his nickname, or so the story goes, involved a jump over a fifty-four-inch pool table. The pool room owner had offered $200 to anyone who could jump over his new table, assuming that no one could make the professional-athlete-grade jump—and if they did, they'd be severely injured. Titanic took up the bet, dragged a mattress to the table's side, and proceeded to flip himself over the table and onto his landing pad.

The modern prop bet is (usually) a different sort of beast. The old masters were, in a sense, cheats. Sure, they didn't outright cheat. But they stacked the deck and set up their victims. It wasn't an altogether fair bet because the information was asymmetric. They knew something you didn't. They couldn't lose. The new prop bettors are more interested in the uncertainty of the gamble: testing the limits of control. The push-ups, a bike ride from Los Angeles to Las Vegas in under forty-eight hours, a quest to stay in a pitch-black bathroom without phone or music for a month, a swim between two Caribbean islands: the modern prop bettor is looking for the proposition that will push him to the edge.

It is, in a sense, the other side of the von Neumann approach: the nerd and the cowboy. The mathematician wants to control chance. The gambler knows he cannot actually do so, not at the poker table, so he creates a new game where he can push the limits on his own terms. It's the computation and the human, one against the other. The combat is constant. And the ultimate victor remains unknown.

"I don't want to see you getting into this degenning." Erik laughs as he sees my bewilderment. Degen, short for degenerate gambler, can be a verb, I've learned, not just a noun. To degen is to gamble a little harder than one should, to push an edge a little beyond where that edge actually happens to lie. If you hit the craps table on your way from the tournament, you're degenning. If you're playing a turbo tournament that's a little above your pay grade—in turbos, the value of skill is diminished given the fast structure—you're degenning. If you're placing your winnings on a sports bet, you're degenning. "I know it can be tempting in Monte Carlo," he says. "But keep a clear head, and go get 'em."

I nod. That part will be the least difficult. To me, degenning doesn't seem tempting in the least. The world of prop betting and slots and sports bets scares the crap out of me. I have no interest in getting any closer than I already have. "I'll come check in on you during a break," Erik says. "Make sure to write down any interesting hands." And with that, he sends me off into my first €1K.

By two a.m., I'm elated to find out that I've not only made day two; I'm officially in the money! The structure of the tournament is such that the first day plays until 12 percent of the field remains, and everyone is guaranteed a min cash, that is, a cash for the minimum payout in the event. In this case, the min cash is €1,540, for a profit of €440. One thousand two hundred fifty-two unique players have entered the tournament (there are more entries in total because the tournament permits reentries, so some people have entered multiple times; I'm not one of those, as I can't afford to be). Two hundred ninety-three of them have survived to the second day. And I'm one of them. I text Erik the happy news and stumble into the night, in search of my hotel down the road. Normally, I'd be a bit scared walking by myself on a deserted road near the water. But earlier, Erik told me the story of how he'd had to carry many, many thousands of dollars from one Monte Carlo casino to another in the middle of the night. He'd asked about security and received a boisterous laugh. Apparently, in the tiny postage stamp of space that Monte Carlo proper occupies, you could safely leave the pile of cash anywhere and no one would dare touch it. Must be nice, I think to myself as I roll into bed.

I bust soon enough the next day—193rd, to be precise, good for the same min cash. Had I lasted through two more players, I would have hit what's called a pay jump, when the payouts increase. An extra €320. I could sure use it. But I'm not yet adept enough at tournament strategy to have paid attention to that in advance. I'd lost a big hand, found myself down to two big blinds, and promptly shoved all my chips into the middle on the next hand, rather than wait a few hands for my extra money.

"You'll learn," Erik tells me as we walk to dinner that night, to celebrate my first "big" cash. "You did well. You should be proud."

We're walking from the Monte Carlo Bay up the winding road, etched into the side of the cliff, to the Italian restaurant that Erik discovered a few years back. In a sea of phenomenally overpriced and sadly underwhelming food—the twenty-six-euro meh pizza that is about an eighth as good as my corner Brooklyn slice, or the thirty-euro burger that leaves me craving Shake Shack? Or perhaps the appetizing-sounding *cold spring* *rolls* for eighteen euros?—it stands out, he tells me, for being crave-worthy even back in New York. On our left is the sound of water. I'll have to picture the water itself, as it's currently hidden behind a large billboard with water drawn along its side. Apparently, the Monegasques have run out of room in their tiny jewel box and are building themselves an island in the Mediterranean, just off the coast. The billboard is meant to hide the unappealing view of cranes and construction but just manages to make the whole thing feel even sadder. As we round a corner to higher ground, the water appears. There's the bay. There's the pair of abstract expressionist–looking yachts I noted earlier. I looked them up and found out they were a Philippe Starck design, owned by a Russian billionaire. There's the outcropping with the nightclub where PokerStars is hosting its players' party, Jimmy*z. Asterisk and *z* original to its 1970 founding.

"That place was here on my first trip," Erik says. "Did I ever tell you about it?"

I shake my head. "Were you here for poker?"

"No, it was the backgammon championship. I was just a kid, had no money to speak of. It was a huge deal for me," he recalls. "I had to rent a tux to play. It was a big production."

I've never even seen Erik in a suit. A tux seems totally unimaginable. I raise my eyebrows.

"Oh, yeah. They were super fancy back then. You couldn't play without one. Anyway, so one of the first nights we're here, a group goes to Jimmy*z. I didn't really drink, and I didn't have the money to pay for anything, so I just sit and order an orange juice." I picture a young Erik surrounded by clubbers, drinking his OJ. It fits.

"They bring the check. I don't remember exactly how much it was, but it was around twenty-five euros. I couldn't believe it. It was a fortune to me." He shakes his head, remembering. "The good news is, I don't think the prices have gone up much since then. The juice should still be the same."

I decide I'll be skipping the players' party.

One more turn to the right, past the gas station and the vaguely Asian place on the corner, and here it is on the left, La Piazza. A neon pink sign spells out the name over a white awning that covers some outdoor tables. There are clear curtains drawn around the outside seating area—it's chilly in April. Simple tables, pink-beige tablecloths, matching chairs, a check pattern on the floors. "You'll love it," Erik says. "One of my favorite restaurants in the world."

We're shown a table inside. The place is full. To my left is the window. To my right is a mother-daughter duo fresh from shopping the latest *Vogue* lookbook. They have identical straightened blond hair, identically made-up red lips—I know there's a specific name for this shade, but this is outside my personal or journalistic area of expertise—identical tall pointed stilettos, in shades of pink. Their skin is touched by an identical golden glow. They are speaking Russian. Of course. I've been here forty-eight hours and I've already realized that the Russian speakers seem to outnumber the French. I try my best to forget that I speak Russian after realizing their topic of conversation. Daddy, it seems, is involved in some business that is not exactly of the legitimate kind. I practice my best poker face and try to focus on the menu.

"Erik!" comes a booming voice. I look up to see a large, smiling man making his way over.

"So glad to see you're back." He gives Erik a hug. "Sorry we're just on our way out—otherwise I'd ask you guys to join."

I see another large, smiling man behind him.

"Hey, Falafel!" Now Erik is standing up. "I didn't know you were in town!"

The three briefly catch up, and the two jovial Zero Mostel look-alikes depart. "Dinner's on me!" the one who isn't Falafel declares. "Make sure you get the lobster pasta. It's the best."

"That was Slobo," Erik tells me. "He's the one who introduced me to this place. I think he eats here every night. And you might have heard of Falafel. I know him from backgammon."

Of course. Falafel. Hearing Erik say "backgammon" triggers the memory that started stirring when I heard the name. I know him from a *New Yorker* profile some years ago, the homeless backgammon wonder who captured the world from Washington Square. Everyone here has a nickname, it seems.

"Right, that's the one. He's a fascinating guy. I think you'd enjoy talking to him. I didn't know he was back in Monte Carlo."

Our food arrives—a beautiful lobster-and-avocado salad and the lobster-and-tomato pasta Slobo made us promise to get, because when in Monte Carlo . . . —and Erik catches me up on his old backgammon friends. Apparently, they *do* degen it up quite a bit—I make my acquaintance with multiple prop bets of the past, including weight loss, weight gain, and everything in between. (There is, it turns out, an in-between: what you eat, how you eat, when you eat, when someone else eats, when and how you go to the bathroom—one bet involved a stipulation that any step be a lunge, resulting in a tournament disqualification for the player involved, who decided to pee in a bottle rather than lunge to the bathroom.)

"Speaking of prop bets, I want to ask you something." I've been meaning to ask Erik about a strange game, or at least I think it's a game, that I overheard on one of my breaks the day before, as I walked past the high roller tables to see how he was getting on. A bunch of people were throwing out numbers, and it seemed to have something to do with guessing the distance between Earth and Jupiter. I try to explain as best I can, and luckily, Erik almost immediately knows what I'm talking about.

"That's Lodden Thinks!" he tells me. "It's such a great game. So much fun, and so good for your thinking. I think you'll love it."

Lodden Thinks was created one day in the mid-2000s, when two poker pros found themselves bored at a televised poker table. The Magician and the Unabomber—Antonio Esfandiari and Phil Laak, the former nicknamed for his past profession, the latter for his affinity for hoodies pulled low over his face and sunglasses shielding his eyes—soon came up with a way to pass the time. At the table was Johnny Lodden, a Norwegian pro and mutual friend. They would take turns asking him a question—and then bet on what he thought the answer was. Lodden would then supply his own response, and the person who'd been closest to Lodden's answer would win the round. The game took off, and soon, players around the world were betting anywhere from a dollar or two to tens of thousands on a single question.

The beauty of Lodden Thinks is that the real, factual answer to any given query doesn't actually matter. The game is all about perception and psychology: What does Lodden (or whoever is the target in this particular iteration) *think* the answer is—and can you be the one to see the world from his perspective more closely than your opponents? In a sense, it's the heart of not only poker but many a social situation. How good are you at figuring out how others see the world—and at gearing your own actions accordingly? Remember: objective reality doesn't actually matter. Subjective perception, and your ability to tune into it accurately, is key to the win.

On one episode of *Poker After Dark*, a popular television show of high-stakes cash games, two high-profile players, Phil Ivey and Doyle Brunson, played a round of Lodden Thinks for $10,000.

"I want to bet on Clint Eastwood's age," Doyle says to open this particular game. Daniel Negreanu volunteers to guess. He'll be the Lodden. Once he's "locked it down"—that is, has thought of his response and locked it in—the guessing can begin.

"I'll play this one," comes Phil Ivey's voice. He turns to Doyle. "Will you play this one with me? For ten thousand?"

Doyle nods. "Yeah."

"OK."

"OK."

Doyle starts at twenty-one. Ivey can now either accept the under or propose a higher number. He counters with forty. Now Doyle can either accept the under or go higher. Immediately, he counters with sixty. Now things start getting more serious. Ivey stares him down a bit before offering, "Sixty-two." Sixty-four, counters Doyle with a smirk. Sixty-six. Sixty-eight.

Phil reflects. "How dumb is Daniel . . . let's see." He knows his edge is to read his Lodden. He doesn't need to have a clue as to Eastwood's real age.

"You're not signaling him, are you?" asks Doyle.

"In some way we are," Ivey responds. Because of course, part of the game is watching the Lodden's reactions and seeing what you can extract from his responses. Like so many things in life, this is a game of people, not hard truths.

There's a slight pause as Ivey shoves all his chips into the middle of the table with pocket sevens—they are playing a high-stakes game, after all, and the pot is now over $8,000—and then counters with sixty-nine. Seventy-two, says Doyle, as Ivey sees that he is up against a superior pair of eights. Ivey comes back with seventy-three. Doyle ups it to seventy-four. Ivey accepts the under and they turn to Daniel. "You lose," Doyle says confidently to Ivey as they wait for the answer.

Negreanu laughs. "I had seventy-three."

Ivey loses the pot in the middle but wins ten grand all the same.

Doyle shakes his head in disbelief. "He's seventy-seven." It's like he can't believe that someone could possibly not know that.

As Ivey departs—with that hand, he's lost his $20,000 buy-in—Phil Hellmuth chimes in, reminding him that he owes him from their Lodden Thinks bout earlier. One dime. Not slang—actually ten cents.

Ivey rummages in his pocket and throws a dime over the table. This round of Lodden Thinks is at an end. Doyle knew the answer, but Ivey knew his man.

Sometimes, though, knowing your man may not be enough if you're not careful to observe the specifics of the interaction—and too much personal knowledge can actually get in the way of winning. Erik recalls one of his own most painful Lodden moments, against the Lodden master himself, Antonio Esfandiari. It was 2014, and Erik had come to South Africa for a $100K. He hadn't particularly cared to play that tournament, but Dan Harrington had been trying to complete his quest of traveling to fifty countries, and they had already travelled to Australia for the Aussie Millions, so the timing seemed opportune. And so they made their way to Johannesburg. The tournament was a bust—only nine players, all pros—but the trip was proving to be eventful. A safari planned, a stay in Cape Town, some tours of local sites, a little time spent away from it all. That morning, Erik, Dan, Jungleman (the nickname of poker pro Dan Cates; he happened to have taken down the $100K a few days earlier), and Antonio found themselves on a bus on their way to a lion park. It's not surprising that they were soon playing Lodden Thinks—at the time, it seemed Antonio would take any opportunity to engage in the game he'd helped create.

The Lodden on this particular round was Dan Harrington, and Erik and Antonio were doing the betting. The question: How much money would it take for Dan to forgo wearing socks ever again? Soon, the guesses were flying, with Erik quickly arriving at the half-million mark. Erik was confident: he and Dan were old friends, after all; he knew his man. The stakes were high.

"I'm pretty sure it was over five thousand dollars for the question," Erik tells me. "And it wouldn't surprise me if it was eleven or twelve grand."

Antonio quickly agreed to the under, and they looked expectantly at their target. The winner: Antonio Esfandiari. Dan had put his number at around $160,000.

"That's crazy!" Erik remembers telling him. "To never wear socks again?"

Even now he shakes his head. "It was so tilting. I mean, he goes to the gym, he exercises. No socks, ever? Really?"

Erik had done what he was supposed to do: he'd used his knowledge of Dan, their years-long friendship, to decide that something so uncomfortable would command a hefty price tag. Dan certainly didn't need the cash.

But knowing your man in the abstract isn't enough. "I wasn't watching him closely enough to see his reaction," Erik recalls. "Antonio was."

The abstract doesn't matter, no matter how honed your portrait may be. What matters is the moment. His current state. His current frame of mind.

As it turns out, Erik knew Dan better than Dan knew himself—after giving it some thought, Dan admitted that his stated number was likely far too low. But Erik had already lost. "I have to admit I was really tempted to just pay him the one hundred sixty thousand dollars and make him suffer through never wearing socks again," he says.

Erik laughs. "Antonio has probably made millions on Lodden Thinks."

THE REST OF THE trip, I keep playing through the layers of Lodden Thinks in my mind. It's a neat distillation of so much of what I've been trying to articulate about the complexity of poker—and the complexity of the life decisions that it models. It's a constant circle. There's the math, the calculations, the strategy derived from hundreds of thousands of—yes—Monte Carlo simulations for the game-theoretical solutions. But there's so much more. As von Neumann knew, the human always gets in the way of the mathematical model. That's why he couldn't even build the perfect model: he wanted humanity, and humanity could always surprise you. You need to know the base strategy. You need to adjust based on the specific individuals. And then you need to adjust further based on how those specific individuals are feeling in that exact moment, in that exact situation. And what if they don't fully analyze everything themselves and, like Dan, confidently state the wrong guess about their own preferences, forgetting for a moment what such a guess would actually mean? You have to account for that, too. Otherwise you'll lose the bout of Lodden, the hand of poker, the tactical negotiation. Someone can always be confidently wrong, even about their own mind.

I play on. I eat my thirty-euro pizza. I get kicked out of a dining room along with my dining companions because the prince of Monaco has decided to eat there that evening. (We're rewarded with a free dinner. I'll take the prince kicking me out any day.) I get a plate of soy sauce spilled on my only sweater in a fancy beachfront restaurant, only to be told it can't be cleaned for the next three days because of a strike. I learn that the secret to surviving in Monaco is to leave Monaco. A ten-minute walk, and you're in France, where dinner can be had for fifteen euros and orange juice costs just about what you'd expect. I befriend some players who tell me about a local Airbnb that's less than a mile away and costs a fraction of my hotel. They offer me a spot in the house for the following year. A few more days and I'll practically be a native. I'm learning to survive on the tour.

Over ten days, I enter a total of six tournaments and end up cashing in three of them—two more min cashes to follow my €1K debut. Ninety-third out of 624 in the €440 Cup, good for €730, or a €290 profit, and eighteenth out of 138 in the €1,100 six-max, named for the fact that a maximum of six players is allowed to sit at any table, down from the typical nine or ten. That one yields me €1,840, a whole €740 profit! Forgive the exclamation point. I'm thrilled. I can't believe that I'm actually making money at poker tournaments. I've made €1,470 in just over a week. If I cash at this rate, I think, I'm golden. It can't be far to go until Main Event glory.

But Monte Carlo has a few more lessons for me. When I excitedly tell Erik about my rate of cashes at a final breakfast before flying back to New York, I'm expecting something of a standing ovation, or at least a muted declaration of fellow excitement. See how well he's done teaching me the ropes? What I get instead is the kind of "Well . . ." that I've come to associate with the moments where he's trying and failing to extract some sort of positive lesson from a hand I've absolutely butchered. It's the face a parent makes when taking a bite of a cookie his first-time-baker six-year-old proudly presents, only to realize that she's mistakenly dumped in salt instead of sugar. I must admit I'm confused. What's not to like?

"Generally speaking," Erik begins, "your tournament cash rate should be around twenty, twenty-five percent. Not fifty percent." What? I'm cashing too much? How is that a bad thing?

"The way the math works is that the money is concentrated up top. The only people who really make money in this business are the ones who can make it to that final table," he says.

That makes sense, but I still am not sure how I'm doing anything wrong. "You need to be playing for the win, not for the min cash. If you're cashing this much and then busting soon after, you are doing something wrong. You're getting to the bubble short-stacked." I think back on my tournaments and realize that he's right. Every single time, I just tried to hold on until the money. For multiple hours, as we got close, I'd get cautious, fold hands, bow to pressure. I didn't want to be the person who bubbled—that is, bust out of the tournament right before being paid. I wanted the cash. And wanting the cash isn't the same as wanting the win. "Generally, the people who cash the most are actually losing players. You can't be a winning player by min cashing. It's just not possible."

Do the math, he urges me. How much does airfare cost? Hotels? Food? How high were the entries to the tournaments I *didn't* cash? Now how much am I making for this trip?

I'm deflated to realize that far from a €1,470 profit, I'm actually losing money. Compare this with Vegas. Yes, that was a tiny pond. But I won over $900 for a $65 buy-in, more than fourteen times my investment. And my second-place Aria finish? An almost eighteen-fold return. Those fields were small enough that to cash, you all but had to final table. The money was concentrated at the top, just like here, but I'd reached it. This isn't just a better player pool. It's a much larger one. Instead of beating out thirty or a hundred players, you have to get through hundreds, sometimes thousands. The math is completely different. The considerations are different. Sure, I may have learned the basics of not busting early, of slowly building chips, of playing a solid game of poker. But I haven't really learned about the dynamics of multiday events, about bubbles, about the type of aggression you need to exhibit—can't avoid exhibiting—if you want to actually have a shot at finishing well. At this level, it becomes a far different game. I feel momentarily overwhelmed. It all suddenly feels that much further out of reach, instead of closer.

"Don't get me wrong," Erik says. "You're doing really well to be cashing in these events. I mean, four months ago, you hadn't ever played a live hand of poker. You should be proud." But he wouldn't be a very good coach if he wasn't honest and didn't let me know what I was doing wrong. "Now that you know you can play at this level and cash, we need to work on identifying what you're doing wrong leading up to the money. I'd rather you cash less, but go deeper." Be willing to bust more often, take the higher variance lines that might mean I lose all my chips—but if I win, will propel me into a far more commanding position to go deeper, last longer, get closer to that final table. Be willing to be more aggressive even if that means losing more. There's a saying in poker that if you're never caught in a bluff, you're not bluffing enough. I try to think of a time in the last week when I showed down a bluff with pride, confidently flipping over my cards when someone called my final bet even though I knew I held nothing, and I come up short.

"Good players are going to realize if the min cash is important to you," Erik says. "And they're going to take advantage of that. They'll really abuse you."

In poker, I'm experiencing firsthand the learning trajectory that I so often modeled in the lab. The more you learn, the harder it gets. The better you get, the worse you are—because the flaws that you wouldn't even think of looking at before are now visible and need to be addressed. If you want to grow, if you want to progress, you need to always dig deeper. It's fine to be proud at some milestones, like cashing in an international event—but it's also important to stay focused on the bigger picture, and remain aware of how much you have yet to accomplish. It's important not to let a minor victory lull you into thinking you're doing great, when all you're doing is better than before but not good enough to actually make it count. Too often, we settle for the minor tokens that mark our accomplishment—the participation trophy rather than that podium finish—and let them make us feel that *just fine* is good enough. And sometimes, maybe it is. But not now, not here, not for me.

Erik isn't discouraging me. Quite the opposite. He's moving my target ever higher. He's fighting my complacency before I realize I could possibly become complacent. Min cashing is great, and a good goal *before*, just to show that I could actually play in this field. But now I've shown I can. We move the goal higher. We move the target further. We become more ambitious. Fuck participation trophies. We go for the win.

I realize now, too, that on some level, even though Monte Carlo is a validation of my ability to play at a bigger table, it's a continuation of some of the patterns that I've exhibited since that very first hand of online poker in New Jersey in the fall. I'm still playing scared. Maybe not as often, but I still fold rather than take the gamble, try to sneak into the min cash money instead of trying to aggressively accumulate chips to make a real run for the real money. And the good players? I've likely been abused more than I realize, bluffed off a hand, pushed off a pot, made to fold in a spot where I shouldn't have just because I was so fixated on proving that I could last, that I could cash, that I could get that little Monaco flag under my name on my Hendon Mob page.

Do I do that often? I find myself asking. Do I go for the min cash in my life decisions, holding on for the safer sure thing rather than taking more risk for the more uncertain but ultimately more attractive option? Do I lack gamble in my life? Do I let myself be taken advantage of by people who recognize the fright behind my eyes? I'm not sure I'm prepared to know the answer.

"Do you think I'll be ready to play the Main in two months?" I almost whisper.

"Let's see what happens," Erik says. "We'll take a look at the preliminary schedule and see how you're doing." He proposes I play the smaller events, maybe a satellite or two, to see how everything is coming together. I've come a long way in a short time, it's true. But when he originally took me on, we discussed a year of preparation. In his mind, that was a year of playing. Not a third of a year. A third of a year is a high ask for anyone.

I nod. I'll do everything I can.

"You never know," he says. "I know it's important for the book. But you also have to take this seriously. Ten thousand dollars is a lot of money. And if you're just doing it to do it and put it in your book, that's one thing. But if you're really looking to make a go of this, you have to assess where you are and if you have a real skill edge. Don't hold yourself to an arbitrary deadline. There's always next year."

Oh, but I've never missed a deadline in my life, I want to tell him. And I don't intend to start now.

The Art of the Tell

New York, May 2017

*"In the great American game, Draw Poker . . . the 'bluff' plays so
great a role—the attempt to beat your opponent by sheer boldness and self-confidence. The psychic effects of this are significant. It makes the man who bluffs play better and the opponent
play worse. The psychic effects of the bluffer in every day life
only need to be mentioned."*

CLEMENS FRANCE, "THE GAMBLING IMPULSE," 1902

D o you count cards? The man sitting next to me on the plane from
Nice wants to know, once I tell him that I was in Monte Carlo
for a poker tournament. After I finish explaining that he is
thinking of blackjack—and that he is far from the first and won't be the
last to make that mistake—a follow-up is inevitably not far behind: What
about tells? Can I tell when people are bluffing by looking at them?
Surely as a psychologist—and one who has studied deception, at that;
after all, I did spend multiple years with con artists—surely I've devised a
way to stare into the depths of a player's soul? Maybe I can teach him a
trick or two for his next casino visit?

I've learned a lot of things about myself in Monte Carlo. Foremost
among them is that it seems I'm quite the soul reader. It's an unforgetta-
ble moment: I have officially made the money in my first big tournament.

Prop bets are forgotten as I sit, on day two—my first ever second day in a tournament! I can't get over the fact that I'm playing a tournament that has multiple days—and feel like I'm riding on some sort of major break-through. Over a thousand players entered, and we're down to just a few hundred. And me, I'm one of them! I'm revved up. I'm tuned in. I'm feeling it.

A new player arrives at my table. He's wearing a white ribbed tank top. His biceps, covered in tattoos, are the size of small mountains. His head is shaved. *Aha*, I think, *I know just the type.* In my mind, I am already raising him and showing him who's boss. I won't let him push me around, that aggressive maniac. I've learned that the hard way. I've got to show these guys what I'm made of; that's why I'm sitting here, isn't it.

The first few times he raises, I'm in no position to fight back, but the third time—the third time, I've got him exactly where I want him. The maniac raises, it folds to me, and I look down at the beautiful ace-queen. It's not suited, so it's actually not a great hand, but what it does have is wonderful blocker value. (Phil Galfond was right. The terms come far more naturally once I start playing more.) The fact that I'm holding an ace makes it less likely that he has one, and the queen makes queens or strong queen combinations equally less likely. It's perfect for a bluff raise. And so I three-bet. Back it comes to the maniac, and he re-raises me. The nerve! I know he's pushing me around—how else did he get that huge pile of chips but through his aggression?—and this is where I put my foot down. I shove my remaining chips into the middle. Instantly, he calls, the so-called snap call that usually spells doom for hands like mine. And indeed, he flips over one of the hands I so sneakily "blocked" in my analysis, pocket queens. In other words, I'm in absolutely terrible shape. If I lose—which I should do about 70 percent of the time—it will be game over. Oops.

The board is dealt, and I hit the miracle card: the ace, the only card in the deck that can grant me victory. The maniac sends over his chips and departs two hands later, shaking his head. I stack my ill-gotten gains, congratulating myself on my excellent play, suck-outs like this one promptly deleted from memory. (I conveniently forget to review this particular hand with Erik.) For now, though, I'm just relieved that I got saved.

"What were you thinking?" The Irish gentleman to my left is looking at me in wonder. "That's one of the tightest players on the circuit. When he re-raises you, you fold pocket jacks!"

What was I thinking, indeed. Well, I know exactly what I was thinking: I was acting based on stereotypes and incomplete knowledge, all the while imagining that I had a very good read on someone I had no business reading to begin with. I wasn't using tells. I was using my implicit biases. Some were formed from experience, sure—I'd played with plenty a muscled and tattooed bro who'd tried to bully me out of pots over my months in the game; in Atlantic City, they practically rule the felt—but they weren't formed from specific experience with this player, and they were far too broad (and biased) to be useful.

I may have lucked out here, but this is a wake-up call: I'm far too confident about some of the things I think I know. Sure, I may have built up some sense of the general player tendencies in forty-dollar tournaments on the Vegas Strip, but this isn't that. This is bigger. The players are better. And the players come from all over the world. If I'm going to succeed, I'm going to have to become better at the thing I was so sure I was good at—people. Maybe the math actually is the easy part, now that I'm getting it down—it's the adjusting to humans that's harder. I'm glad I've never been challenged to a bout of Lodden Thinks. Methinks I would go down in flames.

We form impressions about someone from the first moment we see them. As Solomon Asch, one of the great psychologists of the twentieth century, once wrote, "We look at a person and immediately a certain impression of his character forms itself in us. A glance, a few spoken words are sufficient to tell us a story about a highly complex matter. We know that such impressions form with remarkable rapidity and with great ease. Subsequent observations may enrich or upset our view, but we can no more prevent its rapid growth than we can avoid perceiving a given visual object or hearing a melody." Indeed, we now know that we don't even need a few words or a real glance: in as little as thirty-four milliseconds—less than the time it takes to blink—we have already formed judgments on things like trustworthiness and aggression. We grow more confident in these judgments the longer we look at someone, says Alexander Todorov, the man largely responsible for refining our knowledge of perception into ever-tinier and tinier fragments of time, but we don't often change that initial reading. The process occurs at the level of perception rather than thinking: it's subconscious, processed by our visual system rather than the part of our brain responsible for logical assessment. And it's remarkably powerful.

I see a shaved head and tattoos, and bingo! I think aggression. I think maniac. I think bully. I see someone in his seventies, smiling sweetly and asking me to translate for him because he's found out I speak Russian and he doesn't understand English—of course! I'm happy to help—and I think, when he raises me in a huge pot, well, I guess I have to fold my two pair because he clearly has me beat. And then, of course, he triumphantly turns over the bluff and I find myself short on chips and feeling awfully sad that the nice old man I helped could have possibly bluffed me like that. There are no friends at the poker table, the saying goes, but I still somehow take it personally. Why did he have to turn over the bluff with quite so much glee? Couldn't he have at least had the decency to pretend he held a good hand?

Our brains, it turns out, are veritable prediction machines. We are constantly making sense of the environment—and making guesses about what will happen. It's called predictive processing: we actively think one step ahead and look at the environment accordingly. Our brains are more proactive than reactive. Whether our predictions are accurate or not, of course, depends on the inputs and the prediction-making process. Whether they improve in accuracy or not over time depends on our capacity and willingness to learn.

The moment someone new sits down at the table, I'm already predicting how he will play. I'm already adjusting my own moves accordingly. I'm already changing my strategy, even at the most subconscious level, simply based on my impression. I don't do this on purpose. I don't do this actively. It just happens. It's on me to notice it and to change it if it's wrong. Otherwise, it will govern my actions without my quite realizing it.

When we make thin-slice judgments of people—the term for the fleeting perceptions our brain creates, first coined by psychologist Nalini Ambady—our inputs are often mistaken. We're governed by things like facial structures and expressions—the things we rely on in those thirty-four-millisecond judgments—as well as our own past experiences, which, as it usually happens, are closer to incidental peripheral noise that has no bearing on the current situation. We decide that a person is aggressive because they have tattooed biceps like someone who bullied us in the past—but we don't actually have any real knowledge of that person. (It turns out that in this particular case, my initial assessment would have likely been made by others, even without my experience, as well: signs of masculinity, like enlarged biceps, have consistently been found to be judged as dominant and aggressive, likely due to their link to higher testosterone.) But the fact that our judgments are not based in objective reality but rather some subconscious, quite biased processing that takes place in our heads doesn't stop us from using these instantaneous impressions to make decisions that should rightly require deep, systematic thinking.

Here's the thing about thin-slice judgments: they are intuitive, and they are based on large samples. As with all things statistical, they break down in accuracy at the level of the individual. The slant of someone's eyebrows may signal trustworthiness in general, but that's not to say that this particular person is trustworthy. Indeed, in a study that specifically looked at the trustworthiness of faces in poker, players were found to overthink their decisions and make more mistakes in betting when their opponent's face corresponded to our intuitive view of what trustworthy features look like. Not only was the "tell" off; it made people play worse as a result.

I've met my share of the trustworthy types. My Russian frenemy from Monte Carlo wasn't the only one. There was the time that hurt even more, back in Vegas, when I actually thought I'd made a friend. It was the first time I found myself at a table with another woman. She floated in a few hours into the tournament—"It's not a real tournament until the antes get big!" she declared to all as she sat down—and proceeded to smile warmly in my direction. "I think we'll be friends," she said. "Show these men a thing or two." I smiled back. She showed me a photo of her kid. She told me about how she'd moved to Vegas a few years ago and how she'd let me in on all the secret local spots that make the town worth living in. She nodded with sympathy at my dwindling chip stack. "You can always just rebuy and run it up," she advised. I confided that I couldn't actually afford to rebuy and this was my only shot. She sighed with heartfelt understanding. And then she bluffed me out of all but eight of my big blinds. I'd raised with queens. She called. The flop had come jack-high. I'd bet and she'd called again. The turn was a card I absolutely didn't want to see—an ace. I checked; she bet a sizable amount. After some thought, I called. The river was a ten. I checked, and she put me to a decision for my tournament life. *She must have the ace. Or a straight*, I thought dejectedly as I folded. She turned over an off-suit king-ten, for a measly pair of tens—but some great blocker value with that king. "Don't you just *love* to bluff the ace?" she told the table. "You guys always think the girl has the ace." Of course, I was not one of the guys. And I had woefully misplayed my hand. But it hurt. Part of the reason I'd folded was that I hadn't thought she would try to bluff me like that. She *knew* I couldn't reenter. Talk about female solidarity! Well, talk about being gullible. Are my years spent studying con artists not enough? Will I never learn? No, looking and seeming trustworthy is a far cry from actually being trustworthy.

What's more, the fact that everyone agrees on what superficial characteristics signal certain personality traits doesn't mean that agreement is actually valid evidence. Take competence. Teacher evaluations, for instance, have been found not to correlate well with actual student learning: sometimes, the most popular teachers aren't the best teachers, and the ones who get worse evaluations are actually far more competent and end up teaching their students far more, based on objective assessments. If consensus meant accuracy, there would be no fraudulent financial management—we'd give money only to trustworthy, competent people. No psychopathic encounters—we'd be able to see a psychopath a mile off and avoid him. No friendships or relationships gone awry because we were charmed by charisma that proved illusory.

Obviously, that's not the case. And objectively, we absolutely know that. But we'll still adamantly deny making decisions based on snap judgments. Tell me that I'm making a play based on a fleeting impression of a face and I'll tell you I know better. Tell me I chose my investment adviser based on a friendly encounter and I'll tell you that, no, actually, I looked at all sorts of objective data to make my decision. Tell me I chose the person I'm dating based on a jawline and I'll laugh in your face.

But our denial belies the fact that we often don't really know why we make decisions—and we justify them with objective-sounding reasons even when, in reality, we were acting based on faulty intuitive reads. That's not so bad if we were to listen to corrections. But instead, we often argue with the truth: if someone gives us our actual thought process, we dismiss it in favor of the version we've constructed for ourselves. In a series of now-classic studies, psychologists Richard Nisbett and Timothy Wilson found that people systematically denied the reason for their decision even after presented with evidence. First, they showed students a video clip of a college professor giving a lecture on the philosophy of education in a European accent. In some cases, he was warm and friendly in answering questions. In others, autocratic and distrustful. The students then rated his likability, his physical appearance, his mannerisms, and his accent. The ones who had seen the warm video not only liked the professor more (a reasonable response) but rated his appearance, mannerisms, and accent as attractive, whereas those who'd seen the cold video not only disliked him but rated those same three factors as irritating—even though the professor and the lecture itself had remained identical. What's more, in the students' minds, the causality for their choices was flipped: they were certain they'd found the professor more or less likable *because of* the other three factors, and not, as was actually the case, the other way around.

Let me tell you, I quickly recast my opinion of the endearingly blundering Russian at that Monte Carlo table. Charmingly confused? I bet the old bastard knows English perfectly and just tried to get me on his side. The tried-and-true Benjamin Franklin gambit that I know so well from my foray into con artist land: get someone to do you a small favor (in Ben's case, lend him a book; in this case, translate between English and Russian) and they will see you in a positive light. It's like I learned nothing from the Fox at the Nugget. True, this one wasn't angle shooting, but I still quite resembled the helpful neighbor I'd looked down on just a few months earlier—and here I was, more experienced than I'd ever been. Older men play more conservatively? Ha. This will teach me to respect their raises. Next time, I'll know exactly what's what, and you bet your ass I'm calling that bet. Did I mention he asked me to take a photo of him for his grandson, and made a point of telling me how far he'd traveled—Siberia!—for a chance to play here, how much it meant to him? It made me think he couldn't *possibly* be risking so much on a bluff; if he's called, it's back to Siberia! Next time, I'm sending him into the frozen steppes myself. I won't be making this mistake again.

More often than not, though, we aren't motivated to correct our mistaken reads. We operate instead by an inflated sense of our own power of person perception. After all, we're social animals! We've had all the practice in the world. And we can always blame our faulty reads on something else—I'm normally so good at this, but here's why this specific case was an exception. One thing we're incredibly good at is making excuses for ourselves and crafting explanations for why we're still as good as we thought. (Later, it turns out that I may have corrected too far. I'm so cold to another blundering seventysomething Russian that I pretend to not even understand the language. He is so frustrated at his bet being misunderstood that he almost bursts out crying at the table, until a floor person who speaks Russian is called. I feel guilty for the rest of the day—and have to pretend to not see various Russian-speaking acquaintances lest the jig be up and I'm unveiled as a coldhearted faker. There's a close call when one starts weaving his way over to the table. I'm forced to drop my phone and crawl under the chairs to retrieve it rather than blow my cover, until he retreats in confusion. For future reference, I do not recommend anyone ever attempt to crawl on a casino floor.)

If your goal is predictive accuracy, it's enough to bring you to despair. Can I soul-read? The real answer is usually a resounding *no*, despite what I might think at the moment. Sorry to disappoint everyone who seems to think that just because someone studies psychology and the psychology of deception, they're qualified to judge when someone else is lying. On the flip side, if there's anything I learned from studying con artists, it's that the better the deceiver, the worse we are at spotting the deception. Paul Ekman, the psychologist most closely associated with studying how well we can discern deception, found that the vast majority of people don't fare any better than a coin toss at deciding whether someone is lying or telling the truth—and even with significant training, people are unlikely to spot the practiced deceiver. The face, in the end, is not a particularly good metric—and the eyes are certainly not the window into the soul. If you try to stare someone down to figure out if they are for real, you're in for a disappointment. So do I just admit defeat and give up on tells?

The answer to that, it turns out, is also a resounding no. Impressions, whether based on a certain look, as in the case of my maniac turned nit, or on certain actions (he's raising me every hand!), can actually be valuable. I've witnessed enough Lodden Thinks, for one, to see that some people really can pick up on seemingly invisible information. Maybe not deception as such. But *something*. It's just that one very specific criterion has to be met: the resulting judgment has to be based on reams of data. Hundreds of hands, in the case of poker, thousands of points of behavioral observation. Countless hours, repeated interactions. It's too easy to read into something because it meshes with your existing perceptions, but the validity of any information is highly suspect unless it's layered in expertise. The cognitive shortcuts that are problematic in isolation become powerful when backed by the kind of data and observation that we simply don't have time to gather at a tournament table—unless we've played with an opponent many, many times, or have studied their game in a televised context over multiple settings.

Luckily, some researchers have indeed looked at those hundreds of aggregate hours to see if there is information out there to be gleaned. And what they found is far more useful than any quick read we think we might have on a newly arrived opponent. After my Monte Carlo fiasco—and what I now realize are a number of other reads gone badly wrong—I turn to just such an expert to see if I can form a more scientifically based approach to evaluating my opponents, when I don't have access to any past experience. In the two months before the Main Event, can I pick up enough data on reads that actually work that I can use it to help make up for some of my lack of technical finesse? I can't beat the wizened pros at the math. But I've been working so much on the foreign technical elements of the game—hell, I even bought PioSolver, one of those solver programs I swore I'd never use—that I've ignored what may be my biggest natural advantage. Can I leverage my psychology background a bit more successfully than I've been doing? It wouldn't be hard to be more successful, given how much of a disaster I seem to have been so far when I've trusted my "reads." But what I want is to become one of those players who really can, it seems, see your naked soul. If the science is out there, I aim to find it.

MICHAEL SLEPIAN STUDIES SECRETS—SPECIFICALLY, what happens when we try to keep them. Does it affect how we act? How we look? How our bodies behave? In 2013, while still in graduate school for psychology at Tufts University (he is currently a professor at Columbia), Slepian was working on the psychology of thin-slice judgments under Ambady. He and a colleague showed students very short videos of people (a few seconds long) to see if the students could guess the intentions behind certain actions. For instance, why was someone moving an arm? What was the intention behind a motion to pick up an object? "We were trying to distill person perception down to its most basic nuts and bolts," Slepian told me. They had a few positive results and decided to move a step forward: videos of people in the real world, picking up and putting down objects with simple arm movements. They were struggling to figure out how they could tape something along those lines when they realized that there was already a trove of secret-keeping motion data ready for the taking: videos of professional poker players placing bets. And so a new line of work was born. "The poker studies were so exciting that we ended up only pursuing that aspect," he said. Indeed, it's those studies that have brought me to Slepian in the first place: that magical research that just might give me an extra bit of oomph as I do my best to ramp up my game in my limited time.

In a series of three studies, Slepian and his colleagues asked undergraduates to look at clips of players from the 2009 WSOP. Some of the clips were unaltered: you could see the full body and face of the player, from the table up, as he made his bet. Some were cut to faces only: you could see the chest and head, but nothing below. And some were of arms alone: you had no idea what a player looked like, but you could see how his arms and hands moved as he handled the chips. In the first two studies, the students were asked explicitly to judge the quality of the poker hand, from very bad to very good.

In both cases, something curious happened. When the students looked at unaltered clips—the way we normally see the world—they were no better than chance at guessing the quality of someone's hand. When they looked at faces, their judgments actually dropped to *below* chance levels. That is, their opinion on the quality of someone's hand was less predictive of the actual quality than a coin flip—suggesting that faces may actually give more false than useful information. (That seems right to me, I reflect, based on how I've been using faces up to this point. Maybe everyone should play in a ski mask to help me out.) But when they looked at the motion of hands alone, their performance shot up. Even people who had no prior knowledge of poker whatsoever seemed suddenly able to tell with some accuracy whether someone had a hand that was strong or weak.

What was it about the hands that was sending this signal? In a final study, rather than judge card quality, the students were asked to reflect on either the confidence of the player or the smoothness of the movement. Slepian found that in both cases, they were better than chance at picking out the players with the stronger cards. The players they picked as more confident and those they picked as executing movement in a more fluid manner were also the players who had the winning hands. (Slepian is quick to point out, however, that the "smoothness" rating is a bit problematic, as there's no way of knowing how students interpreted it. They might have been looking at speed of execution, for instance, rather than overall fluidity.)

In the years since, Slepian has done additional work on hand movement, none of it published. Some of it, though, is suggestive. For instance, your accuracy at guessing the strength of someone's hand will be higher if you have some general knowledge of the game—but experience playing doesn't seem to matter. So it's good to understand poker, but the perception of strength from hand motion appears to be happening at a more basic and instinctive level. And it helps if you score higher on measures of nonverbal perception. That is, someone who's more likely to pay attention as habit—not only following Erik Seidel's advice to put away those cell phones, but being attuned to the physical cues people give off as a matter of course—is more likely to pick up on these cues as well.

Slepian actually makes me more confident in the power of tells than I've ever been. Yes, our own intuitive judgments are often based on incorrect inputs and deeply flawed. But if someone else does our heavy lifting and then tells us where to look—which isn't where most of us would choose to look naturally—we may be more perceptive than I've realized. It's not just poker. It turns out that we're able to make all sorts of accurate predictions about behaviors—not judgments about people, mind you, but predictions about how they might act irrespective of how we might feel about them—if we ignore the cues we normally love to look at (faces) and instead look at bodies. People can predict whether someone is about to cooperate with them or compete with them based on how they reach for a Lego piece. When a rugby runner is about to change direction, intending to deceive opponents, someone looking from the outside can predict the intention at above chance levels. We're making predictions anyway; why not leave our egos and our certainty about what matters aside and instead allow someone else, someone who has been able to sift through the actual data more carefully than we ever could, to direct our gaze?

I vow that, for the next two months, I'll do less looking into souls and more looking into hands. I'll follow the shuffles, the bets, the card checks, the calls, and the raises. And I'll see where it gets me. Will my reads improve? They can't get much worse, but what I'm really hoping for is some sort of live play breakthrough. If I can improve my edge by just a few percent—well, I've already learned the hard way how crucial a few percent can be to the bottom line. Any edge, even a tiny one, is an edge worth pursuing if you have the time and energy. And I will be doing nothing else, thank you very much. Just you watch. I'm going to be the local resident expert in hand reading, of the literal kind.

Slepian's work doesn't just give me another goal: it makes me aware of not only how limited my own intuition might be, even though I may be confident enough in my judgments, but how much of my own behavior I don't consciously pay attention to. I know I'm supposed to have a poker face; people say that all the time, in all sorts of situations. But I'm likely less guarded when it comes to the motions I see as more basic, more mechanic. I worry I might blush. I don't worry that my hands are going to do the proverbial blushing for me. What if people are bluffing me not because they're aggressive idiots but because they are getting a read on my body language, signs that I'm not aware I'm giving off and so don't know to conceal? What if my Russian ruffian simply saw that I was hesitating? What if my female foe read the fear of the ace in my stance, in the way I checked, in the way I eventually placed my calling chips into the middle of the pot once it hit? It seems elementary now that I think about it. But I was so focused on learning to play the game as well as I could that it didn't even occur to me until now that I could be a tell box. How can I control something that I'm not even aware I should be controlling? This, too, will need work—and urgently. The WSOP is filled with pros. If I'm giving anything off, they will be there to catch it.

Reading Myself

New York, May–June 2017

"Sailors have an expression about the weather: they say, the weather is a great bluffer. I guess the same is true of our human society—things can look dark, then a break shows in the clouds, and all is changed, sometimes rather suddenly."

E. B. WHITE, LETTER TO MR. NADEAU, 1973

And that is how I find myself in a Brooklyn café, far removed from the glitz of cards and betting and deception that is Monte Carlo, sitting across from Blake Eastman. While Slepian is a psychologist studying secrets with a passing interest in poker, Blake Eastman is a former psychologist turned professional poker player turned behavioral analyst. It's not-quite summer and the WSOP is not-quite started. I don't have much time, but I'm hoping that in the little window I have may be enough. After all, I don't actually have to make my final decision on when and what I play until the day itself arrives. No need for early commitment—or early defeat. Blake is personable and friendly, an open smile completing the all-American look of blond crew cut and blue eyes. His square jaw, the spacing of his eyes, and the oval of his face would likely put him on the "trustworthy" end of the Todorov stimuli. He leans in when he talks, illustrates points concisely with his hands, makes impeccable eye contact, and generally exudes expertise and confidence—not surprising for someone who, for the past decade, has run an organization called the Nonverbal Group, where he's developed research on nonverbal communication in applied settings. While for many years his main focus was on dating behavior—how does our body language on first dates communicate who we are, what we want, what we're about?—most relevant to me is his work on a project he calls Beyond Tells, the largest ever study of poker players in their natural habitat, the poker table. Over thousands of hands and 1,500 hours of play, he's observed players in cash game after cash game. As an RFID reader—radio-frequency identification, a technology that detects signals from chips in the cards—picks up the cards each player holds, a team of researchers, coupled with software, codes the surrounding behaviors. The data is then aggregated and correlated to yield any potential patterns in the relationship between the way a player acts and the strength of their hand.

Before we talk about poker, though, Blake wants to get one thing straight. "I hate using the word 'tells,'" he says. Not only is it misunderstood in the same way that people seem to think there's a Pinocchio's nose of deception—find a tell, and voilà! you know what someone is thinking—but it gives a far too simplistic view of what the study of tells (I'm going to keep using the term despite his reservations) actually is. It's not one gesture, one tic, one action that yields information; it's repeatable patterns and behaviors, taken as a whole. Tells aren't always a perfect correlation. Even if you spot something that corresponds to a specific outcome, it might not mean that it *always* corresponds to that outcome, or that in its absence, the outcome will likewise be absent. "For the most part," Blake says, "we're just looking at how behavior aids the story that is being communicated by the context." It's just one puzzle piece in a large jigsaw.

And forget the face. The term "poker face" is just silly, he says, because even at a basic level, players know they are supposed to conceal information.

If you spend all your time staring down your opponents, the best you're likely to achieve is to make everyone around you uncomfortable.

"The majority of movement at the poker table is just complete noise," Blake tells me. "It can add to the information process, sure, but you're juggling so many things at the poker table that often it's more distracting than anything else.

So what should we look for? What about the hands? I'm curious to know what he thinks of Slepian's work. It's solid, he says, nodding. His group has also found that a huge amount of information comes from gestures. The smoothness and fluidity Slepian noticed is certainly part of it. "Confident people move from point A to point B quickly. There's not a lot of hesitation," Blake says. "When you're at the top of your range in poker"—that is, at the top of the range of possible card combinations you'd hold in a given situation—"you're often going to do that, too."

But what his team has found goes beyond the strength of your betting motions. It turns out that if you look at enough hands over enough hours, you do start to develop a sense of patterns that may yield meaningful data. The patterns tend to come in two flavors. The first has to do with thought process: How does a person approach and think about the game? "The way people handle their chips when they are more indecisive, or their bet style at the top of their range—these are the sorts of things we pay attention to," Blake says. He gives the example of pocket aces versus seven-nine. With aces, I know exactly what I want to do: raise. My thought process is clear, clean, and concise, and my gestures will likely follow. But seven-nine is more of a borderline hand. It could really go in any direction. If someone has raised before me, I could fold, I could call, or I could three-bet. I can genuinely consider all three strategies—and my gestures may correspond accordingly. I may hesitate in a way I don't with the absolute best cards. Or take more time to act. Whatever I do, I may inadvertently be communicating my thought process through my actions. "You see this type of thing in players' hand movements all the time," Blake says. "I've seen this at the biggest stakes in the world. Sometimes, players have been playing for so long they've developed these subtleties in gesture and they don't really realize it."

The most telling moment is often at the very beginning of a hand, when players first check their hole cards: how they check and what they do immediately after tend to be the most honest actions a player will execute in the entire hand. It's still early; the stakes are still low, since there's not yet much money at play; and so their guard is down. Everyone knows to conceal when running a big bluff. But at this stage, there really aren't yet big bluffs. And so concealment is not top of mind. (I can't help but think of moments in my past, at the table and far from it, when I was likely bluffed but failed to see the signs—either because I wasn't looking or I didn't know where or how to look. It's uncomfortable enough that I don't particularly want to dwell on it. I don't like thinking of myself as a sucker.)

Concealment, or how a player chooses to actively hide what they perceive to be telling behaviors, is actually the second type of pattern that the Beyond Tells team has found. "It's a lot more difficult to process and understand," Blake says. "It's not really about the processing of raw emotion"—the proverbial poker face. "It's about understanding a player's level of concealment and how exactly they are concealing." How still is someone, for instance? Maybe they are very still when bluffing but only partially still with the nuts. "Same strategy, different magnitude," Blake says. Or maybe their hand placement differs. Or their breathing. Find out how they conceal and you begin the process of reverse engineering exactly what they might be concealing.

Blake is hesitant to give out any more specifics, and I don't blame him.

That's the thing about tells: once you say it aloud, the read often stops working. The more specific the behavior, the more likely it is to stop revealing much once a player is aware of it. But I do want to get specific about one player: me. Would Blake agree to break down my nonverbal cues the same way he has in his courses? Am I more of an open book than I think—and if I am, could he give me a pointer or two to render me more inscrutable? Can he make sure that I'm a locked box rather than a tell box before I sit down to take on the summer sharks?

"I love this stuff," he says. "Let's do it."

And so, over the next two months, Blake does what he's been doing for the past six years: he looks at multiple hours of my live play, complete with hole cards, correlates it with the thousands of hands and hours he's seen from other players, and gives me a report.

JUST LIKE BLAKE IS loath to reveal the full extent of his research to me, I'm not overly eager to give out a detailed analysis of every single thing that stands out in my own behavior. But in the interest of the greater good, my ego will have to suffer a hit.

As predicted, the richest area of analysis in my own behavior comes before the flop, when I first check my cards. There's one thing in particular that I do that Blake really doesn't like: I recheck my cards several times. "The moment you recheck your cards, you risk falling into a pattern," he warns. Some players recheck only their marginal hands—it's easy to remember when you have pocket kings, but you may need to double-check if you have five-six suited or six-seven. Some players vary the timing in between checks, sometimes checking moments apart and other times rechecking after a pause. That, too, can correspond to hand strength.

"We really want to break this pattern," Blake says. "The less information I have on you, the better, and the fewer actions you take, the less information I have." If I really want to double-check, he offers—maybe I'm getting tired and my energy is flagging—I should do the second look right before the flop comes. That way, I at least ensure that I do it at the same time, every time. It becomes a part of the routine rather than a potential deviation from it.

Suspect action number two: the way I put my hands on my cards. "Just don't do it. No hands on cards, ever," Blake warns. People tend to place their hands on their cards in different ways with different parts of their range—one style of motion when strong, another when marginal. In fact, he says, don't put anything on your cards. "Almost every time a player puts a chip on a card, it's a tell," Blake says. It's not the placement of the chip as such. It's the style with which you do it. "There's a direct style; there's this sort of shrugging *why not* style—each one means different things," he says.

Suspect action number three: apart from double-checking my hole cards, I may actually be a bit *too* consistent, especially early in a session. As the night progresses and I get tired, I start to deviate from that consistency—and because I was so fastidious early on, the deviations become noticeable and give off information they otherwise wouldn't. I start to move more, my gestures are more dynamic, and I give off more as a result. "A lot of people think that acting robotic at the table is the best way to conceal tells. It's actually the worst way," Blake explains. "The more of a cognitive process you have towards concealment, the more of a likelihood that that's eventually going to be a break and we're going to see more stuff."

Rather than consistency of motion, he suggests a consistency of execution at a deeper level—one that will help me fight fatigue and continue to play better longer, because it gets to the heart of my thought process rather than forcing me to pay attention to yet one more thing (did I bet in the exact same way, say, or place my hand in just the same spot?).

"Before each action, stop, think about what you want to do, and execute," Blake suggests. As long as I always do that, I ensure that I'm thinking through every hand at every part of my range, aces and suited connectors and trash alike. Because I've thought before I acted, I act with confidence every time—and I act with a delay every time. There's no longer the problem of immediate action with straightforward decisions and delays with more complex ones. And the whole process becomes more streamlined and fluid naturally. Sure, my exact hand gesture may not always be identical, but it's unlikely to convey anything meaningful.

It's helpful advice far beyond the poker table. Streamlined decisions. No immediate actions, or reactions. A standard process. These are the tools that help us cool down rather than act in the moment, that help us stay rational and look at longer time horizons. Streamlining my thought process may make me harder to read—but it will also make my thought process easier for me to discern.

I make a plan to practice this standardization. Erik and I will map out some smaller tournaments in May. In June, I'll come to Vegas for the beginning of the WSOP and practice some more. And by the first of July, I'll have this down, I think to myself. No jerk from the tundra or femme fatale from the desert will be able to read me. I'm going to be as solid as they come. I'm fired up.

Oh, there's one final thing, Blake informs me. I talk, laugh, and smile a bit too much. Uh-oh. "It seems natural to you," Blake says, "but I'd watch out for it. You're a very dynamic player. If I was playing with you, I'd definitely want to engage you in conversation to see if I can pick anything up."

He has a point. More than a point. Female foe. Russian ruffian. Boy, did we have some in-depth conversations before they pulled their big moves. And they certainly seemed to have gotten a much better read on me than I did on them. I was being genuine. They may have been, too— but they were also figuring me out. And I was left the naïve one of the conversational duo. I sigh. I completely understand this is likely a big leak in my approach. But even still, I'm torn. I don't think I can—or much want to—cut off that part of my behavior entirely. To me, it's part of poker. Part of what makes the game interesting and alive. Speech play— when you try to trick your opponent into revealing information during a hand—is vastly overrated. More often than not, you give off more information than you elicit. But talking in between hands, showing an actual interest in the people around you—that's entirely different. I will often spend time asking the players at my table for their stories. Why they're here, what they're thinking, what kind of person they are when they're not playing cards. It not only changes the dynamics, making an otherwise cut-throat atmosphere far more enjoyable, but it gives you important insight into who they are and what motivates them. The *why* behind the action. And as I come to understand, that's often the truest tell you'll ever pick up. I just have to be careful that it's not used on me.

WHEN I WAS WORKING with Walter Mischel as a graduate student in psychology, I grew intimately familiar with a specific model for analyzing behavior: CAPS, or the cognitive-affective personality system. For decades, Walter had argued that the Big Five version of personality—that we can all be rated on five major traits, namely openness to experience, conscientiousness, extraversion, neuroticism, and agreeableness—was fundamentally flawed. Instead of embracing the nuance of humanity, it stripped traits from context and gave people global scores on things that made no sense. Maybe I'm conscientious at work but a slob at home, Walter suggested, or agreeable in the face of authority but a sudden bully in the schoolyard. Personality was all about context and all about dynamics, and you couldn't hope to crack its puzzle unless you were willing to go through the work of regimented analysis. Walter and Yuichi Shoda formalized the idea of CAPS in 1995, writing:

> In the proposed theory, individuals differ in how they selectively focus on different features of situations, how they categorize and encode them cognitively and emotionally, and how those encodings activate and interact with other cognitions and affects in the personality system. The theory views the person not as reacting passively to situations, nor as generating behavior impervious to their subtle features, but as active and goal-directed, constructing plans and self-generated changes, and in part creating the situations themselves.

People aren't a combination of traits. They are a mosaic of reactions to and interactions with situations. If you can get a person's behavioral profile—a catalogue of those reactions in an *if-then* relationship, such as "*If* I feel threatened, *then* I will lash out"—you have a far better read on who they are or how they will behave in a certain setting than if you have only a set of trait rankings.

Tells are the hardest poker skill to master because there is no shortcut for experience, for the brutal hours of analysis required to pick up accurate information about player tendencies. Each time you change tables, each time you change opponents, each time you change contexts even with the same opponent, the calculus necessarily shifts. But CAPS is a different beast. It doesn't rely on physical patterns. It's all about psychological and emotional dynamics. And isn't my goal to ultimately predict behavior given a specific situation—the very thing that CAPS was designed to do? Poker is a CAPS theorist's wet dream: it's *all* about dynamics. At the table, you see a range of situations that would take months to encounter in the real world. It's a living drama. It's a game that manages to concentrate the essence of myriad situations and force you through them as the day wears on. You're up, you're down, you're energized, you're exhausted, you're in a position of power, you're in a position of defense: the whole drama plays out over and over, each game, each tournament trajectory like a life story in miniature, a narrative sped up, complete with multiple acts.

How does someone react to winning a big pot? To losing a big pot? To being bluffed? To bluffing successfully? How does someone deal with a streak of bad cards? How does someone deal with a run of good outcomes? If a player wins a flip, what are they feeling? If they lose a flip, what are they feeling? Are they the sort of player who cares what others are thinking of them or no? Afraid to look "weak"? More afraid to bluff—or to be bluffed? To raise—or to be raised?

These are the sorts of tells that are all about reactions rather than actions, reactions that are dynamic. "Each person you're playing goes through different phases," Erik explains to me during one of our lessons. "Very often you see they lose a big hand and then all of a sudden, it's a lot more likely that they're going to try to find a way to get it back and their judgment is not going to be as good. That's a very common thing." Or the opposite happens: they get gun-shy. They want to protect the chips they have and become frightened of running any major bluffs or playing any big hands. It's an if-then pattern, not one based on a sudden slant of the eye or twitch of the nose. You don't need thousands of hours to pick it up, just a few of what Walter would call diagnostic situations.

Who you are comes out at the poker table. Your baggage, your experiences, your confidence, the stereotypes you hold. Eventually, there will come a dynamic where you unwittingly act it out.

Scene: A six-year-old me on the playground in the back of the subsidized housing complex we've just moved into. It's nothing fancy, a swing, a slide, a set of metal bars for climbing, swinging, monkeying around. Those bars are my nemesis. I desperately want to be able to hug the thin rail with my knees and swing down, carefree, hands dangling midway to the ground, seeing the world from an inverted freedom. My older sisters do it effortlessly. And oh god, how I want to join them (though I'd never say it out loud). I feel like a stupid, silly fraud. One of them taunts me. I try, for what seems like the hundredth time. I sit on top of the bar. I slide slowly down so that my knees brace against the top, as I've seen them do. I start leaning back. And I can't let go. My hands won't let me. I'm stuck in an awkward half crouch and must once more admit defeat as I lever myself back up to full sitting position. I can't help it. I'm simply too afraid my legs will betray me and I'll go crashing headfirst to the pavement. All I can think of is my broken neck, and how pointless of a way it would all be to die.

"Scaredy-cat," a kid yells.

I am. I know it. But I just cannot let go. To this day, I've never swung upside down off a monkey bar. I've done headstands and handstands, dives and balances, but the playground remains unconquered. I'm a scaredy-cat. Risk-taking scale score, from zero (never takes risk) to ten (always seeks risk): negative two, give or take.

And yet. When I was in college, I decided that for my senior thesis, I would travel to Georgia—the country, not the state. And I would do so during a civil war. You see, I wanted to observe decision-making psychology in action, to experience how real people and real leaders reacted during real crises, not just ones that had been created in a college lab. And so, notebook in hand, I flew halfway across the world, hired a bodyguard, and made my way into the literal line of fire. What risk-taking score do I get on that one?

How about for putting my career at the *New Yorker* on hold to play poker? Or for being too afraid to ever ride on a motorcycle or fly in a helicopter unless under duress? Or for moving in with my now husband less than two months after we met? Or for never having tried a single recreational drug, not even pot, because I'm too afraid to cause any sort of permanent damage to my neurons? At the end of it all, am I risk-seeking or risk-averse?

The answer, as Walter would tell you, is it all depends on the situation. It's impossible to tell in the abstract. But at the poker table, it turns out, my "profile," or behavioral signature, as Walter would call it, emerges in full. Blake could pick up on some small physical habits that may give off information—and I'm certainly going to make every single effort to eliminate those entirely. But the more powerful tells could well be psychological. I shy away from small risks—in a marginal spot, where a more aggressive player may call or raise, I'll just choose to fold. But given the right circumstances, I'm also apt to run insane bluffs for my tournament life. Observe me over a day at the table, and you'll be able to tell more about my risk-taking proclivities than people who've known me socially for years. It's a full life drama. Years of situations and contexts distilled to one day at a tournament table.

The interesting thing about this dynamic, though, is that it's, well, dynamic: the situation may change simply because of the players involved. A psychological situation isn't stable because it isn't just about cards and actions. It's also about the emotional experiences and people involved. And so it's iterative. I may act differently if I think people are reacting to me differently, and vice versa. I might perceive the risk calculus differently than I did at a seemingly identical moment. It's a process of constant adjustment.

Frank Lantz has developed a poker concept that he calls "donkey space," about the dynamic between two expert players who understand the game at a high level and are playing a heads up match—that is, one on one. There's perfect theoretical play, which is unexploitable by any opponent, and then there's adjustment to that play based on your opponent's strategy. The only time you don't need to adjust is if everyone is playing perfectly— which in the messy reality of a poker table doesn't happen. "The hard part of poker at this level is actually not this incredibly hard thing of knowing what perfect play is, which is as hard as it is in a game like chess," Lantz says. "The hard part is this: How good are you at identifying where your opponent is in strategy space, based on their actions?" You watch them act and react over multiple situations and you try to adjust based on that be-havior, to be maximally profitable against this particular person.

But now, if your opponent is good, they realize what you're doing—and they adjust in turn. It may even be the case that they moved to this particu-lar spot in strategy space on purpose, Lantz points out, so that they can now exploit you better. They've given up equity for a little bit to then kick you once you've moved. "I call this donkey space because a donkey is a fish, a player who is not playing perfectly," Lantz explains. "But these two peo-ple are like fighter pilots, maneuvering around each other, because in a dogfight, what you want to be is on your opponent's tail. That's where you can shoot them." He continues, "You're doing barrel rolls and triple flips, and you're constantly trying to outmaneuver this other person."

In a sense, it's like John Boyd's OODA loop playing out at the table in-stead of in the air. Boyd was a fighter pilot in the air force, and he invented OODA to describe a dynamic that he'd learned through his years in combat: to succeed, you need to constantly observe, orient, decide, and act. OODA. The way to outmaneuver your opponent is to get inside *their* OODA loop. Figure out what they are observing, how they are orienting and deciding, and how they act as a result. That way, you can anticipate them. Because at the end of the day, the fighting, just like the poker table, comes down to information. "You're getting signals when you play, and you're giving off signals. Your actions are both actions in the game that lead to the result in this particular hand, and signals for your opponent to interpret, that explain your strategy," Lantz says. "Someone can look at them and, from them, reverse engineer the strategy book you're using. It's a deep, multilayered problem in information processing."

The first read anyone has on me is a simple one: I'm female. How does that change their CAPS, if at all? I find that certain men want to be gentlemanly; they find it distasteful to take my chips. They will often show me their cards to let me know I've made a good fold. Once I discern that, I can use it to my advantage, folding more when I would otherwise call. Other men don't think I have any business being there. I should be washing dishes or changing diapers. They want me gone. So they bully and bluff and push. Once I see that, I can play more passively and let them give me their chips. Some men don't think a woman could run a big bluff. If I raise and show signs of life, they fold. Now I can bluff more than I otherwise would. And some would rather die than be bluffed by a woman. Now they will call me with next to nothing, only for the satisfaction of seeing me beat. With them, I can bet more thinly for value, but should avoid trying to pull one over. But all of that is only the first part.

Now comes the interactive part of CAPS, the donkey space. Do they know I'm adjusting—and did they do this on purpose to get me to respond a certain way?

I'm in a major hand in Monte Carlo, deep in the six-max that will be my final tournament of the trip, and I have to make a decision that will cost me most of my chips. I've been playing against a certain older Russian gentleman all day (no, not that one; this one comes later, but my impressions of the original Siberian wolf are still plenty fresh). And he has more than conformed to my newly developed stereotype of such gentlemen: to them, I should be in the kitchen, not the casino. Like the Siberian who'd so hoodwinked me, he has gleefully shown me multiple bluffs when he's put me in miserable spots in the past, and I've overheard him boasting about "beating the girl" to a friend during breaks. (At this point, he is happily unaware that I speak Russian.) I've also seen him curse out another opponent for having aces against his ace-king. He doesn't take defeat well. And now we are at the river and he is all in. If I call and am wrong, I'll lose over two thirds of my chips. I have what's known as a bluff catcher: a hand that can beat only bluffs. It's top pair, sure, but by the intense action getting to this point, it's clear that if he is shoving for value, I'm well beat. I don't know what to do.

As I think, he gets up from the chair and starts doing a little dance. He's goading me to call him. "Come on, call already!" he yells. Then he calls the clock on me—that's when a player asks for a member of the floor staff to give you a countdown when they feel you've taken up too much time. I've never had the clock called on me, and I'm miserable. Finally, I decide to make the call. He flips over a set, and I send over my chips.

Did he set me up for that moment? I can't help but feel he did, and I went terribly wrong. I let my developed patterns get in the way of what should have been a stronger signal: the man is dancing and singing. He probably has a good hand. Even Mike Caro, the original master of tells, whose book was the first of its kind in the poker world, would have told you that this behavior screams strength. I say even Caro, because his work was done without any advanced analytic techniques and some of it hasn't stood the test of time. But this is as basic as it gets. In this hand, I'm the donkey.

So where does this leave me? Clearly, my CAPS is more dynamic and complex than I've realized. Despite having worked with the system for years, I've never done the hard work of digging deeper on my own unique nodes and dynamics. I've been so busy focusing on reading the motivations in play for other people that I forget to factor in myself.

I know at every level how crucial it is to read people correctly if you're going to develop beyond a basic and proficient player, into an exceptional one. You don't play against an aggressive player the way you play against a passive one. You don't play against someone who is strong the way you play against someone you think is weak and bluffing. And I know how incredibly difficult a thing it is to get your read right. Through careful observation, you not only have to learn how to tell the difference between your faulty intuitions and real data, but understand how to exploit what you've seen—and how to know if you're being exploited in turn.

That last part is the one I seem to have momentarily forgotten. I've been so busy reading others that I've missed the step of stopping to read myself. Blake can tell me only what I'm giving off physically. He doesn't have enough to go on to unravel my inner psychology and understand the internal tug-of-war that may be governing my actions. In each hand he analyzed, imagine everything that was going on inside my head that I wasn't even aware of. I've done the work of physical profiling. But what about psychologically? What about understanding the *why*?

In turning my mind to tells and reads at this stage in my learning, I may have missed a crucial step: that the first person you have to profile—psychologically, not physically—is yourself. Had I understood that lesson, I wouldn't have found myself, so soon after the stunning cliffs and starlit poker room, out ten grand on the Rio bathroom floor.

Full Tilt

Las Vegas, June–July 2017

*"Gaming is an enchanting witchery. . . . [The gamester] is ei-
ther lifted to the top of mad joy with success, or plunged to the
bottom of despair by misfortune; always in extremes, always in
a storm; this minute the gamester's countenance is so serene
and calm that one would think that nothing could disturb it,
and the next minute so stormy and tempestuous that it threat-
ens distruction to itself and others; and, as he is transported as
he wins, so losing, is he tost upon the billows of a high swelling
passion, till he hath lost sight of both sense and reason."*

CHARLES COTTON, *THE COMPLEAT GAMESTER*, 1674

June comes much faster than I'm ready for. It seems that just yesterday I touched down, fresh from my Monte Carlo semi-triumph. (I've come back around to thinking that I should be more proud than not. Targets move, but having a new one, however hard it may look to hit, doesn't negate that you've reached the first. Plus, I've discovered that the key to harnessing a positive mindset is to seek out other poker players who have done even worse than you. Talk to enough people who didn't even min cash a single event, and you can feel adequately satisfied with your own slightly less negative trip.) And I vowed to work as much as I could on my ability to not only read others but curb their ability to read me, to do everything I could to gear up for the Main, which is taunting me from afar. But where am I, really?

May, as it turns out, didn't pan out. Sure, Erik and I scouted a few more local events for me to try. But when I get back to Brooklyn, I realize that I really don't want to leave. I've been traveling almost nonstop since January. Two- and three-week chunks in Vegas. A week in Maryland. A week at Foxwoods, in Connecticut. Almost two weeks in Monte Carlo. And even when I was in New York, I was in New Jersey more often than not. Hoboken cafés had become my de facto office. Poker has become my life. And my *real* life has, naturally but still somehow surprisingly, taken a back seat. I'm lucky, of course. I have a husband who is fully supportive, who tells me over and over to give this project my all and see where I come out. But as I settle into more than two days at home, I understand that I've also gotten deeply lonely on the road—and that I've forgotten so many of the reasons that I came to poker to begin with. I had set out to understand the limits of control, the nature of luck. I had wanted to make my life richer and better. And I was doing all that, to be sure. But in my nonstop drive to reach the WSOP Main Event summit in an incredibly condensed time frame, I forgot to stop and enjoy it all—enjoy the game, the journey, the new skills that are rapidly making their way into my thought process. I want to stay and spend time with my husband, who is now embarking on his own new venture. I want to watch early spring in New York—my favorite time of year. I want to enjoy the fact that my health is finally back under control and I can actually be outside. I want to visit my family. I haven't seen them in months. I want, in other words, to pause.

Mastery is always a struggle for balance. How much time do you devote to the craft, and how much to yourself? And can you really do one without the other? I have a dual goal here. My poker journey—but also the larger journey that the poker is meant to lead to. They can't be separated. And as I'm learning, the craft of poker certainly cannot be mastered without self-knowledge, self-care, and self-reflection. All your technical prowess will evaporate if your mind and emotional landscape aren't solid. My return from Monte Carlo has made one thing clear: I need to recharge.

I spend May doing just that. I'm still studying poker every day, watching videos, taking notes, thinking through strategy. I'm practicing watching players for those little signs and gestures that Blake and I reviewed. I watch video of myself to see what I need to look out for. Erik is in Las Vegas, but we set up calls a few times a week to go over material. Not my hands, but the hands that others are playing. We watch streams on PokerGO. We discuss strategy videos from Run It Once. I practice riffling my chips in the privacy of my apartment (bonus: the chips are devoid of mystery substances and none of them stick together). I give myself pep talks—June will be amazing. June will be the boost I need. June will bring me the confidence I need to play the Main Event, and the knowledge that it will be money well spent, not money thrown away on a pricey reporting lark.

It's May 30, and I'm on a plane. The plan is to spend two weeks playing the preliminary events, return to New York for two weeks—my best friend has the nerve to schedule her wedding during the WSOP, and Erik warns me that spending the full month and a half of the WSOP in Vegas may not be conducive to full mental health at this stage in my learning journey, with too much stimulation and not enough time to reflect and absorb and adjust—and then make the trip back for the Main Event right after the Fourth of July. Assuming, of course, that these next two weeks in June go well.

"There are lots of events that are at a more reasonable price point and should have good value," Erik has told me. Not just the Ladies. There's the Colossus. The Millionaire Maker. The Giant. I must admit they've done an excellent job naming everything. Who *doesn't* want to play a tournament that promises to make you into a millionaire or that makes you feel like a colossus or a giant? Many people who come to the WSOP never even play the Main. Instead, they focus on the slate of smaller tournaments that surround it. From a bankroll perspective, it's certainly a smart choice. Up first: the Colossus. It costs $565, making it one of the most affordable of the WSOP bracelet events. And, year after year, it boasts a prize pool that makes its winner a millionaire, or close to it. I'm excited. I'm nervous. I'm everything at once. My first World Series event. This is what I've been working for.

It's my first time in the Rio, and the only familiar thing is the huge picture of Penn and Teller on the outside of the hotel. It brings me back to my first trip and that impressive tank. I walk inside, and immediately, I get lost. It turns out I've gone through the wrong entrance. There's the main hotel, and there's the convention center that the WSOP takes over once a year to host all its events. Seasoned players know to come straight to the convention entrance, around the back. Erik forgot to mention that detail—or maybe he mentioned it and I forgot, in the excitement of it all—so I find myself trapped in between something called Carnival World and another something called Masquerade Village. I notice a KISS store over to my right. Does anybody actually go there? I find myself wondering. Not the right mindset or start to my WSOP journey. I feel largely like I did that day back in the Golden Nugget. As I wander past some Vietnamese restaurant, I glimpse the muted yellows of a WSOP banner over to my right. At last, the scent is fresh. I hurry in that direction, past a Starbucks, and follow the red arrow around the corner.

On my left, Hash House A Go Go. On my right, a Mexican place with Guy Fieri's oversize face smiling out in neon. Am I going toward my destination? The arrows over my head assure me that yes, the WSOP is indeed coming right up. As I walk down a long hallway with glass on my right and a series of small stores on the left, I start seeing more and more people. The hallway opens up to a circle of activity. It's a din of voices and bodies. A large banner suspended from the ceiling welcomes you to the 48th World Series of Poker. Up ahead, I see sets of large double doors that are open to a room filled with poker tables. In the middle is what looks like an open store, selling exclusively WSOP merchandise. To the right is a Caesars Rewards registration line, which I need to get in to get my account verified so that I can register online in the future. I read all about it on the website ahead of time, in a frenzy of nervous preparation.

I'm directed to the registration windows, down another side hallway off the main circle. I turn left, and I don't know what hits me. The hallway is overflowing with booths. Each booth is selling something. And it seems like each comes equipped with at least three people who stand not behind the merchandise but in the middle of the hallway, intercepting anyone who walks by and trying to muscle them into the vending area. I was expecting a poker tournament, not a bazaar, but a bazaar is what this most closely resembles. One that seems to peddle quite its share of snake oil. There's a bar with multicolored bubbling cylinders that look to have been taken directly from the set of Doc Brown's laboratory in *Back to the Future*.

"Would you like to try some pure oxygen to clear your head?" comes a chipper voice in my right ear. I turn, ready to launch into the reasons why oxygen bars are a total scam and, far from clearing my mind, will make me feel worse, but decide that I have more important matters to attend to and simply shake my head.

"Chargers! Headphones! Chargers! Headphones! Hey, honey, want some headphones? These are the best."

I try to push my way past a duo of men who seem to really, really love chargers and headphones. At the end of days, they will clutch them like a life raft. And, truly, I hope the chargers do save lives, because a quick glance tells me that the price is about five times higher than I've ever encountered. Woe to the poor soul whose cell phone dies midway through the tournament. (Luckily, Erik has armed me with a tournament survival kit. Water, energy bars, and a mobile charger. I myself have added industrial-strength Purell.)

There's a stand selling crystals—each one has a unique energy, the sign says. Never sit at another poker table unprepared. Ah, just what I've been missing. I text Erik to let him know that my worries are now behind me. I'll pick up some crystals, and the bracelets are sure to follow. "Good plan," he writes back.

There are the more legitimate booths, too. D&B Poker, a publisher of poker books, is advertising a new book by Chris Moorman, about his path to becoming "the most successful online poker player of all time." A huge cardboard cutout of what I assume is Moorman himself stands next to a display of books. I make a note to look him up when I'm back at my hotel. I see a booth for an accountant who specializes in poker. Smart thinking, to be right there for everyone who makes a big score. I don't know whether the accounting firm is any good, but they are certainly savvy. Finally, I see the registration line. I make my way to the back and begin the wait to play.

FIVE BULLETS. THAT MEANS five separate entries. Five times paying the oh-so-reasonable-sounding $565 entry—or at least reasonable in the scheme of $1K and $3K and $5K and $10K events. That's how many times I end up registering for the Colossus, at the end of it all. I was going to play just one time—but somehow, after every bust-out, I wound up back in line hoping for just one more chance. And the next day, and the day after that. From $565 to $2,825. I've been here three days, and I've already blown a big chunk of my budget for two weeks. How did that happen? What happened to me? I'm a reasonable, solid human being, with a reasonable, wise mentor who cautions me over and over about being responsible in my bankroll decisions. What exactly did I just do?

That's what I find myself thinking, in disbelief, as I exit the Rio after the final flight of the Colossus in a daze. Here's something I've never encountered before: the Colossus is a multiple reentry event, with six starting flights over three days. Each flight, you can enter up to two times. This means that if you bust and the entry period for the day is still open, you can enter again—or "fire" again, in poker parlance. And if the entry period is closed, but there's another starting flight? You can simply fire again, up to twelve times. So, if you're really trying to set an entry record, you could conceivably spend $6,780 attempting to run up a commanding chip lead. At least I haven't quite gone that far, but I've come much closer than I ever thought possible.

I can't stop shaking my head as I slump back to the Aria, where I'm staying, to lick my wounds. The simple truth seems to be that I wasn't quite as ready for the whirlwind of the WSOP as I thought I was. I let myself get caught up in the excitement, the energy of the rooms. The joyful anticipation of everyone there that they, too, could emerge in a few days with a bracelet. Everyone at the WSOP has a dream. *It could be me, it could be me, it could be me* is the rhythm that the chips sing as they clink against one another. *This is my shot, this is my shot, this is my shot* whistle the cards as they slide across the felt. And then you get unlucky, and the cards don't go your way, and someone hits their flush when you held top set and you find yourself at the end of the line, ready for the walk of shame out the door . . . except you realize that it's *not* the end of the line. You just got unlucky this time. You should really give yourself a fair shot and try again. And "Are you going to fire again?" comes the chorus from the pros you meet on your way out the door, the pros who've been doing this for years and have bankrolls far larger than your annual income. "You should really fire again. This is such a great field." And so you say, yes, why not, and you fire again—not quite realizing that what makes the field so great, at least for now, is you. You're the great field. You're the one who is going to get slaughtered. Over and over and over. And over and over, if you're me, to round it up to five.

And there it is. The WSOP is its own beast. And it's not the kind of beast I've previously encountered. It's not just the nature of near-unlimited reentry, although that, too, is new to me. It's the aura, the energy, the, yes, peer pressure from players much stronger than I am, for whom it really does make sense to fire again after an unlucky break. I thought I was prepared—and maybe strategically, I wasn't so far off. But mentally, emotionally? I never realized that would be my shortcoming, but clearly, here we are. Once the din in my head has quieted and the hallways of the Rio are behind me, sitting with my Thai takeout at my hotel-standard desk, with my laptop open to the Excel spreadsheet tracking my poker budget, I feel something close to shame. I'm chagrined that I was so easily swept up in it all, that I wasn't strong enough to know my own limits. I'm mad that I let the pros talk me into doing something I wasn't comfortable with. I'm even more mad that, just because they have an edge, I somehow fancied that I, too, have an edge over those silly amateurs. But silly amateur is exactly who I am, and I shouldn't delude myself into thinking anything else. I close my laptop and vow to do better. And I begin that journey in self-improvement the very next morning, during my check-in report with Erik. I catch him up on hands from the Colossus for my next round of studying. He compliments me on how many interesting spots I noted—"There's so much here! A lot for us to talk about." And I conveniently forget to mention the number of bullets I used in order to compile said interesting hands into one lovely narrative.

The remainder of my two weeks passes in what seems like a minute. I enter a six-max event—I now officially love them, after cashing in the only other one I've ever played—and cement my love of the format by notching my first official WSOP cash: 237th, for $2,247. Almost two thousand people entered. And, sure, it's yet another min cash—I bust right after the money, having once more found myself short-stacked on the bubble, despite talking through a new, more aggressive approach with Erik beforehand; there's a difference between knowing what you're supposed to do and actually having the nerve to do it in the moment. But, as Erik tells me over sushi at my new favorite sushi place of all time, Kabuto, it's still a milestone. "It's your first ever WSOP cash. That's really great. The important thing is, you're threatening." He doesn't mean threatening as in I look like a lion newly escaped from the zoo. He means that I'm threatening to make a deep run. I'm getting closer. Just a few more moves, a few more breaks, and it seems like I could almost break through to those real cash numbers.

I enter the Millionaire Maker. Twice. I mean, I did cash in the other $1,500 event, so how bad could one little reentry really be? It doesn't make me a millionaire, but I do cash in 1,063rd place—not impressive-sounding, I know, but there were almost eight thousand entries—for $2,249. I'm still down for the event, but at least I almost recovered both bullets. My final cash comes in the Giant, the $365 event I enter one evening after I bust my first Milly Maker bullet. I earn $1,252 for 595th place, out of 10,015 entries. That's better than a min cash, and it helps salve the pain of the Marathon ($2,620 entry, above my limit but justified in my head because the structure is similar to the Main Event and will help me prepare for the slower, deeper feel of that tournament) and another $1,500 bracelet event, both of which yield zero. Final tally for the two weeks: $11,810 in entries (yikes) and $5,748 in cashes, for a net loss of $6,062. And that's before hotel, food, airfare, and my daily Lyft rides to and from the Rio.

I fly back to New York for my friend's wedding, in spirits far less exuberant than they were when I touched down in Vegas. How do professional tournament players do it? I'm exhausted. I miss my bed and my husband and home cooking. The adrenaline is fading, but the empty pockets feel very real.

The tally of my accomplishments: three cashes in my first ever WSOP foray is nothing to scoff at, as Erik has told me repeatedly. Technically, I'm improving. And while I may not have Blake's tells down to a science, I do think I'm improving on that front, too. At the very least, I don't have any more stories of affable table neighbors who would never bluff me doing just that. I'm more guarded, in both speech and gesture, and I do think it's paying off. And it's true, I'm threatening. But will I ever actually threaten? I can now see why the min cash route just isn't going to cut it. I need to do a serious self-assessment to see if I have what it takes to go deep, to get over that hurdle and really make it all worthwhile. I've played the preliminaries. But am I really ready for the Main Event? And if I'm not, do I want to play it *just because*? Ten grand for a story and a dream?

The me who conceived of this project last summer wouldn't have thought twice of jumping straight in. Wasn't that the point? A journalistic foray into unknown territory, reporter's notebook blazing bright, à la George Plimpton, or more close to home, Colson Whitehead?* But the me who has now traveled this far can't help but feel a little differently.

---

*George Plimpton was known for his journalistic stunts of "participatory journalism"—one even involving a comedic performance in Vegas. And Whitehead entered the WSOP Main Event for a book, *The Noble Hustle*.

If my journey is about understanding luck, about feeling out the boundaries of control, about knowing how to optimize and reclaim power over what you *can* do while minimizing the perils of happenstance that you can do little about, then poker has already done its job well. It has taught me the pitfalls of the gamble, the necessity of selecting games so that you have an edge, so that you have a statistical advantage, so that your skill can win. It has taught me to avoid situations where skill falls by the wayside, where you have to rely on variance alone to break your way because you simply can't measure up otherwise. The Main Event *just because* isn't quite as bad as the lottery, but it surely isn't good. Here's a free life lesson: seek out situations where you're a favorite; avoid those where you're an underdog. This doesn't mean never take shots. Shot-taking is a tried-and-true thing in poker, where someone plays a tournament at a higher level than before, enters a cash game at higher stakes than before, to see if she can hack it. If you never take shots, you never know when you're ready to move up. But in a way, these past two weeks were a shot: they were higher stakes, more intense action, huge player pools. And what they've illustrated is that, while the seeds of success are there, I'm not yet ready. The smart thing is to pull back, play smaller, regroup, build up, and try again—better, smarter, savvier, more skillful in both the ways of poker strategy and the ways of mental strength. If I take the intent of my journey rather than the arbitrary end goal meant as a hook for a book proposal more than anything else, the conclusion is clear. Postpone. Come back for July, sure, but instead of the Main, play more of the smaller side events. Build my bankroll back up. Hone my skill. And shoot for the Main in a year's time. Don't jump into the arms of chance and say, "Please don't let me fall!" Don't play above your weight class after you've just been punched down. It's a question of respect for the game—and not just the game of poker. It's beyond simple journalistic curiosity. It's only a few months ago that Phil Galfond reminded me to always find the *why* behind every move, every decision, every action. And here's one thing I know for sure: no matter the decision, the *why* shouldn't ever be for the simple glory of saying you've done something. At least to me, right now, that's not good enough.

Hindsight, of course, is perfect—and hindsight bias is strong. Of course, knowing that I was doomed to bust at the beginning of the second day, I should have chosen to save my precious cash for a better occasion. But this isn't about hindsight bias. In reality, I should have known going in. I just chose to ignore what I knew. Why?

DANIEL KAHNEMAN LIKES TO recount a story about his ill-fated involvement in an education reform project in Israel. Along with a team of education experts, he'd taken on the task of creating a new curriculum, complete with textbook, to teach decision making in school. During one of the meetings of his team, he decided to try out one of the forecasting tactics they were covering: he asked everyone to predict how long it would take them to complete the textbook. When he collected the estimates, they ranged from one and a half to two and a half years. He then asked the resident curriculum expert, who'd observed similar projects in the past, how long it had taken other similar efforts to finish the job. As it turns out, a good 40 percent of them never finished at all—and those that did took between seven and ten years. "We should have quit that day. None of us was willing to invest six more years of work in a project with a 40% chance of failure," Kahneman writes in *Thinking, Fast and Slow*. But they didn't. He called it irrational perseverance: "Facing a choice, we gave up rationality rather than give up the enterprise."

In what's known as the planning fallacy, we tend to be overly optimistic when we map out timelines, goals, targets, and other horizons. We look at the best-case scenario instead of using the past to determine what a more realistic scenario would look like. And in one sense, I can't be faulted here: there is no base-case scenario for my endeavor. I don't know of any other case of someone trying to learn poker from absolute scratch, having never played a real card game before, and aiming for the World Series. I'm a base rate of one. And yet I am at fault, because I'd mapped out a year from when I first had this idea—but have already seen that I was too optimistic in even getting started. A year from start would put me in the dead of the coming winter, with no WSOP events in sight. If even the start of my year was off, it's not difficult to imagine that the training itself is also off. So how do I conclude that seven months is actually OK?

Instead of learning from my original planning fallacy that has brought me to my "target" almost a half year ahead of an already short schedule, I now compound it by sticking to my guns. I had a plan, a specific goal, and even though the circumstances have changed—and changed significantly at that—I'm sticking to it. The status quo bias: continue with the action you've already decided on, regardless of new information. Erik had warned me that one of the most important things about being a good poker player was flexibility. The willingness to admit you're wrong, to embrace the uncertainty inherent in any decision. "Less certainty, more inquiry": his words couldn't have been more direct. There's never a single right way to play a hand—and there's certainly no single right way to reach a goal. Why not defer for a year? Or change the target to something in six months, sticking to the timeline but changing the specific event? Why not exercise some creative thinking in what my journey is going to be? I am too married to what it is all "supposed" to look like, and not critical enough of the fact that I simply made some decisions earlier on with incomplete information—and now that I know more, I should change course. No one is telling me to quit poker, merely to reassess where I am.

But somehow, I convince myself that swerving wouldn't be a demonstration of my adaptability and flexible thinking. Instead, it would be a hit to my reputation, a demonstration of failure, of a lack of ability. It's the classic sunk cost fallacy in action: you keep to your course because of the resources you've already invested. I've written about it many times. Only it seems that when it comes down to it, I don't quite apply it to myself, right now. In my mind, sunk costs are supposed to be physical. Somehow it doesn't occur to me that they can also be intangible. An accurate self-reassessment would have shown that I was nowhere near ready to take on what I had planned, and that the bigger blow to my reputation might actually be proceeding with my set course. No matter.

It's easy to spot sunk costs in others. This person held on to their investment too long. That CEO didn't switch his management strategy in response to a new market environment. That company didn't recognize that their star product was going obsolete. In yourself, it can become more difficult—especially when you're dealing not with a concrete action but rather a lack of action.

One of the most important lessons of poker strategy, intimately connected to self-assessment, is this: sometimes, it's the hands you don't play that win you the title. We remember the hero calls. What about the hero folds? What you *don't* do rather than what you do—that can be greatness. The art of letting go can be the truly strong one. Acknowledging when you're behind rather than continuing to put good money after bad. Acknowledging when the landscape has shifted and you need to make a shift yourself as a result.

It happens all the time in our lives. We find ourselves in an appealing situation—and then we hold on to it for dear life, even when any objective outside observer would tell us that the appeal is long gone. We start at a promising job, only to be stymied in promotions over and over—yet we cling to the notion that the job is great. We embark on a promising relationship, only to find we have less and less in common with our partner—yet we forge ahead, refusing to admit that what seemed so right is now wrong. Sometimes, the most difficult thing of all is to stop playing. All too often, we stay in a hand long after we should have gotten out.

No matter how good your starting hand, you have to be willing to read the signs to let it go. You are not playing in a vacuum. You are playing opponents. You have to follow the game. My starting hand couldn't be better: Erik Seidel as coach, my background in the psychology of decision making as fuel, all the advice and resources I could hope for at my disposal. But, as I've realized in my assessment after my June WSOP foray, the game has changed. It's no longer about a simple exercise in seeing how far I can go. On that journey, I've already learned the importance of playing well—and that means choosing my battles correctly. I know that, at least for now, it's time to fold, not to double down. I know this, I've thought it through, but somehow, I can't quite verbalize it to myself in the moment. And doubling down is exactly what I do.

This is the exact sort of fallacious, unbending thinking I observed in my failed investors in grad school—the ones who conceived of a strategy and then kept executing it even when the environment changed for the worse, because they were smart, optimistic about their own abilities, and no quitters. And here I am, doing the exact same thing.

Kahneman, of course, wouldn't have been surprised. In a 1977 memo to DARPA that he'd written with Amos Tversky, on how to best reach specific military objectives, he warned that knowing about a bias didn't mean you wouldn't exhibit it; it could still look highly attractive:

"Erroneous intuitions resemble visual illusions in a crucial respect: both types of error remain compellingly attractive even when the person is fully aware of their nature." I might realize that my thinking has been fallacious—but if I still like my plan, I can trick myself into thinking it remains a good idea. Sure, there may be some planning fallacies and status quos and whatnot involved, but I see that, I've taken it into account, and I still think it's a good idea.

Of course, I could easily correct my illusions, however pretty they might be. "In situations likely to produce illusions of sight or intuition," Kahneman continues, "we must let our beliefs and actions be guided by a critical and reflective assessment of reality, rather than by our immediate impressions, however compelling these may be." Ah, but what if my immediate impressions are so compelling that I simply don't want to be corrected?

Here's what I find myself thinking. I've shown I can make it with the best already—wasn't that the lesson of Monte Carlo? (OK, one of the lessons, but who's really counting?) I didn't crash. Instead, I cashed. I played six events and made money in half of them. If that's not good, what is? And before Monte Carlo, didn't I win a tournament? Didn't I final table another? Didn't I exceed everyone's expectations in a short time? I've been working my ass off. I've earned it. I even have three WSOP cashes under my belt (losses conveniently forgotten).

I should know how much this smells of overconfidence—after all, that's what I studied. This is my actual area of expertise. I'm practically dripping with irrational exuberance. The data don't even back me up: I have it, right there, in hard black-on-white Excel. I've been losing money. But here's where something of the Dunning-Kruger effect creeps in. Yes, that one. The one that shows that the less competent you are in an area, the more likely you are to overestimate your degree of competence. That the less you know about a topic, the more you think you know—as long as you know just enough to start feeling a bit fluent in its vocabulary. This is one bias I never thought I'd find applicable to me. I have a PhD in psychology, for god's sake! But here we are. I've had just a taste of seeming success, and suddenly, I'm feeling ready to take on the world.

This is what I'm thinking, and I don't want to be persuaded otherwise. In 2018, Kaitlin Woolley and Jane Risen demonstrated that people will often actively avoid information that would help them make a more informed decision when their intuition, or inner preference, is already decided. They will, for instance, avoid learning how many calories are in an attractive dessert, or how much they will be paid if they choose to take on a boring task instead of a more exciting one. Part of them knows that the information might mean they need to change their decision, so they choose to ignore it.

Wouldn't it be rational for me to ask Erik's opinion on whether I should enter the Main right now? Of course it would. Just as it would have been fitting for me to tell him that I'd fired five bullets in the Colossus, instead of just going through interesting hands. But there's that irrational part of me that wants the praise for my hand selection, the praise for my cashes and my progress, and not the voice of reason that tells me that min cashing isn't going to cut it, that I shouldn't be reentering, that I should be reconsidering. And so instead of asking for the sage advice that I don't want to hear, I decide to inform him of the fact that I'm entering. Wouldn't it be rational for me to do an objective analysis, using the tools Erik has already given me, of where my bankroll is, where my results are, what my ROI is? I decide instead that those numbers don't mean much. I'm feeling good; shouldn't I ride that feeling?

Even on the morning of the Main, I have the opportunity to call it off. One thing Erik has stressed, over and over, is to never feel committed to playing an event, ever. "See how you feel in the morning" is a refrain I've grown used to hearing from him. His point is a simple one: your edge is your edge only if you're playing your best game. To play your best game, you need to be your best you. Rested, sharp, focused. If you're off, a game that would have been a winning endeavor can suddenly become a losing one. An almost sure thing can become a gamble. I thought that it was just his way of letting me off easy, in case I got jittery about playing a big event—but, no, he does it himself. I've seen him skip a major $500,000 tournament—one with quite a prestigious title—because he wasn't feeling his best. He'd done a self-assessment, decided he wasn't quite where he wanted to be at the moment he needed to be there, and calmly bought a ticket to New York, where he spent the week of the tournament seeing the latest of Broadway and taking in art at the Whitney. No regrets. He lives what he tells me. Never feel like you have to do something just because it's expected of you—even if you're the one who expects it of you. Know when to step back. Know when to recalibrate. Know when you need to reassess your strategy, prior plans be damned. Everyone thought he'd play. I thought he'd play. He'd thought he'd play. And then he didn't. And it was all fine. And he went on to play that event the following year—this time, he was feeling just great—and came in fourth place, for over $1.2 million.

"See how you feel in the morning." The words echo through my mind as I feel a slight tingling in the back top right of my head while I get ready. That's where my migraines always start. Same exact spot. Same exact tingle. Over the years, I've come to be closely attuned to their potential onset, lest I find myself in a less than pleasant situation. But I shrug it off. I've slept well, I've exercised, I've eaten—I couldn't possibly be getting a migraine. Of course, the bigger issue is I don't *want* to be getting a migraine, so I decide it's not possible. The desire being conflated with the reality. And I trudge onward to the Rio.

Here, then, is the unvarnished truth. I didn't correct my decision not because I couldn't but because I didn't want to.

AND SO I FIND myself in the Main Event, ahead of schedule and full of illusory high hopes. I'm not the only hopeful one. All around me are people gunning for the dream. Some have a better reason than others. A man at my table is wearing a T-shirt with a photograph on it. He explains that his friend died from cancer earlier that year. His dream had been to play the Main. Once he realized he wasn't going to make it, he left entry fees in his will for each person in his home game to come to Vegas and play in his memory. This man knows he doesn't have much of a shot, but damned if he doesn't have a good reason for playing.

In this room, in this moment, the dream is incredibly real. As I play my first few hands and win some small pots, I notice that I, too, am hoping against hope that maybe, just maybe, I have a shot at a real run. But then the day goes on, the pain is too much, and the chips that had started, however slowly, to accumulate are orphaned and left to fend for themselves, and I'm on a bathroom floor, hopes almost dashed, phone in hand, hiding the fact that I'm a bit less than optimally inclined from the person who has put his trust in me. "Hanging in there," I text him, and as he wishes me luck, I realize that I'm failing at my goal.

I do somehow manage to make it back to the table before the end of the day. And I do manage to find that magic bag of chips for the next morning: 29,500, down from 50,000 to begin the day. Out of the 1,643 players who've made it on to the second day from my flight, I'm number 1,351. It's not great, even I can see that, but I'm in there.

"You made day two. That's really great." Erik is excited and supportive.

And I am excited but guilty. After all, I wasn't exactly playing my best game. Migraine and bathroom go unmentioned.

"A lot of people didn't make it through. For your first time, this is great news," he continues.

"Yeah, but I'm really short," I tell him.

"You still have over thirty big blinds. That's plenty to work with. You'll be great."

And he's right, I reflect as I drift off to sleep, exhausted with pain and nerves. I *did* make it through where so many others didn't. Isn't that a sign of something? Just imagine how I would have fared had I been at full capacity. Could my decision to play have really been so bad? And tomorrow is another day. I still have a chance to shine. I fall asleep to fairy-tale visions of my success jumping like sheep around my head.

I wish I could report that they came true. Alas, on day two my inexperience catches up to me. I get impatient. Despite Erik's assurances that thirty big blinds is plenty, I get nervous that I don't have enough chips and that I need to make something happen if I'm going to survive. And I do the exact thing he told me not to do—compare myself with others rather than focus on how I'm doing on my own.

In every tournament, there's a display clock with relevant information, including how many players remain and what the average chip stack is— that is, the average number of chips all remaining players have. It can be a useful gauge, but it can also be a distracting one.

"Ignore the average," Erik implores. "Just focus on how many blinds you have. The average doesn't matter for your strategy. What matters is how deep *you* are." We've studied what I do when I have lots of chips (deep-stacked), a middling number, or a small number (short-stacked). All I need to know is how many chips I have relative to the blinds, and I can play. I shouldn't worry about how many others have—at least, not the others who aren't at my table. Sure, I should be paying attention to the chips at my table. But the tournament average has no bearing on that whatsoever. Erik knows something important about me that I can't quite see: if I start comparing myself with the average, I'll start panicking. He wants me to focus on what I can control, not the irrelevant noise.

But I want to see what I should aspire to, and so I find my eyes drifting to the clock. Uh-oh. I'm so far below average it's not even funny. I am doing horribly. And so, before the first level of the day has a chance to progress very far, I do something very stupid. I'm in the big blind with king-jack off-suit ("I probably play king-jack less than most players. It's just not a good hand," I can hear Erik saying) after a player in early position opens. The flop comes king-high. I've hit top pair. Normally, when you have fewer than thirty big blinds, top pair becomes an incredibly strong hand. You can safely get all your chips in the middle and not be making a huge mistake. But *normally* doesn't apply to the Main Event.

The Main Event is different in several ways. First, it's the slowest event that exists: nowhere else do you have levels that last for two hours. This means that you can take your time. You don't have to get impatient, ever. It's much closer to a cash game. You know the blinds won't be going up anytime soon, and your thirty big blinds will still be thirty big blinds, not shrinking rapidly, an hour from now. Second, it's the Main Event. For many people, this is their shot. This is what they've been saving up for. This is what they've been working for. This means that the average player—not the seasoned pro, mind you, but the recreational player who has been planning for this for the whole year—isn't as likely to make big moves or run big bluffs that will put his entire tournament at risk. For many people, even those who are usually fearless in building chips, this is the one event of the year where simply min cashing is enough. The goal becomes the ability to say that you cashed in the Main. You don't want to bust if you don't have to.

This is all to say, if there's ever a time to tread a bit more carefully when you're not quite sure where you stand, it's the Main. You should, generally speaking, be a little less trigger-happy in calling off light for your tournament life—that is, in making a marginal call that will end your run. Because, generally speaking, people won't be putting you to that decision as lightly.

So here we are. Back at the table. I've hit top pair, with a jack kicker—the kicker being the second card that will be a tie breaker in case another player holds the same pair; the higher the kicker, the better your chances of winning. Normally, a jack is a decent kicker. When you have an early position raiser, it becomes a marginal kicker. That's because that early player will have raised all of his ace-king and king-queen card combinations—and if he has one of those hands, you're in bad shape, indeed. Let's look at the rest of the board. There's a ten and a nine, both of them spades. What does this mean for me? The raiser could easily have a suited king-ten, for two pair. Again, that would mean I'm in bad shape. I recheck my cards. No spades. If he holds two spades, that means any additional spade would render my top pair dead.

Of course, he could also have worse pairs—queens, say, or jacks. Tens would give him a set, as would nines—and he could certainly have both of those. And he could have something that missed the board completely. Say, ace-queen of hearts or diamonds. But here's the thing. I already have top pair. If he has air or a worse pair, I should let him bluff and give me money. I don't particularly need to protect my king. The only card that could improve him and hurt me in that scenario is an ace, and if the ace comes, so be it. And if he has a draw, isn't it better to just wait and see what develops rather than risk everything now?

That's what I should be thinking. Instead, I see my top pair and feel elated that I've hit the flop. I'm already counting my double up, to a far more comfortable sixty blinds. I check. He bets. And before I even pause to think, the way I've been taught to do before every decision, I raise. My mind, it seems, had decided it was going to check-raise even before I checked. I'm just so excited by the prospect of doubling that I don't pause to consider any alternatives. My opponent isn't as quick. He thinks it over for a bit and then, very deliberately, re-raises enough to put my tournament life on the line.

Let's pause here for a moment to consider what we know. Most people wouldn't pull a move for thirty big blinds with air at this stage. I've sent photos of all the players at my table to Erik and a few other pro friends, and no one recognized this particular opponent. That means he's not a well-known pro—someone who very well might peg me for the amateur I am and not care particularly about losing thirty blinds if he thought I'd fold most any cards. Instead, he's likely an amateur like me, who values his chips and his time playing at the table. He wouldn't be pulling this move off lightly. Then there's the motion of the hands and the deliberation beforehand. If I paid as much attention to my Slepian and my Eastman as I thought I had, I'd know that the gesture is as full of meaningful intent as they come. This player thinks he is very strong. He isn't just pushing me around. And how does my marginal top pair fare against a strong hand? Pitifully. I should, at this stage, realize that the check-raise was an ill-considered mistake and fold. I'll still have just about twenty big blinds, and I can sit and wait for a better spot.

But I don't pause to consider. Rather than take the time to reassess the situation given the new information, I decide to call. I know better. I've played better. But now, this moment, I can't quite access "better." And just like that, I'm out to the nut flush. On some level, even as I'm shoving my chips into the middle, I know I shouldn't be doing what I'm doing. And a fully rational me wouldn't have. But a panicked, ever-so-slightly overconfident me who thinks she knows more than she does? A me who has become so emotionally invested in this outcome that she can't fathom the possibility of failure? That's another story. I don't even have a migraine on which to blame my faulty decision making. The only culprit here is me.

SEVERAL MONTHS EARLIER, I'D gotten a note from someone named Jared Tendler. He'd told me that he was a psychologist and a mental game coach. He'd heard about my project and was reaching out to know if I wanted to do a few sessions with him and hear about his approach. At the time, I'd just thanked him and said I'd be in touch. It's not that he didn't look qualified. Far from it. He has a master's in counseling psychology and a client list that boasts some of the top athletes (I learn he coached golfers before turning to poker) and poker players in the world. His website lists quite the testimonials. It looked like he was great at what he did—it's just that I didn't think I needed it. I'm a psychologist, I told myself at the time. I've never needed counseling for anything. I understand decision making. I have a handle on my mental health. Why would I need a coach?

Now that I've ingloriously busted the Main—it's hard to describe the deep disappointment that envelops you from toe to head once you realize the dream of the Main is at an end—I realize that maybe a mental coach is just what I need. A coach who can help me take a step back and critically assess myself. Not someone who spends time running solver simulations or talking through the specifics of bluff frequencies and bet sizing.

One who can help me with the mess of data inside my head. I realize a beat too late that a bad run in the Main Event doesn't mean my journey is over; no one ever said I had to end with the Main. That had always been arbitrary. I'd just forgotten it. What this is is a wake-up call. A chance to reflect, reassess, and see how I can improve. I may have busted the Main, but the process has certainly opened my mind. I have my decision-making strategy coach in place. Why wouldn't I also want someone to help me through the mental elements that I seem to have left to fend for themselves?

Jared and I first meet over Skype, after I've returned from Vegas—we're in different cities and time zones. Even on a computer screen, Jared is easy to like. He has that clean-cut, wholesome look that comes from easy confidence and affability. He smiles often and genuinely. He listens well. He empathizes and reflects. He sounds like someone who wouldn't let you down.

What, I wonder, can he do for me? What is it, exactly, that he does for others?

Jared gets right to the point. "To go straight for the jugular: it all comes down to confidence, self-esteem, identity, what some people call ego," he tells me. This is at the heart of what he needs to identify. Who are you? What's important to you? "When you sit down to play, you put yourself on the line. What you have to understand is you're always a person first and a poker player second." The key to figuring out where your emotional leaks will be as a player is to identify where they are as a human and what it is that brought you to the table to begin with. "How do you feel about yourself? Do you want to prove you're not an idiot, or overcome pain, or fulfill visions and dreams of yourself as someone capable of playing at the highest levels?"

The poker table, Jared explains, brings out the fears that I already carry with me and pushes them to the surface: fears of failure, pressure—it all gets exaggerated and brought forward during the course of a game. "What I look to do is see all of that as symptoms of deeper flaws. And what we're trying to do together is get at those deeper flaws."

Identify the weaknesses and you start the process of responding to them in the moment rather than after the fact. "If you're at the table under extreme pressure, you'll often revert back to mistakes you wanted to avoid even though you consciously realize it. You need to train yourself, remove your triggers so that you don't have that emotional response in the moment." Here's what Jared proposed to do for me: work through my underlying emotional holes and teach me to be a one-woman bomb squad, defusing the emotional bombs and getting rid of them before they show up and cloud my judgment.

We talk. And I tell him about my end goal. "This WSOP didn't go as well as I'd hoped," I acknowledge. "So what I want to do is work on figuring out where I'm going wrong emotionally. And then I hope I'll do better next year."

Jared stops me. "That word you just used."

What word?

"Hope. Hope has its place in the world, but when it comes to poker, it really doesn't belong," he says. "As far as hope in poker, fuck it."

Interesting. I'd thought hope was a tenet of mental health.

In some sense, yes. But not in the sense of making me a mentally strong player. "You need to think in terms of preparation. Don't worry about hoping. Just do." That phrase resonates. It's what Erik was getting at with his admonition about bad beats—the worrying about what could and should have been, the hope that replaces analysis and actual reflection. It crystallizes why I shouldn't have played the Main, not this year—it was a decision based on hope. The doing part of me knew I had a lot more to accomplish before I was ready. I find myself nodding in agreement. It's time to stop hoping and start doing.

And so we begin our work.

THE CONCEPT OF TILT in poker is one that's remarkably malleable: it applies to all sorts of situations. It means that you're letting emotions—incidental ones that aren't actually integral to your decision process—affect your decision making. You are no longer thinking rationally. It can be used as a noun (I'm on tilt), verb (I tilted), or adjective (that guy is so tilting), and it's a pithy way to recognize and describe when your decisions are not what they should be.

We tend to imagine the tilted player as the angry cowboy with a raging temper. "It is well known that [gamblers] have eaten up cards, crushed the dice, broken tables, damaged the furniture, only to end in fights with each other," writes Andrew Steinmetz in his 1870 treatise on gambling, *The Gaming Table*. In the throes of emotion, Steinmetz reflects, men are capable of anything. One man once jammed a billiard ball so far into his mouth it had to be surgically removed, while another became stuck to a wooden table after biting it with too much fury.

But everyone tilts differently. And while tilt often is a negative feeling—anger, frustration, and the like—it can also be a positive emotion—being very happy at winning a hand, liking someone at the table, and so on. All it means is that you're experiencing an emotion that is not, strictly speaking, related to your decision.

When it comes to making solid decisions, emotions aren't inherently bad. They can be useful markers for making the correct choice. Antonio Damasio, a neuroscientist at the University of Southern California, has found that the absence of emotion—the actual clinical inability to experience emotion caused by lesions to an area of the brain called the VMPFC, the ventromedial prefrontal cortex—can cause people to go broke on a gambling task. Not caring about the negative emotional effects of large losses, they don't learn to distinguish the better decisions and instead go for the larger wins and larger swings.* Likewise, Norbert Schwarz and Gerald Clore, social psychologists who spent multiple decades studying the varying effects of mood on our thoughts and outcomes, have argued that in the right context, emotions can be powerful drivers of correct choice: the emotion just needs to be integral to the decision, rather than incidental to it. Touching a hot stove makes you feel pain and anger—and you avoid touching the stove in the future. By anticipating the negative emotion caused by pain, you make a more prudent choice the next time around. We experience emotions for a reason, and the goal is not to stop experiencing them.

Instead, the goal is to learn to identify our emotions, analyze their cause, and if they're not actually part of our rational decision process—and more often than not, they aren't—dismiss them as sources of information.

In Schwarz and Clore's seminal study on the phenomenon they term "mood as information," they called people in various zip codes to ask them how satisfied they were with their life—a simple question rather than an elaborate decision task. The zip codes were chosen alongside weather reports. Some people were experiencing a sunny day, and others a rainy day. On average, people expressed higher life satisfaction when the sun was out. But the effect disappeared when the experimenter drew their attention to the weather, by asking, "How's the weather down there?" In other words, if our attention is drawn to the actual cause of our mood, it stops having an effect.

---

*More recent work has questioned the validity of the exact measure Damasio used, the Iowa gambling task. Nevertheless, other researchers have found similar decision-making deficits on tasks that have more consensus on their validity.

Schwarz and Clore's findings have been replicated in multiple settings. Stock market returns have been found to be lower on days with greater cloud cover—and higher when a favorite sports team wins. Over and over, incidental events affect decisions they shouldn't actually influence, simply because they affect how we're feeling. Tell people what's going on, though, and they can often overcome it.

Which is great news for dealing with tilt—at least up to a point. If I start to understand the sources of my tilt, I have a chance to stop misattributing the emotions I'm feeling to other things and instead to dismiss the emotions as irrelevant. If I'm upset about losing a pot, I can acknowledge that fact and realize it's not technically relevant to the next hand.

Unfortunately, that remedy seems to work only for the kinds of emotions that are more subtle than not—more priming effect than visceral storm. When it comes to emotions that are stronger, you often can't get away. Anger. Jubilation. The emotions that have a powerful magnitude—they are visceral and strong—tend to creep in no matter what. Knowing you are acting emotionally rather than rationally isn't enough: the knowledge can't protect or prevent you from the course you're on. It's unlikely that telling Steinmetz's gambler that he's a bit angry before he bites into the wooden table will prevent that table, or his teeth, from breaking all the same. All it would likely accomplish is catch you in the crossfire.

In those cases, it may help to learn to anticipate the emotion before it arises, thereby cutting it off at the source. Walter Mischel often said that he couldn't keep chocolate in his house. He knew himself too well: if it was there, he would eat it, even though he had spent his life mastering self-control. The chocolate caused positive tilt. A longing so intense it couldn't be denied. That's why preventing that emotion in the first place was so essential. You need to learn to anticipate how something will make you feel in the future and act accordingly in the present.

Early in my poker training, I read a book called *Every Hand Revealed*, Gus Hansen's account of every hand he played on the way to winning the Aussie Millions, a major poker tournament. Hansen has quite the reputation as a gambler: he is beyond aggressive and has lost his bankroll (and then some) many times in the past. That's why one hand in particular stuck in my head: it was a hand so outside the typical Gus that I couldn't help but notice it long before I understood its implications.

In a dramatic moment of the tournament, Gus puts in a healthy raise with one of the best hands in the deck, ace-king, only to find himself in a bit of a predicament: a subsequent player goes all in. Gus has him covered, that is, he has more chips than the aggressor. He knows that his aggressive image means that his opponent might have worse cards than one usually does on an all-in move. (That is, because people know Gus is aggressive and likely to raise with mediocre hands, they will themselves play a wider range of hands in response—the OODA loop in action.) He could very likely call and come out ahead. But one thing stops him: before he makes the call, he thinks through the implications of a loss. He will no longer be the table chip leader. He will not be able to play the way he wants to—he will have to move more to the defensive. His mindset will likely be off for the rest of the day, making him play worse than he otherwise would. So Gus does something that most people never could: he folds one of his strongest possible hands.

It's here that his true experience as a player shines through. Most of the time, we're horrible at anticipating our emotions. We aren't sure how we'll feel. What we'll regret more. Self-awareness is a learned skill, and in this particular moment, Gus shows a level far beyond the norm, and certainly far beyond mine. What I wouldn't give for some time travel, to channel Gus just a bit with that ill-fated king-jack (which, I can't help but reflect, was also the hand that caused me to bust from my first ever live event).

Tilt makes you revert to your worst self. Think of your game as a resting inchworm divided into three sections, A, B, and C, Jared tells me. A is my best game. It is infrequent—I have to be at my peak to achieve it. C is my worst game, which should, at least in theory, also be infrequent. The B game is the bell curve part of the inchworm. It's the longest and most visible part. To improve my game, I need to move my bell curve the way that an inchworm moves, slowly pushing so that my C game becomes my B game, my A game drifts to B, and an even better A game takes its place. Tilt not only stops the process but reverses it—and unless I work on it, I won't see the sort of improvement I need.

"The only thing you can truly expect is your worst," Jared tells me. "Everything else is earned every single day."

What we need to do is optimize my thought process in the moment. Erik can give me all the actual strategy advice I need before and after the fact, preparing me to play and analyzing my hands. He can even prepare me for the fact of tilt. "You really have to make sure that you're still thinking clearly and still going through the process of thinking through things in a way that's not influenced or impacted by the fact that you just lost or won a big hand," he's told me before. But in the moment, as hot conditions rise, I need to prepare myself to deal with the emotions that will inevitably bubble up. How do I control them in order to be able to go back to my rational process, the one that Erik and I have constructed? To do that, we need to do some emotional digging. I already know that I have emotional triggers—I've said as much. It's time to think through the past, identify specific situations that have stuck with me, and see what we can learn.

Jared gives me an assignment: I need to map out my emotional process so that I can start finding ways to solve each problem. I need to actually sit down and make a spreadsheet. Each time something happens, write it down in the situation or trigger column. In the next column, write a description of the thoughts, emotional reactions, and behaviors that the situation or trigger causes. In the next column, give my best assessment of the underlying flaw or problem, and finally, write a logic statement that I can use in the moment to inject some rationality into the issue.

Later that night, I sit down and I start thinking through the last six months. What has stuck with me? When do I remember being most uncomfortable? Angry? Upset? It's not long before I start seeing patterns.

The first one doesn't require much depth. It's been clear to me for a while. I just didn't realize quite how strong or ubiquitous it was.

I remember one of my first bigger events, at a major casino in Las Vegas. A man in a bright green, shiny tracksuit sits down to my right. He has a strange accent, part Chinese, part Texan twang. He explains, unasked, that he is a businessman from China who's been living in Texas for some years.

"You are very pretty," he tells me.

I half smile noncommittally. I've learned that it's best not to ignore comments like this completely—that tends to make people angry, which is not ideal when they are sitting mere inches from you and playing the same game—but I have no desire to engage.

"How about a drink?"

I tell him I'm married and don't drink when I play. Not that it's his business.

"A drink when this is all over?"

I shake my head. Somehow the married part didn't seem to register.

He keeps leaning in closer. I keep trying to move my chair. But there isn't much room at the tables. I'm starting to lose my concentration, and still he will not let up.

"I'm married, too!" He produces a phone and shows me a picture of an infant. "That's my son. He died."

"I'm so sorry," I say, because what else can I say.

"The only bad beat that matters. Losing my son."

I nod.

"So about that drink?"

This is getting to be too much. Using a dead son to get me to take a drink is a low I haven't encountered before. I decide to go into complete *ignore* mode. It has little effect. He continues to try to engage me even without a reply—and has ordered a second drink for himself.

Soon enough, I lose a large pot. I'm not sure if I look upset or if he's just using any excuse, but he leans in so close that I smell the cheap rum and cigarettes on his breath, and says with a smile, "Oh, baby, someone so pretty shouldn't be sad to lose. I'll happily give you a few buy-ins after we're done here. I'm staying right upstairs, room 3205."

Did that just happen? Did I just get propositioned?

My mouth drops open. There's silence around the table. And I'm in some liminal state between anger and crying. "Can I speak to the floor, please?" I finally manage.

I explain that I need the man to be moved to another table. That I can't play like this. And they refuse. He hasn't done anything so terrible, they decide. It's not like he called me a cunt, they suggest in so many words (that, too, has happened, and it didn't matter nearly as much). No one speaks up to support me. Soon after, I bust the tournament.

OR THERE'S THIS ONE. I'm playing at Foxwoods, the Connecticut casino, a few months into my training. It's late in the day. I'm tired. And a guy sitting at the other side of the table won't leave me alone. "Hey, little girl," he yells when I sit down. "You ready to play with the big leagues?"

A bit later: "Oh, little girl, you must have a big hand."

Later: "Your husband play, little girl? Is that why you're here?"

Little girl. Little girl. Little girl. Each time he says it I cringe. *I'll get you, just you wait and see*, I say to myself.

"I'll check, little girl, let's see what you do," he says when we're in a hand together. Got him, I think, as I shove my chips into the middle. He has the nuts, and instead of my getting him, he gets me.

NOW I'M IN THE newly opened Live! casino in Baltimore. And I'm actually having a great time. There's no smoke here and never has been. Everything is new and shiny. People are friendly. Everyone is chatting. I learn about a guy who usually plays in the local tournaments but isn't here today because of two broken legs—apparently, he jumped off the newly installed smoking balcony on a prop bet a few weeks back. The jury's out on whether his injury means he forfeited the cash. We're laughing. All is well.

The man to my right leans over conspiratorially. "Hey," he says in a friendly tone. "Can I just offer some advice?"

"Yes?" I ask.

"You're stacking your chips wrong. The way you do it, I can see right away you're an amateur. You want to do it like I do it, see? Just some friendly advice."

He's oozing well-meaning, but somehow I find the evening ruined. Did I ask him for some friendly advice? And what's so wrong with looking like an amateur, anyway? I'd love to look like one now.

THIS PARTICULAR TRIGGER, IT turns out, is actually the easiest to deal with. I don't wear a hat or sunglasses when I play—I find you miss more information than you hide, and you potentially give off even more by the way you handle them, when you take them off, when you put them on, and the like. But I do have a pair of Bose noise-canceling headphones that I gave myself as a gift after that Foxwoods adventure to drown out the *little girls*.

What I have to start doing is being proactive rather than reactive. When I react, it's already too late. The tilt is on its way—and even knowing my reaction is based on incidental emotion isn't enough to stop it. The feeling is too intense. If I see a situation that may turn sour—and let's face it, many of them potentially could—I should put on my headphones as a way of controlling my surroundings. I don't actually have to listen to music. But now I have a socially acceptable way to selectively drown out conversation. I can still hear everything at the table, so I don't miss important information, but I no longer have to acknowledge hearing it. I have an escape plan, one that gives me a degree of control that's otherwise missing. Because whether I'm receiving unwanted overtures or condescending needles or patronizing good will, the thing that unites my encounters (apart from the obvious gender implications) is the lack of agency they foist on me. I'm placed in a position where I'm forced to react. Putting on my headphones reclaims some of that space for me.

The other emotional areas will be tougher. Over the next few months, Jared and I systematically go through a host of emotions I didn't realize I was feeling. There's the persistent impostor syndrome lurking underneath the veneer of confidence—I'm a fraud who doesn't deserve to be playing the events I'm playing in. Over and over, I feel like I don't belong.

We finally get to the root—the real root—of that one. I'm in kindergarten. It's the first day of school. I'm five years old, and my name tag is missing. Every kid has one, but my name is absent from the table. There is one name tag left, and the teacher insists on putting it around my neck. I shake my head. That's not me, I want to scream. Why are you insisting

I be someone else? But I can't. I don't have the words. I speak no English. The only thing I know is how to write my name. My identity, the one thing I'm certain of, and now it's being questioned. I can't say any of this, of course, and so I cry. Loudly and with abandon. I want to do the same thing now, whenever I feel out of place, like I can't control what's happening, except crying has become a less socially acceptable response. Jared calls this moment my Freudian breakthrough.

THERE'S THE CONSTANT ANXIETY that I'm letting people down—the players who believe in me, the people who back me, myself. It's a fear of high expectations that I'm afraid to subvert. The fear of making mistakes that has never quite gone away. Often as I play, I can see myself from afar, a fly observing what's going on below. There I am, knowing exactly when I'm supposed to bluff and how, and not quite having the guts to pull the trigger. And I know that I can't actually pull that trigger unless I'm feeling it. It works only if your mind and heart are behind it. Otherwise, people will spot the fake, the weakness, the half-heartedness. That's what I'm supposed to spot in my opponents, not the other way around. When I overcome the jitters and just go for it is when I play the best—when I start winning. But I somehow can't summon that inner strength at will.

Jared calls this one my beaten dog syndrome. "You don't want future Maria to beat the shit out of you, and so you're instinctively cowering to future Maria's power." I don't have the guts because I'm afraid—still—of looking stupid, of making mistakes, of being judged and judging myself. Here's how to deal with that beaten beast, he says: "Tell yourself, sure, I may be wrong, but cowering to future Maria is the bigger mistake. The bigger mistake is not taking the aggressive line, even if I'm wrong. And future Maria has to learn to be OK with that." Future Maria sounds like a real bitch, I tell Jared.

Slowly, we work through it all. We set goals. We practice visualization: planning out how I want to play so that it's easier to execute, holding my future self in my mind's eye before the fact. We discuss my optimal stress level: how to push myself so that I'm stressed enough to perform well, but not pressure myself so hard that I lose all confidence. I learn how to sit up and take up space and hold my head to project a confidence I might not be feeling—the techniques of self-deception that are often the first step to making you feel the confidence that was lacking. It's a process known as embodied cognition: embody the feeling you want to express, and your mind and body will often fall into alignment. Channel your outer warrior and your inner one may not be long in coming out.

And I start to see the results. Even as I'm working with Jared, I'm developing my new plan of attack with Erik. We decide that I need to retrench a bit, back to smaller events, series where not so many big shots are out, where the buy-ins are more often in the three figures. I also decide, with Jared's help, that being all in on poker means also being all in on my emotional well-being. So I make sure that my schedule includes multiweek stretches in New York. It's a delicate balance. Stay away from the tables too long and all the work and progress you've made is threatened. But stay at the tables too long and the same thing could well happen—as it did to me in my frenzied Colossus outing. You lose perspective, you lose emotional stability, you lose the ability to accurately gauge how well calibrated your decisions actually are. It's like that damned timer ticking down on my first glimpse of online poker—and while I realized how much decisions suffer under time pressure when the timer was in my face, I somehow failed to realize that I'd made a big red blinking timer in my head leading up to the Main. No wonder I couldn't think straight. I was my very own experimental subject.

So we make a plan where I don't go more than three weeks without playing—but I make sure to recharge fully in between. That, too, is crucial for learning the game. The recharging is also a part of playing well. It's funny that it's taken a mental coach to help me see that. I've always been a proponent of stepping back during any endeavor. Of taking breaks. Of taking a breath. Hell, I even wrote a *New Yorker* piece about the benefits of a four-day (or even three-day) work week. But as you dive into a new undertaking, it's easy to lose perspective and, in the process, lose part of yourself and part of your reason for doing what you're doing.

The sense of displacement that I've realized I was feeling for the past six months starts to dissipate. Sure, there's still the stream of interchangeable hotel rooms and casino carpets, but I feel more grounded in between. I return to Vegas. I go to New Jersey. I even combine a summer vacation with a stop at the European Poker Tour in Barcelona. Out of those, I have only one cash—a 109th-place finish in Barcelona, for €3,790—but I'm feeling much more optimistic than I was. I feel like I'm playing better, like I'm thinking better, like I'm being less reactive and more proactive in the choices I'm making. Now that the time pressure is lifted, the brain fog that came in its wake lifts as well. I have the room to think—and have been given the permission, first by Jared and then, through repetition, by myself, to do so.

It doesn't hurt that I'm starting to feel more comfortable in this world. The more I play, the more familiar the faces become. I start making friendly acquaintances. People start asking me to dinner, to drinks. Some of the poker media has noticed my project and has featured me in a few articles and videos. People recognize me from those clips and ask about how my book is going. It feels good, and I feel a new sense of determination to make this journey count for more than I'd originally planned.

Soon, I make my first final table of an international event, taking second place in a turbo at the PokerStars Festival in Dublin. It's a €170 buy-in, a level Erik and I can both agree to. It's in a city I'm excited to visit. I'm armed with my spreadsheet of emotional triggers. I've been pushing my inchworm forward. And I feel good. Sure, I'm playing against an opponent, a Swede, who is not only drunk but volubly so, taking every chance to hurl some invective or other in my direction. Sure, I should rightly beat him by the time it's down to the two of us, given his impaired thinking, but I'm simply proud that I didn't let him get to me and that I made it this far to begin with. Old me would have likely tilted my way out the moment he sat down at my table, hours earlier. I celebrate my almost-victory with a FaceTime call to Erik, recounting most of the hands that brought me to second place—the Dublin stop is a bit too small for him and he's back in Vegas. His "Well done!" is so genuine, so full of pride, that I can't help smiling for the rest of the day. Of course, he has some criticism—but it's clear that he's happy. That night, I have drinks with a group of Irish players and someone I'm told is quite important—Stephen Hendry, a former snooker champ and legend of the game. I have to look up what snooker is. I've never heard of it before. I decide to keep that to myself. Just like I decide to hold back the comment that it simply looks like a weird game of pool to me. The trip is light, fun, and—at last—actually profitable. When I get back to New York, I don't feel the usual drain. I'm starting to get the hang of actually *enjoying* this.

I take another second place soon after, back in Las Vegas. It's my biggest score to date—almost $6,000. And to get there, I even agreed to that thing that had so hurt my ego back at Planet Hollywood: a chop. It's four a.m., I'm exhausted, and I recognize objectively that the variance may well go against me. I was chip leader not too long ago, and now I'm in second place and fading fast. So when a six-way deal is proposed, I say yes. I don't take it as a personal insult. I perform a self-assessment that's far less biased than it ever has been, and do what is better for my ultimate bottom line. Sure, I may be forgoing a trophy. But I am also protecting myself against the downside of sliding even further in the chip counts. It's smart risk-mitigation strategy given how tired I am, not a blow to my ego.

I travel to Prague and place twentieth in a €2,200 buy-in event. It may not be a final table, but it's far better than I did on my prior forays into the European Poker Tour—and my best ever result at that level. I don't beat myself up for failing to do better. Instead, I pride myself on finally making it so close in a truly large international arena. I've never even reached the top hundred at this level before. This is a major leap forward.

My confidence—my actual confidence—is slowly building. And I start looking forward to my next event, one that I've been hearing about for months. The PCA, or PokerStars Caribbean Adventure. The PCA is one of the oldest live poker tour stops, going on thirteen years, and has grown to be among the most prestigious. It certainly doesn't hurt that it's set in the Bahamas. I'm excited to have the chance to play in something so iconic. And it's coming on my one-year anniversary in the poker world—that moment that was originally slated for the WSOP summer, before the reality of my schedule made that an impossibility. Now that the real one-year mark is upon me, I'm eager to see just how far I've come.

Glory Days

The Bahamas, January 2018

"Fortune always will confer an aura of worth, unworthily, and in this world the lucky person passes for a genius."

EURIPIDES, *THE HERCLEIDAE*, c. 429 BCE

The Bahamas are beautiful—or so it appears during the brief few minutes I spend walking outside between my room and the casino. I'm actually glad that it's been raining up a storm, as that makes me feel slightly better about having no time to enjoy the beach. And, of course, the more sightseeing you're doing on a poker stop, the worse you're likely playing. If you're doing well, you don't have time for the great outdoors. And that is precisely what is happening with me, to my great delight.

Two days ago, I flew in from New York. I got my bearings. I entered my first ever PCA tournament the next morning—the National Championship—and was sad to bust late that day. Luckily, there was another turbo flight that evening, and I somehow managed to make it through—a day of play that ended up lasting some sixteen hours. And then I stumbled into bed, only to realize I couldn't actually sleep for more than a few hours. The adrenaline rush was too much. I entered the familiar spiral of *I need to sleep to play well, oh, no, I'm not sleeping, this is terrible* that anyone who has ever dealt with insomnia knows so well. The moment your mind becomes preoccupied with sleep is the moment sleep escapes for good.

Today has been caffeine-fueled chaos, my mind a sort of sleep-deprived muddle battling on its last fumes. But my inchworm made progress. We made the money. I made some hands. And somehow I didn't bust. Which means that—drumbeat—I have managed to make the final table. I'm excited beyond words and exhausted beyond imagining. And I must admit to some concern: I know just how important this is, and I know that I need to sleep, and I know that I have adrenaline and caffeine coursing through my body. It's a trifecta that doesn't bode well for a good night's rest. And it's weighing on my mind. Erik's "See how you feel in the morning" doesn't quite work for a multiday tournament, when you have to come play, whether or not you're feeling up to it.

I make my way from the tournament room and pass by Plato's, one of the lounge areas at the Atlantis. I spot familiar faces—it's a gathering of many of the players I've come to know. It turns out that Scott Seiver, a cash player who is rare to find at a tournament, is having a little get-together to celebrate his foray into the tournament scene. "Join us!" he says, waving me over. Part of me wants to get into bed as quickly as I possibly can, but another knows that I will inevitably fail to sleep anyway—so I might as well ask some of the best poker minds about their coping strategies. This is all new to me, but for the dozen or so high rollers gathered at what seems to have evolved into a whiskey tasting, it's second nature. Their entire careers seem to be one deep run after another.

"I can't sleep," I say to no one in particular as I'm handed a tumbler of my own. Perhaps this aged bourbon (neat) will help. "How do you guys do it, with all the adrenaline? My mind just won't stop."

"Oh, here, I've got you!" One high roller is helpfully holding out a bottle of pills. *Melatonin*, I read. It's an interesting thought. But I'm skeptical whether I should try something new at such a major occasion.

"I really like these, actually," and now I have a second container appearing magically by my side, from another pair of hands. CBD tablets. Definitely not up my alley, but I appreciate the thought.

Another player offers his advice. "I have some Valium in my room if you need? It can be really helpful to just calm you down a bit."

"We're going out to smoke now if you want to join?" comes a fourth helpful voice. Pot, of course. "Mellow you out, sleep like a baby."

The scene seems almost made-up—except it never would have occurred to me that something like it is actually possible. I shake my head in disbelief. Here I thought I was learning almost all I needed to about the poker world, but I seem to have underestimated quite the level of dedication I'm encountering.

Poker players, it turns out, command one of the best-stocked pharmacies you're likely to find for most any occasion. Need a boost of energy? Caffeine pills of all doses are on offer. An even bigger boost? Nicotine tablets to the rescue. Trouble focusing during your deep run? Adderall, Ritalin, you name it, it's there. That's not to mention marijuana in all its forms and copious amounts of psychedelics. ("I swear by microdosing," one player who shall remain nameless tells me. "I won my last WCOOP title that way." WCOOP, I've learned, is the World Championship of Online Poker. WCOOP titles are hard to come by, with or without a little psilocybin thrown in.)

It's not that high-level poker players are particularly drug-loving in the sense of chasing a high. It's that the endless selection of pharmaceuticals is evidence of something bigger: these pros approach nearly everything as a game-theoretical model to be optimized. To serious players, poker is as much of a sport as they come, and they will use every tool at their disposal to make sure they are fighting fit.

What they are trying to do is optimize their bodies—and do it in the most optimal way. I'm quite surprised, for instance, to learn that Ike Haxton—he of the philosophy major and Harry Potter looks—starts every morning off with a pill.

"I take a caffeine pill," he tells me when I ask him about his usual routine before a big tournament. "And then I have to roll around delirious in bed for thirty to forty-five minutes. Then I meditate for eight minutes, shower, and go play the tournament."

"Caffeine pills? Really?" I make a mental note to ask about the precise timing of the meditation and the decision to skip breakfast, but the caffeine pills are my biggest surprise. I love my morning tea ritual and would never want to give it up for a pill. To me, drinking tea is meditative—and so, of course, when I spot something that is so different from what I, personally, would do, I find myself in disbelief.

"Well, I used to have coffee," Ike explains. "Then I started spending so much time in hotel rooms that acquiring coffee started to feel like a bad ratio of work to the quality of coffee I ended up with and how enjoyable the whole experience was. So I decided to just start taking caffeine pills."

Quality ratios. Weighing benefits versus costs, calculating the best use of time, evaluating quality of life with different factors tweaked: welcome to the mind of a true poker player when it comes to most any decision. The only time I've ever encountered this approach before is in the psych lab, when someone is being asked to go through an explicit benefit-cost calculation, usually after making multiple poor decisions that illustrate one bias or another, in an attempt to de-bias future tries. What you typically find, however, is that the moment the lab is left behind, the old frame of mind reasserts itself.

But that sort of body hacking is on display among the most dedicated players. They have expertly calibrated diets—some travel with personal chefs. Keto is common. Veganism. Meditation. Exercise regimens. Erik has even picked up yoga in the year that I've known him. Mind and body in unison. One recent study showed that elite chess players can burn up to six thousand calories a day during tournaments, exhibiting metabolic patterns reminiscent of elite athletes. Professional poker players, I suspect, would exhibit many of the same effects. (On this particular trip, I'll somehow manage to lose eight pounds in a week without any effort. "I should rethink this book and call it *The Poker Diet*," I tell Erik. "Instant bestseller," he replies.)

I appreciate the efforts on display to hack my sleep in preparation for the big day tomorrow. But I can't quite get myself to pull the trigger. I've never been one for sleeping aids. I'll try a midnight meditation and hope for the best.

When I get back to my room, I, of course, don't manage to sleep for more than a few minutes at a time. The one moment where I do drift off, I jerk awake with the sense of dread that comes from a particularly disturbing nightmare. I think back to try to recapture what it was that had such a profound effect. And when I realize that the nightmare was actually me playing out a poker bad beat in my head, I start laughing, a hint of hysteria creeping in. Maybe I should have taken them up on that melatonin.

IT'S MORNING. AT ELEVEN a.m., my phone pings. It's Erik. "Job today: relax, focus, think. You worked hard for this. Don't allow distraction."

I nod, forgetting for a second that he can't see me.

My phone pings again. "I'm very excited and so is Ru."

I'm more nervous than anything else, but I will absolutely do my best. I gather my things and walk down to the casino. And I can't believe I'm here. The final table. One of only eight players remaining. I've been to final tables before, but never at a major event. Never something like this. When I look around me, it seems like I must have entered an alternate timeline.

There's Chris Moorman sitting to the left of the dealer. The one of the life-size WSOP cutout. I still don't know him personally, but I now certainly know his reputation. A feared tournament crusher who has been ranked in the past as the number one online tournament player in the world. That WSOP booth wasn't lying. There's Harrison Gimbel, two seats to my left. I don't know him, either, but I do know that he has won the coveted Triple Crown of poker—a WSOP bracelet, a WPT (World Poker Tour) title, and an EPT title. Actually, he won the main event at this very stop. He's on familiar turf. To my right is someone I don't recognize. But I know who he is. When I looked him up the previous night—a basic step in preparation—I learned that he is a chess grandmaster and Dutch chess champion, Loek van Wely, who was once ranked in the top ten chess players in the world. One player is a Canadian pro with almost a million in earnings, another a pro from Chicago with over a million in earnings. I'd say I have my work cut out for me, but that's not quite right. I feel like a total impostor, a fool who lucked into a room where she surely does not belong.

Jared wouldn't approve of my thinking, but I can't help myself. We worked on this very thing. "Remember," he tells me. "You haven't seen those players in the lead-up to their peak. You don't know that they were staked in their first hundred-K. You don't know the serendipity that happened to get them there." I try to remember this as I look at the table and feel like everyone deserves to be here except for me. "Everyone got lucky at some point. Strip down the mythology around their greatness. They still have weaknesses. They are humans first, players second."

I try to collect myself. I take deep breaths. I reflect on how far I've come. Improbably, I'm second in chips. Over seventy big blinds to work with—exactly where you want to be heading into a final table. And I've just gotten a big surprise. When I walked into the tournament room, Erik was there to greet me. He hadn't told me he'd come, but has woken up early to offer moral support and encouragement. He has a final table today, too, but not for a few hours. He could be resting, but he wants to see me off on my first real tournament triumph—even if I don't do well, just getting here is already a win. I'm chuffed. I tell him that I'm so nervous I couldn't eat breakfast and I'm worried I might actually vomit if I try to do anything at all.

"One hand at a time," he says. "The nerves go away when you are paying close attention to play. You've got this."

Easy for him to say, what with his countless final tables and titles. I put on a brave smile and ask him if he has any last-minute advice.

He does. "Don't be a fish."

And with that, he's off to start his day and to watch the action from afar. Final tables are hell to watch in person. You see the cards only if you watch the action unfold from your screen. Live, they are about as boring as you'd expect, with no hole cards to be seen—and no strategic advice to be offered.

Don't be a fish, I repeat silently as I sit down and smile for the cameras. Don't be a fish. Don't be a fish. But, oh, a fish is precisely what I feel I am. I am out of my depth.

And it's not long before I prove to be just that. Not even thirty minutes into the biggest poker day of my short career, I am dealt two beautiful red aces under the gun. I raise to just over two big blinds and am saddened to see everyone folding in turn. But the player in the big blind, Van Wely, the chess champion, defends. I am ecstatic. I have the best hand in all of poker and I am going to win big.

Here comes the flop. A king of hearts, a queen of clubs, and a jack of hearts. Not the most pleasing flop in the world to pocket aces—this is what we call a wet board, or a board with many draws available; it is also a board that improves a lot of hands that I had beat before. When the big blind calls a raise from under the gun—by far the strongest position—he often has a fairly strong hand himself, at least at this stage in the tournament. A lot of high cards. A lot of suited connectors. A lot of things that match nicely the cards on the board. But I don't think of any of this. Instead, I think of my lovely, lovely aces. I bet close to half the pot. Van Wely calls. So far, so good.

To the turn we go. It's a six of diamonds, a blank if ever there were. None of the draws have improved. After Van Wely checks again, I decide to fire out another hefty bet. *Aces, aces, la la la.* Except now, instead of calling, he raises, and the raise is a sizable one. Uh-oh. Red flags should be waving, horns should be blasting. And I should be folding. I am beating exactly none of his value hands—his straights, of which he has many flavors, his two pairs, even his sets. And is he really bluffing? I hold the ace of hearts, which blocks the nut flush draws, a big part of his bluffing range. It's hard to see just what would compel him to risk over half his chips with such huge pay jumps ahead unless he has a hand that I really don't want to see. But none of this enters my mind. I hardly pause a second before calling. *Aces, aces, aces!!!*

The river pairs the board with another king. Van Wely checks again. And somehow, some part of my mind wakes up to the idea that maybe, just maybe, something is not going according to plan. I check behind. And he flips over his nine-ten, for a flopped straight. There go my chips. In a single hand, I've managed to lose over a third of my stack. I've gone from one of the chip leaders to one of the shortest stacks at the table. I know I've messed up, and I'm crushed.

Erik texts me soon after—he's following along online—and confirms what I already know: I screwed up, badly. But then he types something else: forget it ever happened. "Put it out of your mind and back to work," he writes. We will discuss strategy later. For now, just focus on the next hand and forget the chips you've lost. Reset mentally, and play your short-stack game. One hand at a time.

One of my favorite books about writing is Anne Lamott's *Bird by Bird*. The title comes from a story she tells about her younger brother. When he was in elementary school, he was assigned a big project about birds. He'd had weeks to work on it but had put off doing it until the very end. Now the report was due the next morning and he was sitting at the table crying. How was he ever going to finish it? "Bird by bird, buddy," she describes her dad telling him. "Just take it bird by bird."

Bird by bird has become a sort of inner mantra for me whenever I'm feeling overwhelmed. When it seems like it's just too much, I'll never finish, I'll never get something accomplished, I close my eyes and tell myself, *Bird by bird*. And then I start working on the next bird on the list. Bird by bird. Hand by hand. It might feel overwhelming, but I can do this. I take a deep breath, close my eyes, and press the reset button, just like Jared and I discussed.

One hand at a time. Reset. Reset not just strategically (how do I play a short stack?) but also emotionally (no anger at myself, no frustration with myself, just focused energy, forward-looking momentum; I may make mistakes, but I am still competent). I do my best to slow my breathing, let go of my blunder, and look ahead.

The next two hours pass quietly. I don't play many big pots. I take it slow. In the past, I may have wanted to up the aggression now—get those chips back to my stack, where they belong. Now, mental game in hand, I wait for the right moment. My chips dwindle, but I cannot allow myself to panic. Especially at this stage of the tournament, patience is key.

Chris Moorman, one of my most feared opponents, busts in eighth place, taken out by a pair of aces that fares better than did mine. That's one less shark for this little fish to fight. "Moorman out!" I text Erik in excitement. "Yay," he writes back. He knows that I was dreading this particular opponent. Yay, but don't dwell on it. There's still a long way to go. Alas, Moorman's chips have gone to Harrison Gimbel—my other most-feared opponent—and not to the older gentleman two to my right, whom I've pegged as a weak link in an otherwise formidable lineup. I played with him all day yesterday and have him tagged as Aggro Oldie. He's been far too aggressive, in my mind, playing the older gentleman card a bit too liberally. People often assume players over a certain age are tight and conservative in their play—and some of them, I've found, love to take advantage by upping the aggression. This one seems to have grown a bit too confident in his ability to push us, especially me, around. I make a mental note to bide my time. This isn't personal.

We take a twenty-minute break. Jared has created a routine for me, and I now follow it by the minute. First five minutes of break: off-load and brain dump. I write down some of the key hands so that they don't occupy any of my headspace going forward. I'll analyze them later with Erik. For now, the important thing is to get them out of my system so that my mind is ready for new information. Then a few minutes of contemplating my decision making. Asking myself: How was my thinking? Were there any emotionally compromised decisions? Again, I'm not analyzing now, just noting for the future. Next ten minutes: nothing. No poker talk. No thinking. Just walking and relaxing. And then, right before the end of break, a few minutes of warm-up for the next level. Get myself mentally ready, psyched, in gear. My goal is to keep my mind as clear and fresh as possible, for as long as possible. With every break, that will get harder and harder as fatigue sets in. For now, though, I'm ready.

WE SIT BACK DOWN. I don't even have a chance to properly adjust my mind back into the game when there they come again, oh, those bittersweet aces. This time, though, the story plays out differently. A Brazilian player—I don't have to guess his nationality; he's wearing a colorful Brazilian flag T-shirt—pushes his remaining chips into the middle. I look down at the hand that did me wrong, or, rather, that I did wrong. I call. Antunes, the Brazilian, turns over ten-eight of clubs. I'm feeling good. The flop: two queens and a six. Safe enough, at first glance—except then I notice that both the six and a queen are clubs. Uh-oh. His chances of winning just skyrocketed. I don't have an ace of clubs, so if another club comes, I will lose a healthy chunk of my chips. *Please hold*, I tell myself silently, the sort of prayer I imagine many a poker player makes in her head under the circumstances. May the gods of poker be just. Or, in less colorful terms, may the variance go my way. This time, it does. I hold through the off-suit ten turn (but now he can make trips! more outs, or cards he can hit to make a superior hand) and the nine river. He is out in seventh place, and I rake in a much-needed boost. I am still one of the two shortest stacks at the table, but at least I'm moving up.

"More of the AA strategy" comes the text from Erik. I smile. Some humor is well advised in the midst of all the nerves. "Even KK is ok" comes another one, "but AA smarter." I smile again and put down the phone. Focus, focus, focus.

Another hour passes. I've once again dwindled down to just over twenty big blinds—still playable, but not particularly comfortable. Nothing major; just bad cards, bad boards, and not many spots to do much but fold and wait. But now I'm far more comfortable doing just that. Waiting. Picking my spots, just like Erik has always said. The theory always made sense. My mental discipline has now caught up at last.

The Grandmaster, as I've started calling Loek van Wely in my head, makes a raise. I call with the pretty ace-five of spades. It's marginal; I could fold, I could shove, but after considering my chips, I decide to take the less aggressive road and see how the hand unfolds. The big blind, who just so happens to be Aggro Oldie, also calls, and the three of us wait for the flop to be dealt. The cards fan out: a nine of hearts, a six of hearts, and a five of diamonds. I have bottom pair. Not bad. As many a poker announcer loves to remind you every time you turn on a televised game, it's hard to make a pair in hold'em. It's even better because I have position in the hand. I'm last to act, so I can see what everyone else does before I make any decisions. It's one of the best decision-making aids you could possibly have: maximum information prior to acting. Aggro Oldie checks, Grandmaster checks, and I decide to check along with them. There's no reason to turn my hand into a bluff. I have plenty of showdown value: my hand may easily win without bluffing. And what happens if someone raises me? There are lots of cards that would make a raise attractive, and I would hate to have to throw away a winning hand. Better to check and see what happens.

The next card is another six. Aggro Oldie bets, Grandmaster gets out of the way, and I have a decision. Should I call, or is it better to fold? I don't have many chips, eighteen big blinds, and the call will take away three more of them. He doesn't like to fold, so he could very well have a six in his hand—a card I'd discount from tighter players who won't play many hands after two other people have entered a pot. He could also, of course, have the seven-eight for a flopped straight. But something tells me he would have bet that earlier. He's not one for slow play. On the other hand, I've seen Aggro Oldie bet the turn every single time a flop checks around. He's as likely as not to have absolute air, or a draw. I decide that, in the context of what I've seen, I will risk it and call. The river is the jack of diamonds. All the obvious draws have missed—the flush, the straight. He throws in a hefty bet. Over a third of my remaining chips. If I call and am wrong, I'll have under ten big blinds. The real danger zone. The fewer chips you have, the worse your ability to maneuver. You basically have one tool left in your arsenal: to go all in. The complexity of play is all but taken away.

I'm torn. I try to think through the logic of both decisions. Would he play his really strong hands this way? Would he play a marginal hand this way, after I've already called twice? After all, I lose to even the marginal hands, with my bottom pair. A nine, a jack, those all beat me. I almost fold. But then something pushes me over the edge. I remember what Phil Galfond told me all those months ago over dinner in Vegas. Retell the story from the beginning. Does the narrative flow—or are there logical gaps? I'm a detective. I'm a storyteller. What does the expertise I bring to the table outside of poker tell me now? I slow down and rewind, not just the story of this hand, but the story of the gentleman's play over the past three hours. How did he play his strong hands? What did he do when he was bluffing? My poker strategy knowledge is exhausted, so back to doing what I know best: looking for inconsistencies across behavior that can help me.

My mind goes back to an earlier hand that also started multiway. As now, my adversary bet the turn after a checked flop and was called. On an innocuous river, he hemmed and hawed for some seconds before saying, "OK, OK, I check." His opponent checked back, and a visibly frustrated adversary turned over the flush. "Why didn't you bet?" he demanded. "I was obviously weak!"

Of course, I know very well that one data point does not a pattern make. But I also know he likes to push people around. Not just me; I've seen him force multiple folds from Gimbel, a much stronger player than I am, and from Moorman while he was still in the game. Aggro Oldie likes to play his oldie image. Taken together, the data push me over the edge. I call. And when he turns over a naked ace-high—no pair, nothing—I'm rewarded with the pot. I breathe a sigh of relief. I'm up to just over thirty big blinds and I'm alive.

Two hands later, I flop trip jacks—a very strong hand—and am able to rake in another pot to get up to forty-five big blinds. Finally, I am no longer the shortest stack at the table. I can play a little, be more adventurous, start enjoying myself a bit, even.

The next hour is uneventful. I lose some small hands, don't win much, and hover at the table average. I get lucky with pocket queens against pocket jacks to eliminate another player—no skill to that one—and we are down to five.

Our older gent gets the better of me soon enough. After I check a flop, he barrels the turn and river, and I decide to just let him have it. It's five o'clock, and the day is getting to me. I'm tired. I haven't eaten. I'm running on pure adrenaline. I can't fight every battle, and I make the strategically suspect but personally necessary decision to wait for another moment to strike. I need to refuel, and quickly: I'm now once again the second-shortest stack at the table—soon to be shortest, when Harrison Gimbel falls to the Grandmaster an hour later.

The break can't come soon enough. When it does, I forgo my usual walking routine to get some green tea and an energy bar. Brains need fuel. I know of players who fast their way through tournaments, but I have no idea how they manage to do it. What's more, the science seems to be against them.

While it's quite fashionable in the modern productivity culture to fast, and many a productivity guru swears by it—Twitter CEO Jack Dorsey, for one, has talked about the "focused point of mind," whatever that may be, and the drive that comes from his fasts—the science is decidedly more negative when it comes to decision-making ability. Fasting has been shown to affect our delay discounting ability: we start to prefer smaller rewards sooner rather than waiting for larger rewards later. In effect, we become more impulsive. Indeed, even work that has shown some benefits of fasting on certain tasks also admitted that the thought process involved was reliant on "gut feelings"—an appropriate choice of words for decisions governed by the stomach. And while that's all well and good for someone like Erik, whose "intuition" is actually decades of careful expertise that he doesn't necessarily have conscious access to, for the rest of us, our guts are just as likely to be wrong than right—and we have no way of telling the difference. We become reliant more on our reflexive thinking than on cool, measured reflection. And we become more emotional: we often interpret the cues of hunger that our bodies send as negative emotional states—hence the term "hangry"—and so, all the negative decision effects that occur when we misattribute mood as information may very well now enter into our thought process.

Maurice Ashley is a legend in the world of chess—the first black grandmaster in history. In recent years, I've learned, he's been teaching chess to kids at the Hunter College High School. He and other grandmasters gather on weekends to watch eight-year-olds play and analyze their moves. One weekend, Kevin Slavin, Frank Lantz's cofounder of the game-design company Area/Code, observed Ashley at work. One thing struck him: how from a single list of moves, he can deduce a seemingly infinite amount about a child's mindset. Slavin recalls one particular interaction that Ashley has with a little girl.

"This is not your game," he tells her after glancing at her sheet.

"Yes, it is," she counters.

"OK. What did you have for breakfast?" he responds.

"Nothing. We were running late and didn't have time."

"There you go. You're playing like a hungry person. Next time, you have to eat."

I, for one, don't want that to happen to the clarity of my thought process at this crucial stage. I need to, quite literally, refuel.

I don't know if it's the movement, the caffeine, or the snack, but when we sit down to play twenty minutes later, I feel like a different person. I can do this. Enough with the surrender. I may be the shortest stack by far, but that makes me powerful, too: I can pressure players without fear of getting bluffed. All I need to do is push my chips into the middle, and they know I have nothing left to lose.

Very soon, I do just that. I'm in the big blind, and Grandmaster raises from the small. I look down at two sevens—a beautiful hand when you have twelve blinds and a dream. I'm well ahead of Grandmaster's range here, and very happy with my decision. Very happy, that is, until he snap calls and flips over . . . two aces. I shake my head in disbelief. He was the villain when my aces withered to start the day on the wrong foot, and now he'll finish me off with the same hand. The flop comes all spades: a nine, an eight, and a six. I suddenly have more life: any ten or five will make my hand into a straight. As long as it's not a spade, of course, as Grandmaster holds the ace of spades in his hand. The turn: a miracle off-suit ten. If I dodge a spade on the river, I'll stay alive. The river is the beautiful two of clubs, an absolutely harmless card. In a moment that I find filled with symbolic symmetry, I have managed to suck out against

Loek to stay in the game. I couldn't have gotten my money in much worse than I did—and I couldn't have gotten much luckier than I did. As they say, to win a tournament you absolutely must get lucky. Skill alone won't take you over the finish line. ("Did you just double?" Jason Koon yells at me as he passes by the rail. He's at the final table with Erik and is on his break. I nod. He gives me two thumbs up and a big smile. "Go, go, go!")

Soon after, the Grandmaster bids us goodbye in fourth place, and it's down to three. I feel pumped, filled with a renewed sense of purpose. I'm focused and confident. I'm the shortest of the three stacks—but I never could have imagined getting this far along to begin with. My victory with the sevens makes me see the rest as just a bonus. I shouldn't even be sitting here.

I pick up chips. I double up against Aggro Oldie when he tries to bully me pre-flop and I take a stand with a suited king-jack and hold against his queen-ten. And then I deliver him the fatal blow. He raises from the small blind, and I find myself in the big blind with the ace-king of hearts, a monster hand under any circumstances, especially so now. I three-bet. And he decides he's had just about enough of me and shoves. I, of course, call instantly. He has ace-deuce, off-suit, and I'm in great shape going to the flop. The board runs out jack-eight-seven-queen-ten. I make a straight. And it's down to just two. I am at my first major final table, and I am heads up for my first major title.

How do you play heads up? It's a different beast from a full-ring game. It requires different qualities. Patience is no longer the virtue it was. You can't afford it. You have to be ready to play quickly, play well, play confidently. There's no time to sit anything out.

Heads up play is to poker as a first date is to the raucous bar party that led up to it. And not just any first date—this is not a match made in swipe heaven. It's a first date of the increasingly rare, absolutely-must-impress kind, where you spent the prior evening saying and doing just the right things so that the person now seated across from you would accept the invitation. The party was the warm-up—full-table poker. You have your friends, drinks, props, a support system. You can be quiet for stretches of the conversation, until the perfect repartee comes to mind and you can dazzle everyone, target included, with your brilliant wit. You can pick your spots, make sure you're shining in the best light. And so you do.

And here you are, heads up, one on one, sitting over the drinks you hope will become dinner, at the start of an evening filled with promise. This time, though, you're on your own. If you can't think of the perfect thing to say, you can no longer sit back and let others do the talking for you. If there's a question you don't quite feel like answering, you can't pass the baton to your trusty wingman. He isn't there. It's just you, and you must act, constantly and without pause.

And so act you do. Your best self. Your best stories. Your best lines. If you don't have much to say, you fake it. If you aren't feeling witty, you fake it. First dates aren't simply about honesty. Silence and awkwardness have to be earned. First dates are about dazzle. You play each hand, even when you'd rather fold and crawl back home, admitting defeat.

In heads up play, you're forced to play cards you'd never dream of playing at a full table. Easy folds become raises. Calls or raises, all-in confrontations. The game is blown up and morphed. And a whole new set of skills and expectations emerges.

Luckily, this time I'm ready. I've spent the past two months working on this exact part of my strategy, practicing heads up play almost exclusively. The reason? That second-place finish in Dublin to my drunken Swedish opponent, with his Guinness in hand and his shades at the ready. I wasn't upset to lose, but I sensed that I could have won if I'd only had the requisite skills. This time, I fully intend to:

Before we restart play, I text Erik. "Heads up! I'm chip leader." I ask him if I should consider talking about a deal. "If you think he's good," he writes back. After a pause, he adds: "You've been practicing though."

He's right. I have, indeed. "I think I'll stick it out for now," I write back. I'm feeling this.

"That's the spirit!" Erik replies. "We are walking over! So damn exciting." He and Ruah are making their way over to the casino to cheer me on, and just that thought gives me an energy boost.

An energy boost that propels me for the next few hands, until I face what could be a tournament-changing decision. I raise, holding the ace of clubs and king of spades. Alexander Ziskin, my heads up opponent and a professional player from Chicago, calls. The flop is two tens and a seven, with two spades. He checks. I decide to continuation bet: my hand is still very strong, and even if he has a pair, I have plenty of opportunity to improve. But instead of folding or calling, the easy options, Alexander raises, to almost three times my bet. I hesitate. Does he have a ten? If he does, I'm in bad shape. I decide that he would call a ten instead—on a board that dry, why not let me hang myself? I have two overcards and a backdoor flush draw. I call the raise. The turn is the deuce of spades, putting a third spade on the board. "All in," he announces. Oh, no. I have just ace-high. What do I do?

My brain starts calculating. If I call and I'm wrong, he has the chip lead and the momentum. This is a huge decision, especially without so much as a pair in my hand. But I do have a spade, and that's something. That means I could improve to the best hand, even if I'm now behind. I agonize for several minutes, counting the combinations of possible bluffs he might have and whether or not they outweigh his value hands, before deciding that I simply can't fold. The pot odds are in my favor. The math is on my side. And he probably knows how hard this is for me, making him that much more likely to try to pull a move. He's the pro. I'm the amateur. He's been here. I haven't. I call.

Alexander turns over the jack of diamonds and the eight of spades. He has a gutshot straight draw (one card can give him a straight) and a flush draw—but my hand is still best. And my flush draw beats his. All I have to do is hold on, to avoid one of the eight cards that will give him the winner (a nine, a jack, or an eight, as long as they are not spades). The cameras rush closer. The reporters huddle around. I look for Erik and Ruah, but everything is happening so quickly that they haven't yet made it to the table. The dealer waits until the floor manager tells her she can flip the next card.

We sit and wait. It seems to drag on forever. And finally, she gets the signal. The river is dealt. It's the king of hearts. I can't believe it. Alexander is getting up and walking over to shake my hand, and I still haven't quite registered it. I've just won. $84,600 is mine. I'm the 2018 PCA National champion.

· · · · ·

T HIS IS WHERE THE story should rightly end. Me, hoisting a trophy in stunned triumph, almost exactly a year since I first started playing. A victory I could have never anticipated—the ultimate act of agency, my life back in my own hands. I've set off on a journey to learn about the limits of chance, and I've proven something that I needed to prove to myself: that with the right mindset, the right tools, you can conquer, excel, emerge triumphant—even through the setbacks, even when the original road map proves faulty and needs to be replaced.

Yet I can't help but feel that ending here lets me off too easily. It's too elegant. Too clean. The classic hero journey from adversity to triumph. And even though it's real life—this happened! I can pinch myself all I want, but it did—something still nags at me. What if I'm a fraud, a one-hit wonder, a flash in the pan, a mayfly about to learn just how short my flight is destined to be? Have I actually learned something that will show sustainability—that, in the long run, I really can be on the right side of variance, that my skills have improved beyond the helplessness I felt what seems like only yesterday? Or am I just feeling better because life improved and I got lucky—and things seem much rosier when everything is going your way?

Sure, I've worked hard, harder than many. Sure, I have a background that has let me accelerate the learning process, an outsider's perspective joined by guidance from the best of the best to help me optimize it. But haven't others worked just as hard, longer, and never reached this pinnacle? A different runout with the sevens, after all, and instead of hoisting a trophy, I'd be an also-ran, an almost-but-not-quite success story. There's something about that trophy, about actually having the title, that sets the result apart. And it wouldn't have ever happened had I not gotten lucky. I understand that.

"Luck is not something you can mention in the presence of self-made men," E. B. White wrote during World War II. "The Society of Movers and Doers is a very pompous society, indeed, whose members solemnly accept all responsibility for their own eminence and success." I know enough to know that I'm anything but self-made. I know just how lucky I've been.

If I'm to finally crack that puzzle, establish, in White's words, "an honest ratio between pluck and luck," I need to go that extra step: keep going and confront the goddess of luck head-on. Otherwise, how will I ever know: Am I really good—or did I just get lucky?

The Heart of the Gambling Beast

Macau, March 2018

"Can one even touch a gaming table without becoming imme-diately infected with superstition?"

FYODOR DOSTOYEVSKY, *THE GAMBLER*, 1866

The day of my victory is auspicious in more ways than one. Not only have I won a major international title; it is also my wedding anniversary. In my excitement over my win, I almost forget about the date, until later that night, over a celebratory Italian dinner with Erik and Ruah. Ruah happens to mention their upcoming anniversary, and a lightbulb goes off in my head. "Excuse me," I tell them. "I need to go call my husband." They laugh. I call. And disaster is averted. At least I'm bringing home quite the anniversary present. "I'm so proud of you," he tells me. "I always knew you could do this." And once again, I feel like the luckiest person in the world.

Things accelerate quickly after that night. Victory changes things in a way that second-place finishes don't. And it turns out, the poker world loves my story. From nothing to champion, all in a year. She was working on a book, and look what happened next! The clickbait headline almost writes itself. It doesn't hurt that Erik is my coach, and everyone wants a bit of that Seidelian wisdom to rub off on them. ("I promise I won't give away your secrets," I tell him. Because, I add in my head, they are impossible to give away. Erik is the consummate jazz musician. Constantly evolving, constantly improvising, constantly responding. You can teach classical music technique. You can't teach someone the spirit of jazz.) The interview requests start coming in.

One day, I wake up to find that I'm trending on Twitter. It turns out that *Deadspin* has run a story on my victory and that story has prompted a broader media storm. From all over the world, the reporters come a-calling. The *Times* of London. *Le Monde*. The Brazilian press. *Newsweek*. *Columbia Journalism Review*. I make my first ever magazine cover: *Bluff Europe*. *Glamour*, the German edition, does a photo shoot. "You know you've really made it when you're in the *Daily Mail*!" my best friend, she of the summer WSOP wedding, texts me.

I'm still basking in my newfound poker fame when PokerStars, the host of the PCA, offers me a formal sponsorship. I'll be the newest addition to its roster of professional players. *Team pro!* The words sound foreign and wondrous in my mouth. A pro. Could I really be a pro? Why yes. Yes, I think I could.

There's an entire new vista of possibility in front of me. My options have expanded. I can travel more. I can play higher buy-ins. I can rebuy without fear of bankrupting us. At least for the smaller events. Sponsorship gives me legitimacy. It gives me a platform. It gives me a cushion. It gives me confidence. As I sign on for another year of full-time poker, I feel like everything is finally coming together in a pattern I could have never foreseen but am only too happy to embrace.

But something is still nagging at me, the something that has never disappeared after that first taste of victory: the feeling that I still don't know quite how skillful I've become. I don't want to be a one-hit wonder.

I don't want to claim false proficiency if I'm really more of a fraud who has luckboxed into an international title. And so, for me, this new chance at a more fully immersed poker life, without as much stress and pressure as the prior year, becomes something else. Not just the opportunity to serve as an ambassador for a game I've grown to admire and love, but the opportunity to test out my real prowess on a wider stage. If I'm to really embrace the title of pro, and really feel like I deserve to be called champion, I'll have to prove, if only to myself, that I can keep the success going. That I can triumph repeatedly. Then, and only then, can I call skill ascendant over luck. Otherwise, I'll have to bow down to that lovely lady, thank her for her help, and step back onto the sidelines.

When Kevin Slavin sold his first company, Area/Code, he moved to Beirut. It was 2011, and Beirut was hardly the hot "it" destination for newly minted tech millionaires. So why go there?

Slavin is tall and wiry, with a boyish excitement and energy that animates every sentence that comes out of his mouth. He seems almost balloon-like in his enthusiasm as he bounces from topic to topic. But this part of our conversation sees him visibly deflate. We're talking about the nature of games, of luck, of uncertainty. It's his specialty, after all, as the founder of multiple ventures focused on designing and developing games in new ways and new environments.

He never expected to sell his company, he explains. He was so immersed in running it—eight years of working "really fucking hard" and taking care of forty-five people can get to you—that he didn't see it coming. He had never had a lot of financial security, and suddenly, there was this "unexpected windfall. Without setting out to be powerful or whatnot, we made something that was successful enough. And I walked away from the company with a couple million dollars, which was not something I ever anticipated."

As it turns out, having money did not make him feel particularly good. "I felt conflicted about it. I gave some to two museums I cared about, to my old college, to some other charities, but it wasn't actually about wealth distribution." What it was about, at the bottom, was luck. "This transformative financial life event—I didn't feel like I deserved it," Slavin explains. "Yes, I worked like an animal, and we did do something that was innovative, but that was also true of lots of other people I knew, and I knew other people who worked harder and nothing happened for them."

It was a chain of reasoning oddly similar to the thoughts that went through my mind as I took my trophy: Did I actually earn this, or did I get lucky? Or, rather, did I earn this *more* than I got lucky—or the other way around?

Beirut, then: a "shitty hotel," a place where no one knew him, a way to "rebalance something psychically." He spent his time in Beirut exploring, but also playing a game called Quadradius, "basically checkers on a grid," except with special powers that can let you do things like move twice or destroy everything in a column. It's a game that Slavin considers "very clever when you go deep" but "something that feels really stupid" when you're playing. Yet he found himself playing it obsessively. "I realized that what I was doing in playing is trying to metabolize my sense of feeling lucky," he reflects. "I don't think back on it frequently, but feeling lucky actually made me feel bad about myself in a weird way."

In that shitty little Beirut hotel room, playing a game he didn't actually enjoy all that much, Slavin started thinking about games—especially games that melded chance and skill, where the outcome of what you did was inextricably linked to the random noise of the uncontrollable—on a level he had never considered before. "That's when I first started really thinking about the role of games in metabolizing luck," he says. "They let you really get your arms all the way around this idea and say, *Yeah, luck exists.* And I think it's really necessary to do that, both as individuals but also collectively." He pauses for a second to reflect. "Denying luck individually is to suggest that we have much greater agency than we really have over outcomes in our lives." Games give us a chance to confront luck in a manner that allows us to process it in life in a way we're not always forced to do. And sometimes, it's the games that incorporate luck most explicitly that push us to the limits of understanding just how far agency can take us—and where it inevitably breaks down.

To UNDERSTAND WHAT LUCK looks like when you worship it, hold it in your hands, make it real, one need look no further than Macau. If Vegas shouldn't exist, Cotai actually did not: it was built from scratch, rising out of the water on sand and soil that had been dumped there especially for its birth. And it now hosts the epicenter of gambling in the Eastern Hemisphere, and, many would argue, in the world.

For months, everyone has been telling me that I can't understand the true essence of poker, the battle between skill and chance that rages under its surface, if I don't make the trip across the world. That Macau is what Vegas once was, except more—more intense, more real, more primal. I haven't wanted to listen because, in a way, I didn't want to see what I might find. Gambling, real gambling, not the high-level poker I've become accustomed to, frightens me. And it frightens me that people I respect, some of the high-level poker players I've come to call friends, can so often embrace it with open arms. To me, poker has been a way of reclaiming my agency over chance. But Macau shows the other side of the equation: that one way of admitting the role of chance in life is by abandoning yourself completely to it, worshipping full-throated at its altar. Macau is the world of the gambler. So perhaps it's inevitable that to test the extent of the seeming agency I've discovered, I will at last find myself here. Macau is *my* way of metabolizing the feeling of being lucky. It is my confrontation.

It's fitting that in order to get to Cotai, you must go through a profound displacement, not only in space but in time. One of the longest nonstop flights in the world, from New York to Hong Kong, followed by an hour-long ferry ride over the South China Sea to old Macau, followed by yet another trip over the island and to its new gambling home on Cotai. The City of Dreams, a large, stand-alone complex of hotels, restaurants, and entertainment venues, seems like an odd, almost alien-looking Vegas. There are all the same hotels and landmarks, but with a Martian quality. A stillness and humidity to the air that make it hard to breathe, coupled with a faint tinge of sewage—a new hotel has just opened across the street and seems to be experiencing difficulties in its first days. Futuristic new constructions. And the feeling that something is hiding underneath the surface—but not necessarily something you'd really want to drag up into the open.

It is Vegas, only bigger and weirder and without any of the things that make Vegas livable. Here, it's all big business. The Venetian here is the single largest casino property in the world. Its annual profits exceed many countries' GDPs.

But the rest of Vegas is strangely, palpably missing. There are not many shows. Not much beyond the experience of the gamble. They've tried, to be sure—China has even linked the relicensing of each casino (many license renewals are coming up in 2022) to efforts to diversify into non-gaming. They want Macau rebranded as a family-friendly paradise.

But family-friendly is precisely what Macau avoids. Indeed, anything that isn't directly related to gambling has a long battle to fight. When the Wynn opened a version of its Tryst nightclub, it closed after four months. The space now houses baccarat tables. When Sands tried its hand at diversifying by partnering with the established and revered Cirque du Soleil—a perennial moneymaker around the world—it ended up breaking their ten-year contract after only three years. When Melco tried a cabaret show, *Taboo*, that, too, closed. Its annual losses: over $3 million. Lawrence Ho, of the mogul Ho family that has run much of Macau's gaming for multiple decades, once put it this way: "Non-gaming is hard in Macau. That is the simple truth of it."

There is no pretense that this was created for anything other than gambling, pure and simple. It is fascinating, but it is cold. Macau feels as if it doesn't have a heart. The players who end up here are the sharks who see dollars, precise and calculating in their quest to maximize financial value at the expense of everything else. They will feast on the fish who are compelled to come, and find, once here, find they lack the will to leave. Because Macau saps you of energy for anything else. It's a frightening place. The belly of the beast. And the beast makes you see the ugliness that is easy to overlook in the rest of the poker world.

There are the barely legal (one hopes) prostitutes who dare not stop walking lest they be arrested for solicitation. As long as they keep moving to avoid confrontation, they are free from prosecution. At the Grand Lisboa, they move in circles on what's locally known as the racetrack. Pick your merchandise where you may. There are the businessmen on their junkets from mainland China. Not only is gambling illegal there, but so is the transfer of funds to this den of vice—or, rather, the transfer of quite as many funds as the hardened gambler would like. And so they go on tourist trips instead. For hard cash, there are a few clever systems in place.

There's the junket itself, where companies loan the money to play and later collect debts that can go into the high millions of dollars. And there's the pawnshop. Buy a watch or piece of jewelry in China. Pawn it at the proper shop for cash. After gambling, arrive back with cash (if any is left) to pick it back up (or upgrade if you've been lucky), and then exchange one last time by returning it to the original store. Or forgo the merchandise entirely: some pawnshops allow you to withdraw large amounts of cash without actually purchasing anything.

Everything about this place makes me recoil. On my own, I would have never come. But I've listened to the voices who told me that what I'll find here is beyond what I'd find anywhere else. They were right, and here I am. It doesn't hurt that Erik is here, too. The APPT—Asia Pacific Poker Tour, hosted by my new sponsor—is known for its juicy high roller events, and he wouldn't miss it. Especially since it gives him the chance to travel to Japan afterward.

It's seven in the morning, and I've been awake since four, or at least I think it was four—this is jet lag more severe than I've ever experienced. I drift in and out of sleep. I don't know what time it is. I feel like that kid who decided to atomize himself in Willy Wonka's factory in an untested prototype, reappearing reassembled, seemingly OK, but severely shrunken. Like him, I thought the machine looked cool—and had no idea what I was getting into. I feel all wrong, as if the pieces haven't quite fit back in the right way.

I decide that the battle for sleep is lost and go out to explore my new surroundings. In the casino, it may as well be midnight: the number of people exceeds what you'd find in most any Vegas establishment at any time of day. Some look like they've been here for days. People are screaming—I learn that the proper baccarat etiquette practically demands it. If you don't scream loud enough, your card may not have the right energy to magically shift into what you want it to be. The din is deafening. People are compiling lists of numbers—but not the statistical charts and range calculations of poker; rather, the runs and other minutiae of certain wheels and tables to figure out which numbers are the lucky ones to play. Red is everywhere—red glittering tracksuits, red hats, red shoes, red dresses. Red is the lucky color; you'd be remiss if you weren't wearing it. It's an atmosphere unlike any I've encountered. It makes a typical Vegas casino floor seem pale and downright rational.

A color. A number. A motion. An outfit. A word. Lucky numbers. Lucky charms. Lucky outfits or jewelry or hats or glasses. Lucky seats at the table—indeed, lucky tables to begin with. Lucky ways of checking your cards or placing your bets. Lucky portents, totems, baubles, signs, mantras. Macau is a shrine to the goddess of chance. And it's where many of the great poker minds have come to embrace her power.

"I actually cultivate some superstitions just on purpose," Ike Haxton explains to me as we wind ourselves through the City of Dreams. I've noted how many of the gamblers were wearing red and how prevalent the number eight (also lucky) seemed to be wherever we turned. Ike has pointed out some nuances I'd missed, like the long pinky nail. "It's a way of signaling wealth and status, because you can't grow out your long pinky nail if you're doing manual labor," he explains. "You'll notice a decent number of long pinky nails here—and that tells you the guy is here to gamble." I just shake my head in disbelief.

I'd come to Ike for an antidote to the feeling that everyone around me seemed to be losing their minds, and his words catch me off guard. Ike Haxton? One of the most mathematical, logical minds I'd encountered in or out of the poker world, purposefully cultivating superstition?

"You don't actually believe in all that, do you?" He can clearly see the disbelief and near-existential dread on my face.

"Well, I feel like the brain just doesn't cope well with luck," he explains. "And just really struggles to latch on to things to associate with good or bad luck. So I'm just taking the reins on that."

It's like the story that's apocryphally attributed to Niels Bohr, a Nobel Prize–winning physicist. A friend of his was visiting his office and kept looking up at the horseshoe over the door. Finally, he could no longer contain his curiosity. Could it really be that a mind as remarkable as Bohr's believed that horseshoes brought luck? Of course he didn't believe it, Bohr replied. "But I understand it's lucky whether I believe in it or not."

So Ike is making the rational decision to be irrational, in an attempt to make that irrationality more . . . rational?

Something like that, he says.

Give me an example, I ask him.

"Well, it's mainly lucky objects and articles of clothing," he tells me. "Like the shirt I was wearing when I won the Prague twenty-five-K one-day tournament is now my designated twenty-five-K one-day tournament shirt. I had a lucky quarter in my pocket for about a year and a half a while ago. I think I have a lucky dollar bill in my wallet right now."

He furrows his eyebrows and reaches into his pocket for his wallet, to check whether the bill is in fact in place. It is.

"Why is it lucky?" I ask.

He explains that he got it from another professional player, Nick Petrangelo, when they had a 5 percent swap in a tournament in Florida. Nick left for dinner break one hand early. "He was texting me about it to needle me, because I'm extremely anal about not missing hands," Ike recalls. "That's really unacceptable." So, while Nick was off having his dinner, Ike ran some quick calculations. How much expected value had Nick cost him by his decision to leave early? It turned out to be a dollar, give or take. Ike told Nick as much, and after dinner break, Nick ceremonially offered him a single dollar bill. On the next hand, Ike stacked an opponent—that is, he took all of his chips.

"It was the most ridiculous pot I'd played in quite a while," he remembers. The opponent in question had returned from dinner with the following words: "So, who else got drunk on dinner break?" Silence. "Huh. I guess just me."

"He sits down and 5-xes under the gun," Ike says—that is, he raises to five times the big blind with eight players to act behind him. A standard raise would be two or two and a half times—and you'd better have good cards to go along with it. Ike is on the button and looks down at pocket kings, one of the best hands you can have. He makes a sizable three-bet, raising the original player for over three times his bet. Mr. Drunk on Dinner calls. The flop comes king-seven-deuce, with a flush draw. Drunk on Dinner checks to Ike, who bets rather large (naturally; he has top set—a monster hand). Drunk decides to raise. Ike, of course, is going nowhere. The next card is an ace. Our inebriated hero decides to shove his remaining chips into the middle. Ike calls. Drunk on Dinner had just punted off his entire stack with an off-suit nine and three.

"He just goes, 'It's a rebuy,' and staggers away from the table. This was for one hundred fifty blinds, two and a half starting stacks, six hours into the day." Ike went on to run deep in the tournament, and the dollar was deemed extra lucky. "It's been in my wallet since."

So what would have happened, I ask, if he'd checked his wallet just now only to find the dollar missing? Or if his lucky shirt got ripped in the wash?

"The dollar, I think I would be mildly distressed for a few minutes and then get over it. The shirt, I might just wear it anyway."

I object that he's purposefully avoiding the point of my question. Isn't attaching himself and any part of his mental well-being to random objects potentially dangerous? Sure, you might feel in control, but really, aren't you just adding one more factor that you might not ultimately be able to control?

In one study conducted in Italy, for instance, seven hundred students were randomly assigned to seat numbers during a written exam. Some of the numbers were tagged as culturally lucky—that is, according to Italian cultural reference, they brought good fortune--and others unlucky. It turns out that students who were in the "lucky" seats were consistently overconfident in how they would do—and those in "unlucky" seats were actually expecting lower grades. Confidence is an important factor in how you play. Wouldn't you want to minimize the potential confounding variables?

On the one hand, I recognize the power of the placebo effect: if you believe it's working, it may well work. If you think an object brings you luck, you are more confident. And yet what the Italian students in the "lucky" seats showed wasn't confidence; it was overconfidence. They thought they were doing better, but the evidence didn't actually back them up. And then there's the flip side of the placebo, the nocebo effect: the belief in evil signs or bad luck. It turns out people can literally scare themselves to death. If you think you've been cursed or otherwise made ill, you may end up actually getting sick, failing to improve poor health, or, yes, dying altogether. In one medically documented instance, a man was given three months to live after a diagnosis of metastatic cancer of the esophagus. He died shortly after. When his body was autopsied, doctors realized that he had been misdiagnosed: he did indeed have cancer, but a tiny, non-metastatic tumor on his liver. Clinically speaking, it could not have killed him. But, it seems, being told he was dying of a fatal illness brought about that very outcome. In another case, a man thought he was hexed by a voodoo priest. He came close to death, only to recover miraculously after an enterprising doctor "reversed" the curse through a series of made-up words. In yet a third, a man almost died in the emergency room after overdosing on pills. He'd been in a drug trial for depression and decided to end his life with the antidepressants he'd been prescribed. His vitals were so bad when he was admitted that doctors didn't think he would make it—until they discovered his blood was completely clear of any drugs. He'd been taking a placebo. Once he found out he had not in fact taken a life-threatening quantity of pills, he recovered quickly. The effect our mind has on our body makes for a scary proposition.

Belief is a powerful thing. Our mental state is crucial to our performance. And ultimately, while some superstitions may give you a veneer of false confidence, they also have the power to destroy your mental equilibrium. I like to think of this as the black cat effect. You see one cross the parking lot as you walk to a tournament. You brood about the bad luck. Your game is thrown off. You blame the cat. You bust. You feel validated. Superstitions are false attributions, so they give you a false sense of your own abilities and in the end, impede learning. What do you do if your lucky charm falls down the drain or the cleaners lose the shirt that led you to victory?

You may think you'd deal with it with grace, buying a new shirt or donning a new lucky charm, but the research disagrees. In that moment where the lucky object is lost, a degree of mental equilibrium often goes with it, consciously or not. You may feel off your game. You may push your edge a little less as you recover. In a sense, you lose your control, because something outside your control has disrupted an object you'd imbued with power—even if only jokingly. There's one Olympian who would always wear a charm around her neck. At the start of the Winter Games, where she was expected to perform quite well, she misplaced the necklace. Soon, she felt like everything was going wrong. She fell on a practice run. She came down with a flu. She fumbled. And she didn't win any medals. Was the lost charm to blame? Probably not consciously. But what happens when something that has seen you through so much, that is symbolic of so much, is no longer with you? Can you honestly predict the limits of your subconscious so accurately as to say it really won't matter? (For some Olympic athletes, the link is far more explicit. Back in 2012, runner Sanya Richards-Ross blamed a third-place finish on her failure to wear a lucky bullet necklace her mother had given her. When she wore it, she won.) In my mind, this isn't a harmless enough pastime. It's something with implications that are potentially troubling for optimal performance in the long run.

Ike doesn't quite agree. "The point of the practice as I see it is to acknowledge and accept that my mind is going to make these associations no matter what, and try to take ownership of that process," he tells me. "And also, to be honest, I think it's funny to talk about it because people find it very strange. Like, I don't *really* believe it, but I do put a medium amount of effort into keeping track of my lucky objects and making sure I have them."

And his unlucky ones, it turns out. He was recently forced to part with a favorite shirt because, well, he just couldn't win when he wore it. "The first time I wore it was for the final table of a hundred-K and I was out in, like, four hands. And then the second time I wore it was for another final table at a different hundred-K, and I went from, like, chip lead to last place almost immediately and out in fourth. And then I decided I would try to wear it in a low-pressure situation, wore it for day one of the PCA main event, and busted in, like, six hands." And that was that. "It has a big bomb on it and things just explode when I wear it." So, no favorite shirt for Ike.

A modified Pascal's wager: You don't really believe it, but what's the harm? Perhaps. Perhaps not. Either way, Ike has been doing it for far longer than he's been playing poker—since middle school, at least. ("I had a lucky pair of boxers that I wore to soccer games. They had polar bears on them." Um, lucky boxers? "I think I just kind of liked them, and then I wore them to a soccer game and we won, and I decided they were lucky.") And it's not just objects that Ike has tried to tame. His approach also entails reining in routines, actions, habits. Like the summer of 2017. He made the final day of the $50,000 Players Championship at the WSOP, one of the series' most prestigious events. At the end of every tournament day, he'd go to El Dorado, a Mexican restaurant near the Rio, and order carnitas. "One day I missed it, but I had it delivered." He has routes that he walks, lucky spots, lucky routines that must be repeated if they led to success the time prior.

Jane Risen, a psychologist at the University of Chicago, calls this kind of thinking from people like Ike—"smart, educated, emotionally stable adults"—a form of acquiescence. We can recognize that something is wrong and irrational, but then consciously and purposefully choose to let the false belief stand rather than correct it. "People can recognize that one course of action is rationally superior yet choose to follow a different one," Risen writes.

You know the sports team you support won't lose if you don't wear your lucky jersey—but you put it on anyway. You may not actually believe in astrology, but can it really hurt to read your monthly horoscope? And you know that your shirt doesn't actually affect the cards you're dealt, but you wear it—or don't wear it—even with that knowledge.

Ike is far from alone. Johnny Chan is known to play with an orange—the fruit—at his side. Sammy Farha has an unlit cigarette. Doyle Brunson has a *Ghostbusters* card protector—and apparently even rents it out to those in need of a lucky boost ($200 if you want it for a half hour). More recently, Frank Stepuchin, who won the WPT Gardens Main Event in 2019, has taken to bringing a chicken wing to the table, for the lucky wings that propelled him to his Gardens win. At the WSOP, I played with one man who lugged a stuffed penguin to every tournament. You'd be right to question my choice of "lugged," but let me assure you, "lugged" is indeed the word. The penguin was large enough that the man was threatened with disqualification from one event if he didn't remove it from the table area. As far as I could tell, he never made it very far in any event, but the penguin remained faithfully by his side throughout. (I later learned that the player in question was a successful one from Hong Kong, Sparrow Cheung.)

Then there's the player who won the EPT Monte Carlo Main Event back in 2014, Antonio Buonanno. In an interview during his incredible run, the interviewer asked him if he was superstitious. Not at all, came the reply. You see, he went on to say, he had tried all the superstitions he could over the years and nothing seemed to work, so he gave it up. Of course, it goes without saying that he was wearing the same shirt he'd worn the day prior because it had brought him this far in the event and he was scared to try his luck with any other outfit. And he had his lucky glasses. Naturally. But no, no, not at all superstitious.

Later in the tournament area in Macau, I spot one of the best players in the world—currently considered by some to be the best tournament player of them all—donning a necklace with a tiny animal figurine under his shirt. His wife explains that it's his Chinese astrological sign. She's bought one for him and for several of his friends—other exceptional players. Surely, someone who is as engrossed in the mathematical as this particular player—he is known for his precision, his seeming encyclopedic knowledge of every permutation of every hand, his ability to spend countless hours running simulations with PioSolver—would be immune. But perhaps it's more of the same acquiescence: I recognize the fallaciousness, but I choose to do it all the same. And I refuse to acknowledge that it may actually be causing some harm.

It goes beyond objects, to a sort of magical thinking that you wouldn't expect in a high-level player. Phil Hellmuth often talks about his "white magic"—an ability to see into his opponents' souls and hole cards to make huge plays. Daniel Negreanu has often claimed to be able to know what card is coming next—something he has said repeatedly on many a poker stream. Even Jason Koon has admitted to having a "lucky feeling" that he was going to win an all-in during a major event, even though he was far behind. He just knew the card was coming. Vision boards, that New Age–y pastime of pasting your desires onto a board so that they come true, have turned into Ouija boards.

"I forgot about my best lucky object!" Ike texts me later that day, after our walk through the City of Dreams. "For about 6 months I kept a small clay doll of Steve O'Dwyer"—a very successful tournament player—"on the felt in front of me at every tournament." The doll is no longer with him, but it lives on the mantel over the fake fireplace in his Vancouver apartment, along with another lucky doll and an antique Korean vase. (Ike is not the only person enamored of the lucky O'Dwyer doll. One went to Scott Seiver. One to Bill Perkins, a businessman and recreational player often found at the high rollers, who told *PokerNews* back in 2016, "The power of Steve is needed so I got the doll." Unclear if he then went on to win.)

When you see unsuccessful players embrace the mythical, it raises an eyebrow but not much else. After all, about a quarter of the American population actually admits to being either somewhat or very superstitious. In a 2019 poll, 27 percent reported that a four-leaf clover is lucky, 23 percent thought breaking a mirror was unlucky, 22 percent will knock on wood, 21 percent won't walk under a ladder (actually, that one seems eminently reasonable; show me someone who regularly walks under active ladders and I'll show you an idiot without basic safety training), and so on. Even the rabbit's foot is a lucky object for 14 percent—and a black cat will ruin the day for about 11 percent. That's not even getting into the significance of numbers. The number thirteen, especially if paired with Friday: unlucky for some cultures, lucky for others. Hotels and airplanes often go to great lengths to avoid floors and rows and rooms of any offending number. Same with sports jerseys: some numbers can never be used; others are held in certain veneration by virtue of their history. The ultimate compliment: a retired number.

But at the higher levels, even with all the rationality in the world behind a practice, it can be jarring. Because even at the highest level, the mind craves control. We are on an endless quest to put our stamp on the things that couldn't care less about our existence. Even if it's not altogether rational, just let me be.

"It tilts me so much" is Erik's reaction to my musings on lucky objects and magical thinking over dumplings at Din Tai Fung. It's the go-to place for pre- and post-tournament meals, close enough to the poker room that it fits into any length break, but far enough away that we can't hear the ear-piercing eighties and nineties covers that a live band blares out of the Hard Rock Cafe from afternoon until late into the night, every single day. As Ike put it when I complained that, even with headphones, I couldn't block out the noise, "It had probably never occurred to you to imagine what the Goo Goo Dolls would sound like if the lead singer had a Chinese accent and the band couldn't play their instruments at all." Now I know.

This dumpling place is quick and tasty, but Macau fatigue is beginning to set in in earnest. As another plate of yet more dumplings arrives, I think to myself that if I never see another dumpling again, I'll die happy.

"You look the right degree of miserable here in Macau," Erik says.

"Ha. Do I really look as miserable as I feel?"

"Yup. I feel you. Well, once you've done Macau, you've survived the worst," he says. "Everything is better from here. The Rio will feel like the Four Seasons Bali after this."

I break open a soup dumpling. Erik looks thoughtful as he picks out a wilted piece of greens and returns to our previous conversation.

"Any form of delusion should be punished in poker," he continues. "It's really tilting to see it rewarded." He's talking less about the lucky objects that Ike espouses and more about the *feelings* and the *I knew the card was coming* bits that get bandied about. But the lucky objects, too, at least a bit. He has zero patience for any of it. "It's just cultivating the wrong mindset," he tells me. "Eventually, that's going to get you in trouble. That's not poker."

Perhaps he's in a particularly dismissive mood because it's been only a few days since his old mentor, one of his first ever teachers in backgammon, died. And that was someone who was as rational as they come, except with some indulged delusions that ultimately ended his life earlier than it should have rightly ended: Paul Magriel, or X-22 as he's better known, for the name of the winning player in a sixty-four-entry imaginary tournament that he once played against himself. Or, to Erik and his other students and close friends, simply X.

Before he was X, he was just Paul. A mathematically gifted boy who loved games, loved to play, loved the world that surrounded him. And it was quite a world: his parents, an art dealer and an architect, were friendly with the likes of Walker Evans, the famed photographer, and Edmund

Wilson, the equally famed critic, and private viewings of prominent art all over the United States and Europe punctuated summers at their home on the Cape, away from their other home on the Upper East Side. Games brought Magriel to math—he became interested in probabilities, odds, percentages—and it grew clear early on that he was quite gifted in both. Dalton, Exeter, NYU, Princeton: Magriel's academics were stellar. Along the way, he graduated from nickel games of draw poker to backgammon. He started playing at the Mayfair Club, where he'd eventually meet Erik, and soon earned enough to supplement a meager income teaching at the New Jersey Institute of Technology.

He quit teaching. He divorced his wife. And he devoted himself to backgammon, rising quickly to become the highest-ranked player in the world. He wrote a column for the *New York Times*. He wrote a book. He taught some of the greatest players—including Erik, who soon ranked at the very top himself. He famously beat George Plimpton while playing blindfolded.

I met X back when I first came to Vegas. Erik had wanted to introduce me to his earliest teacher. It had been a long time since they'd seen each other, and the meeting didn't go according to script. It was in the Sports Book bar of the SLS Hotel. X chose the spot. He was late and flustered. He'd forgotten his phone in the cab. He alternated between awkwardness and aggressive hustle. And it was clear that the years hadn't been kind. I was somewhat prepared. Erik had told me that X had battled a serious drug addiction, a gambling addiction, ill health. But I still couldn't quite square the man whose hands were shaking and who couldn't stop talking, one word after another spilling out in a ramble of not-quite-connected thoughts, with the dashing playboy who was once known to date models all over the world. The debonair, tuxedoed gent who dashed around the globe in private jets with royalty didn't seem to have anything in common with the bowed, sickly figure eking out a living playing cash games for one-dollar and two-dollar blinds. The conversation didn't go particularly well. X alternated between talking about his past glory, making vague attempts at hitting on me, and showing a bit of a hustling spirit—he wanted, for instance, to charge me for access to a library he'd built up on my book topic. "I have lots and lots and lots of very important observations about luck and skill and the relationship between luck and skill in life. So I have a lot of material for you," he told me. After seeing my face he added, "I guess I won't charge you for it."

I didn't want to dwell on the encounter. It was awkward and strange and uncomfortable and, more than anything else, very sad. It had all but taken the fire from my desire to enter the world of poker, and it had taken Erik explaining over and over why X was a special case for me to move beyond it.

But he's on our minds now. And it's fitting that it's in Macau where X comes back into focus. That it's this place, not Vegas, where he made his home in his final years, not Monte Carlo, which saw his glory days, but an island I don't think he ever even visited, that brings him to mind.

Erik tells me a story that, to him, is the essence of why acquiescence isn't a harmless beast.

It was at a casino. Erik was there with X and their friend Billy. X and Billy shared an insatiable yen for gambling, but the nature of their attraction was quite different. X was hyper rational. He was a Princeton-trained mathematician, after all. He knew gambling for what it was. He knew that, unlike poker or backgammon, he couldn't control the outcomes of the table games around him. But he couldn't help himself. He acknowledged his folly, and he gave in to it all the same. Billy, on the other hand, had an inflated sense of his own abilities to spot when a table was running hot, when he was likely to start winning. On this day, the two of them were at the craps table. Erik was watching. And X turned to him and said, "Which is sicker? Billy standing at the craps table, who thinks he's going to win, or me, who knows he can't win and still plays?"

At our meeting in Vegas, Erik reminded X of the story. "Yeah. I enjoy the action too much," X reflected. "I splurged a lot of my money away. I made mistakes." He paused for a moment. "It's the opposite of how I want to play poker and how I trained myself to play. I have very bad management in life. But in poker I try to maintain good discipline, in terms of losing and still playing tough."

Before he left, though, he wanted to make sure Erik knew he was OK. "By the way, Erik, it's been over ten years since I've done any serious casino gambling," he said by way of goodbye.

"That's good to hear," Erik replied.

In parting, X told us of his plans for the future. "I'm going to be writing a lot. I'm getting old, and I have a game plan for five or ten years. Write a book a year for the next ten years."

That was the only time I ever saw him. The chaos of life is far greater than the chaos of games. And now X is dead, and all his future books remain unwritten.

"He changed my life and the lives of many others," Erik says now. "It's hit me today more. He was very special. But so many of his great qualities were degraded by the drugs."

And the gambling?

Yes. And the gambling, too. It was all the same demon. It's always tricky to use the slippery slope argument, but it seems that with X, something of that nature really did happen. A genius for games, a mind fascinated with the nuances of mathematics, and a temperament that never learned to slow down. That wanted action and excitement. A person who knew that gambling was stupid and irrational, that drugs were likewise not the way to success, and who did it all the same, with the full knowledge of his own folly.

"I wish more people knew him in his prime," Erik tells me. "He was such a generous spirit."

"He seemed so lonely," I say.

"Very much so."

We eat a bit in silence.

"I'm glad you met him anyway. Hopefully, you still got some kind of feel for the ex-X."

I'm glad I met him, too. And I'm glad to be reminded of him now. Poker is about precision. Poker rewards the logical and the rational, and, yes, the creative, but with a reason behind it. Gambling is about chaos. It rewards the illogical, the irrationally exuberant. It preys on weakness. Unless you're playing baccarat with an edge-sorting technique to guarantee your eventual win—noting subtle differences in patterns on the backs of cards that some decks unintentionally have—or counting cards at the blackjack table, you're out to lose.

It's why I have such a strong instinctive dismissal of any superstition whatsoever. It's inviting the chaos. It's opening you up to the very elements poker is meant to control. Acquiescence is not harmless. Because the moment you acquiesce, you give up a bit of control, however tiny, to the process of superstition. And if you *actually* believe in it, you become a gambler in the real sense of the word, ready to gamble with fate in a way that is the very antithesis of everything poker has taught me about approaching life. Macau, it turns out, is pretty much my idea of hell.

I MAY NOT BELIEVE in superstition. But I am coming to appreciate the power of belief in a broader sense. As it happens, there may indeed be something to the hot hand: thinking you're on a streak may not be a fallacy after all, at least not always. Here's what more recent analyses have shown. Yes, a basketball player who seems to be on a winning streak may not always be making more baskets—but sometimes she is. Her confidence translates to her execution, especially in the immediate term. A human being is not a robot. How you feel affects how you act. And while a hot streak of cards or dice is actually *not* possible—the gambler's fallacy remains eternally fallacious—streaks that require actual human performance may indeed exist. The more the realm is subject to individual action, such as creative careers where mindset is one of the central elements, the more this is the case. A 2018 study in *Nature* found clear evidence of hot streaks in artistic and film careers, as well as in scientific trajectories. The streak "emerges randomly" and inevitably comes to an end, but while it lasts, it has a self-reinforcing effect.

That self-reinforcement can lead to a performance boost in most any field—and poker seems to be particularly well suited as a demonstration. Because at the poker table, perceived confidence often translates to incorrect assumptions on the part of your opponent: if you look self-assured and act with conviction, your actions will garner more respect. People may fold to you more often—and you will win more often. It's a self-fulfilling prophecy of sorts.

In Macau, I am hot off my victory. I'm feeling triumphant and capable. Sure, I may be questioning the extent of my skill, but no one can deny that I've had quite the run. Over the next ten days, I end up making not one but two final tables—and though I don't add another title to my name, I do add a second-place finish, for almost $60,000. And the hand I lost? It's not the misplays of yore. Instead, I have the bad luck to run a nut flush into a full house—a monster-into-monster cooler of a hand that is rare in heads up battle. Of course, I know that my sample size is still far too limited to tell whether I'm lucky or good, unlucky or bad—but the evidence seems to be that it can't all be luck. And I didn't even need a lucky doll to make it possible.

I've gotten what I came for.

· · · · ·

M ACAU WILL BE MY last hurrah for some time. My moment of glory may propel me to the dream of being officially considered a poker pro—but Macau will be my last final table for now. It's not a downswing as such, just a bit of a reversion to the mean. I lose my hot hand, but I retain some of the skills I've picked up along the way.

For one, I finally do cash the World Series Main Event. The second time around, it turns out, the WSOP feels quite different. I know the correct entrance and can direct my Lyft confidently around the back. I even know the shortcuts that will shave a good four minutes off the drive. I know to avoid the vendors. I know to come early and load money into my online account so that I never have to wait in line for an event. I skip the Colossus, or the Colasshole as I've taken to calling it in my head. Likewise the Crazy Eights and all the other unlimited reentry extravaganzas that seem like great value until you realize just how many pros are sitting at every table, taking every marginal spot because they know they can rebuy infinitely. I know to avoid the chatter—the peer pressure, the drone of the bad beats, the stories of would and could and should have. My headphones are my best friend.

And my head is clearer than it's ever been. I've rented an apartment for the summer. No more hotel displacement. No more sense of being lost in space. I make myself lunch every day and try to go home for dinner as often as I can. My husband comes out for a few weeks—and this time, I know all the places to go that will give us a more genuine Vegas experience. Here's a cheat sheet. For sushi, Yui and Kabuto. For dinner close to the Rio, the Fat Greek, Peru Chicken, and Sazón. For when I'm feeling nostalgic for the jerk chicken of my local Crown Heights spots, Big Jerk. Lola's for Cajun. Milos, but only for lunch. El Dorado for late-night poker sessions. Partage to celebrate. Lotus of Siam to drown your sorrows in delightful Thai.

And it's the Main Event again. I've coasted through the first two days without much trouble. No more king-jack off-suit. No more worried glances at the clock. I've got this. And here we are, near the money bubble. It's late in the evening, and I'm this close to doing it: cashing my first ever Main. I'm happy to say that I'm not particularly short-stacked. Sure, I don't have a massive chip advantage, but I'm not in any danger, either. I'm comfortably average. "Get it!" texts Erik. He busted earlier with a gross hand where his set of jacks fell to a set of aces—I had to drag the hand history out of him, so adamant is he about avoiding bad beats, but this one actually did have some interesting decision points—and is now cheering me on.

During a break, I walk outside—fresh air, always, whenever possible—and spot the tall frame of Patrik Antonius, the Finnish phenom who has been an absolute beast on the live scene for the last fifteen years. He waves me over and asks how everything is going. "The bubble is my favorite time," he tells me. "You should go crazy. Play any two cards." I look at him like he's slightly insane. This is the Main Event, after all. "I'm serious," he says. "No one wants to bust on the bubble. Now is the time to gamble."

I laugh. I don't have much of a reply.

"I don't know if Erik agrees with that," he follows up. "But I think it's the best strategy."

The floor calls us back in—the break was an unscheduled one, to get the exact count of players left before the money. Twenty-two.

"I mean, I did bubble the high roller last month," Patrik says as we walk in. "But otherwise, you can just push everyone around."

I thank him—I don't plan on following his advice at this exact moment, but he is a phenomenal tournament player. And I promptly text some conversational highlights to Erik. Even though Patrik probably has no idea of his enduring influence in this throwaway conversation, "Patrik mode" will become our shorthand for relentless bubble aggression. "Think Patrik," Erik will text me during another bubble. A full year later: "Channel Patrik." Patrik mode, baby. No one wants to bust.

Twenty-two left until the money, and I'm still in. "Keep me posted," Erik texts. "Want a play by play."

Somehow, Patrik rubs off. Twenty off the money, and I find myself all in with pocket queens. The theory that no one wants to bust doesn't quite hold up, as I get called. But luckily, the caller has tens. I double. "Yay!" comes Erik's text. Ten left. Six left. "Go MK!" texts Erik. "Shove AA!" He's urging me to play, not to fold into the money. And I do. Two left. One left. We are on the stone bubble of the Main Event. And . . . the floor announces a twenty-minute break. I am not amused.

"One left and they send us on a fucking 20 minute break!" I type.

"Terrible," Erik writes back. "Still shove AA."

"Will do," I respond.

We return from break. It's three thirty in the morning, and our restart is at eleven a.m. The bubble hasn't burst, and we've been told the starting time for day four will not be pushed back. I wait. The tension is real. One of the players at my table has taken the occasion of the break to get rapidly drunk. He starts to belt out Kenny Rogers. "Know when to hold 'em . . ."

The table bursts out laughing. He moves on to Louis Armstrong. The bubble still hasn't burst, but at three thirty in the morning, you could do worse.

At long last, it happens. Someone busts. And it hits me. I did it. I've officially cashed the Main Event. "In the money!" I text Erik.

"Yay!!!! Congrats!" comes the reply. "That's huge. Amazing accomplishment."

And it's true. I do feel a sense of amazing accomplishment. It feels good.

I don't final table—maybe one day!—but I almost make it to day five. And I have the satisfaction of knowing that maybe, in the end, I haven't let Erik down, after all.

TWO WEEKS LATER, I'M at the European Poker Tour in Barcelona, where I notch my best ever EPT finish. Thirty-fourth place out of over 1,500 entries, for €9,200. Far from a min cash. When my husband comes to join me for a post-EPT vacation, I have enough to pay for the whole trip with some left over. The day I return from Europe, I take a bus to Atlantic City for the WPT Borgata. I'm still on European time, but I'm playing well. I make the final three tables—not a final table, but pretty damn close, and pretty damn satisfying. Twentieth place, from 1,075 unique entrants. That's a real run, and real money. Almost $25,000. My first year's salary as a writer in NYC was $23,000. Not a bad payday, this. I'm not winning more titles, but I seem to have gotten over the hurdle of simple luck. Some skill appears to have seeped through. I settle into a rhythm. When the Global Poker Index, or GPI, awards are announced, I find that I'm a finalist for the award for Breakout Player of the Year. I don't win, but it feels incredible just to have been in contention. I end 2018 ranked in the top five female tournament players.

There is, of course, the inevitable downturn: in the summer of 2019, I realize that I'm losing money for the year. I may have profited over $100,000 the year before, but now it's going in the other direction. Luckily, I have the tools to understand what's going on, the ability to not panic, to analyze, to study, to move on. I'm willing to leave my ego at the door and revisit my thought process, over and over. I get into the habit of writing down the results of every all-in confrontation to see if I'm running at chance levels, and realize that I'm on the wrong side of variance—I'm losing more than my share of flips. It's reassuring: variance plays both sides, and at least I'm not losing despite being on the right side.

There are, too, the moments of simple beauty. I've now learned to pause, wherever I am. To appreciate the contrast between the table and the rest of it, to absorb and not just dread the travel. There's the synagogue in the late winter, snow covering rows of tombstones, in the old Prague cemetery. A hint of my past, of the luck that it's taken for my bloodline to continue to the present day. There's the stooped figure of the grandmother with weathered hands as she grabs a fistful of newly caught razor clams in a tiny alley in Barceloneta and brings them up to my face with a smile. There's the soft tufted head of the wide-eyed deer standing in our path in Red Rock one early morning, when my husband and I take a hike before the start of my tournament, so that I play with a clear head and ready mind.

And there's this, too: Though pokerwise 2019 was not a good year for the Konnikova clan, personally it is somehow as good as they come. My mother may not have gotten another job in programming, but she has learned the power of the career pivot and is teaching young children how to code. My husband did land on his feet soon after his last venture had shut its doors—more than on his feet: a job at one of the best-regarded investment businesses in the world. But after a while, he realized he was deeply unhappy, and in 2019, he made the plunge I'd long suspected he was destined to make, into starting his own business. He told me that my new confidence, my transition to the poker world, the way it has changed my abilities, was what finally pushed him over the edge. I don't think that's altogether true—he's the one who has inspired me, over and over—but I appreciate the thought. Whatever poker has done for me, it has been all to the good.

"*Nu*"—the all-purpose Russian interjection of impatience, of motion, of readiness to move on, from, of course, my grandmother. Her ninety-fifth birthday is right around the corner, and her granddaughter seems to have taken longer than expected in the poker caper. "*Nu*, can't you stop playing now? Maybe you can start teaching?" Some things, it seems, never change, no matter how much I may accomplish and how far I might come. Some minds are not meant to be changed. I smile at her. "Not yet," I reply. "I don't think I'm ready to stop anytime soon." And she sadly shakes her head.

"But you gave such a beautiful talk at that conference." She is talking about the World Economic Forum in Davos, where I was invited to speak about poker and decision making that winter. I'd like to tell her that no one knew who I was in Davos back when I was just a journalist. It took poker for the invitation to come—and my talk was all about my time on the tour. Instead, I just smile again. "I'm so glad you enjoyed it. I've learned a lot."

I keep going. One more tournament. One more game. One more stop. It's a sort of steady state—and I'm not quite sure where I should draw the line. When do I decide I've learned enough? When is my mission accomplished?

As it turns out, poker has one final lesson up its sleeve. I may not know when to draw the line, but life has a way of deciding for you.

The Ludic Fallacy

Las Vegas, June 2019

"In every tablet there are as many grains of luck as of any other drug. Even intelligence is rather an accident of Nature, and to say that an intelligent man deserves his rewards in life is to say that he is entitled to be lucky."

E. B. WHITE, 1943

My hearing goes first. Then my eyesight. I manage to grab the bathroom counter before I fall onto the hard tile of the floor, and can formulate only one thought: stay conscious. I must be having a stroke, I think, or an aneurysm, or something else equally bad. And if I don't get help, I may die or have permanent brain damage. Whatever happens, I cannot pass out. I try to yell and don't know if any sound at all has emerged. I try not to vomit as a big wave of nausea comes over me, somehow still conscious of the danger of choking. And then, what feels like minutes later but is actually mere seconds, I sense someone entering the bathroom—I've made a sound after all, it seems, and my husband has heard me.

I grab in the direction I think he'll be, and say a single sentence. "Something very bad is happening."

THE MORNING STARTED OUT simply enough. It was, once more, the World Series of Poker, and this year, newly minted pro that I was, I was spending the entire summer in Las Vegas. My husband had come with me, and we were living some ten minutes from the Rio, where every day I would go to play whatever tournament was on the schedule.

I no longer hated Vegas. I had gotten into its quirks, its rhythms, even its beauty. Sure, I still hated casinos—more so than ever; Macau made certain of that—but the life around them was vibrant and full. There was an entire world off the Strip. A world of amazing food, amazing people, stunning nature. We had settled into a rhythm of work and rest—my husband working on his business while I played, coming together for dinner, finding the time to get out of the din for weekends away in the canyons, or, once, the beaches of Malibu. Everything was going well. Until it wasn't.

The day before, I played late into the night. I woke up feeling run-down and a bit achy, but I couldn't take the day off or even sleep in—it was a day two, and my chips would be in play the moment the clock struck noon. I spent the entire day battling a migraine. I didn't have much to eat. And I busted the tournament right at the end of the playing day, around midnight. I came home and collapsed into bed.

When I woke, my husband had long since been up. I walked out to the living room to tell him I was awake and then went to take a shower. And that's when whatever was happening started happening, and how I found myself sitting on the living room couch not knowing whether I was going to get through this.

I sit on the couch. My hearing is partially back—the rush of blood to my ears is less of a din and I can just about make out words. But I'm completely blind. It's one of my worst fears realized. I've asked to be taken into the full sunlight of the living room so that I can tell immediately if I'm starting to see again. We sit, and I wait. Those moments are the scariest of my life to this point.

It's twenty minutes but it feels like hours. I start to see spots. Gradually, outlines, and at last, my vision is back. I'm drenched in sweat. My husband tells me later that my pupils have dilated to the full size of my corneas, like two black saucers. I get on the phone to my doctor back in New York, and then I get on the phone to schedule an emergency MRI and MRA.

AUTHOR AND STATISTICIAN NASSIM TALEB distrusts the premise of my entire project: he believes we cannot use games as models of real life because in life, the rules derived from games can break down in unforeseen ways. It's called the ludic fallacy. Games are too simplified. Life has all sorts of things it can throw at you to make your careful calculations useless. And that's true enough. After all, that knowledge is precisely what brought me to poker. That life is uncertain. That we can't know everything. That we can't control it all, no matter how much we think we may be able to.

But one thing that poker has given me are the very skills necessary to deal with the chaos that can be thrown at you from outside the poker table. Experiencing smaller one-off events over and over during play has taught me both the mathematical and the emotional forbearance to accept them for what they are—and to emerge on the other side. There's simply no denying real life at the poker table. It always breaks through, whether in your emotions and reactions or in a more blunt way—that summer, there's an earthquake that forces a momentary end to the WSOP tournaments for the day; the year before, I find myself in Barcelona during a terrorist attack that puts our casino on lockdown.

Life happens, and through it all, we play. We play, gaining perspective, survival skills, the strength and knowledge to be the conqueror rather than the conquered. We play, and we acknowledge, with the full force of the outside world, just how lucky we are to be sitting at the table, to have the chance to even play the game.

"Most people are never going to die because they are never going to be born," Richard Dawkins writes, in *Unweaving the Rainbow*. "The potential people who could have been here in my place but who will in fact never see the light of day outnumber the sand grains of Arabia. Certainly those unborn ghosts include greater poets than Keats, scientists greater than Newton." It's mind-boggling to even consider. "In the teeth of these stupefying odds it is you and I, in our ordinariness, that are here." We are here, and we have the chance to experience life, in all its vicissitudes, all its unfairness, all its noise. Out of countless billions—trillions, quintillions, more than the mind is capable of imagining—of possible people who were never to be, we are the ones who are allowed to play at the table.

We have won the impossible, improbable lottery of birth. And we don't know what will happen. We never can. There's no skill in birth and death. At the beginning and at the end, luck reigns unchallenged. Here's the truth: most of the world is noise, and we spend most of our lives trying to make sense of it. We are, in the end, nothing more than interpreters of static. We can never see beyond the present moment. We don't know what the next card will be—and we don't even know when we see it if it's good or bad.

There's a Buddhist proverb. A farmer loses his prize horse. His neighbor comes over to commiserate about the misfortune, but the farmer just shrugs: who knows if it is a misfortune or not. The next day, the horse returns. With it are twelve more wild horses. The neighbor congratulates the farmer on this excellent news, but the farmer just shrugs. Soon, the farmer's son falls off one of the feral horses as he's training it. He breaks a leg. The neighbor expresses his condolences. The farmer just shrugs.

Who knows. The country declares war and the army comes to the village, to conscript all able-bodied young men. The farmer's son is passed over because of his leg. How wonderful, the neighbor says. And again the farmer shrugs. Perhaps.

You can't control what will happen, so it makes no sense to try to guess at it. Chance is just chance: it is neither good nor bad nor personal. Without us to supply meaning, it's simple noise. The most we can do is learn to control what we can—our thinking, our decision processes, our reactions. "Some things are in our control and others not," writes the Stoic philosopher Epictetus in *The Enchiridion*. "Things in our control are opinion, pursuit, desire, aversion, and, in a word, whatever are our own actions. Things not in our control are body, property, reputation, command, and, in one word, whatever are not our own actions." If we cannot do it ourselves, we cannot control it. We control how we play the hand, how we react to its outcome, but that outcome itself—that, we don't control.

There's an awful lot of time for reflection when you're lying in a tube for two hours, an IV in your arm, and in your head the knowledge that if you move even the slightest millimeter you will have to perform the entire procedure over again. As the machine whirs and clangs, almost unbearably loud even through the earplugs the technician has helpfully placed in your ears, the mind has the freedom to wander wherever it pleases, certain in the knowledge that there will be no sudden interruption. The words of the Stoics come home now with full force. I've controlled what I can. But my body has, for a time, gone beyond me. All I can do now is manage how I react.

My family has a dinnertime tradition. Every time we gather together, no matter the occasion—birthday, anniversary, New Year's, Thanksgiving, whatever else—there is one toast that is always given place of honor. We say it first, before anything else. And then we pause for a moment of quiet, clink our glasses, and move on with the meal and the other celebratory toasts to mark the day. *Пусть все будут здоровы.* May everyone be healthy. *Прекрасный тост!* What a wonderful toast! someone will always say right after, in choreographed call and response. The only toast that truly matters. May everyone be healthy.

"You were conscious for the entire time?" My doctor is baffled. That is the strangest part of the whole thing. Had I passed out, it wouldn't be nearly as scary—they could write it off for one of those sudden moments when your blood pressure falls and you along with it. Had I been panicking, it wouldn't be nearly as scary—they could chalk it up to a panic attack. The fact that I'm conscious and can narrate it all: that places it in the realm of something to be truly concerned about.

And I can't quite believe that I managed to stay calm. That I accepted what was happening and formed a plan for how I was going to deal. This was a very different me from the me of two years back. A poker-faced me. A me who had learned, finally, to embrace uncertainty.

It turns out that it's a very good thing indeed that poker has made me more comfortable with the unknown: the scans come back inconclusive. There are some neural changes consistent with a lifelong migraine sufferer but nothing else that can shed much light on the situation. At the end, the consensus seems to be that I had some sort of one-off horrible migraine, which I exacerbated by playing too long on too empty of a stomach, coupled with a vasovagal event—a sudden drop in heart rate and blood pressure. It wasn't a stroke, but it wasn't good.

IN SOME WAYS, POKER is a poor substitute for life. You can lose, but you don't get blown up; you can bust out of a tournament, but you (usually) don't end up in an emergency room. And no one is asking that poker replace life. You don't want to eliminate uncertainty—it's presumptuous to even believe you can. You simply want to understand it.

In 1979, Carl Sagan wrote about the awe of the universe in his notebooks, as a counterpoint to the irrationality of superstition and false belief. "We live in a universe where atoms are made in the stars; where life is sparked by sunlight and lightning in the airs and waters of youthful planets; where the raw material for biological evolution is sometimes made by the explosion of a star halfway across the Galaxy," Sagan reflects. "How pallid by comparison are the pretensions of superstition and pseudoscience; how important it is for us to pursue and understand science, that characteristically human endeavor—imperfect and incomplete surely, but the best means to understand the world that we know." Admitting to unknowing, accepting a lack of agency without resorting to gimmicks, and instead attempting to analyze the unknown as best we can with the tools of rationality: those are some of the most powerful steps we can take.

I'm glad I pushed myself to go to Macau, to stay in the game, to confront the limits of reason and keep playing despite it all. Because it makes it even more clear just how essential it is to step back from that void. "Those afraid of the universe as it really is, those who wish to pretend to non-existent knowledge and control and a Cosmos centered on human beings, will prefer superstition," Sagan concludes. "But those with the courage to explore the weave and structure of the Cosmos, even where it differs profoundly from our wishes and prejudices, to those people belongs the future. Superstitions may be comforting for a while. But, because they avoid rather than confront the world, they are doomed. The future belongs to those able to learn, to change, to accommodate to this exquisite Cosmos that we have been privileged to inhabit for a brief moment."

Nothing is all skill. Ever. I shy away from absolutes, but this one calls out for my embrace. Because life is life, luck will always be a factor in anything we might do or undertake. Skill can open up new vistas, new choices, allow us to see the chance that others less skilled than us, less observant or less keen, may miss—but should chance go against us, all our skill can do is mitigate the damage.

And the biggest bluff of all? That skill can *ever* be enough. That's the hope that allows us to move forward in those moments when luck is most stacked against us, the useful delusion that lets us push on rather than give up. We don't know, we can't ever know, if we'll manage or not. But we must convince ourselves that we can. That, in the end, our skill will be enough to carry the day. Because it has to be.

Most people think of poker as a way to get wealthy. And it is. Only not the way you think. I didn't make millions. But the wealth of skill I acquired, the depth of decision-making ability, the emotional strength and self-knowledge—these will serve me long after my winnings have run dry.

· · · · ·

ERIK AND I ARE walking in Riverside Park. The summer is done. The World Series is behind us.

He turns to me. "I hope you'll keep playing after this is all over."

I smile and nod.

He reflects a bit more. "I hope I can keep playing for a very, very long time," he says finally. "I don't want to have to retire. This game is just too damn interesting. It's such a beautiful game."

And it is. It really, really is.

Glossary of Poker Terms

Note: These terms are explained in ways specific to No Limit Texas Hold'em, the game described in this book. In other game variants, connotations may vary slightly.

All in: A bet for all of your chips. Also *shove* and *jam*.

Ante: A forced small bet that each player must pay every hand of the tournament in order to receive cards. Previously paid by every player every hand. Now more commonly paid in the form of a *big blind ante*, where the player in the big blind pays for the entire table.

Bad beat: A run-out where a player loses despite being an overwhelming statistical favorite to win beforehand. A classic example: a player holds AA and is beaten by KK when a king appears on the board, giving the dominated player a set.

Bankroll: The total amount of money you have with which to play.

Blinds: The forced bet two players pay each hand, putting in money "blind" to start the action. The *small blind* is typically half the size of the *big blind*. In cash games, blinds stay constant. In tournaments, they go up in each level of play.

Board: The cards in the middle of the table. To *play the board* is to declare that the five community cards are better than any hand you can make with your hole cards.

Bullet: An entry into a tournament. *I fired two bullets* can be translated as *I entered the tournament two times.*

Button: The position to the immediate right of the blinds, denoted by a dealer button. This will be the last position to act after the flop.

Bust: To lose all of your chips. A related term, *to go bust*, usually refers to a player who has lost her entire bankroll and is broke.

Call: To match the amount of the prior bet.

Cash (v): To be one of the people in a tournament who is paid, typically somewhere between 10 and 15 percent of the field. Also known as *to make the money.*

Cooler: A run-out where one premium hand clashes with another. A classic example: two players make sets, with one higher than the other.

Deal: The cards given to each player. In hold'em, they are all facedown.

Degen: Someone who likes to gamble too much, usually without an edge. Also used as a verb, *to degen.*

Draw: A hand that is not yet made but needs certain cards in order to be completed.

Edge: An advantage.

Equity: The future value your hand has.

EV: Expected value of your action. Can be positive (+EV) or negative (-EV).

Feel: Playing by intuition and experience. A feel player.

Fish: A losing player.

Flop: The first three community cards dealt.

Fold: To discard your cards.

Flush: Five cards of the same suit.

Freezeout: A tournament style where you only have one chance to enter. If you bust, you are out. This is in contrast to a *re-entry tournament*, where you are allowed a specified number of re-entries, from one to unlimited.

Full house: Three of one card and two of another. *Aces full of tens*, for instance, would mean three aces and two tens.

Full ring: A table with every seat filled.

Grinder: Someone who plays, or grinds, many cash games or tournaments over the year, usually lower or middle stakes.

GTO: Game Theory Optimal. A style of play where, theoretically, you are unexploitable and have no incentive to deviate from one specific strategy.

Hand: The cards that you're dealt. Also one completed turn of the game. *We played one hand against each other.*

Heads up: One on one poker.

High Card: A hand that has not made a pair or any sort of other "made" hand. For instance, ace-high means you have no pair, no straight, no flush, no full house.

Hole cards: The two cards a player is dealt facedown.

Odds: The chance of a player making specific hands.

Outs: The number of cards that can improve a player to a specific hand.

Jam: To bet all of your chips. Also *shove* or *all in*.

Limp: When a player opens the action by just calling the amount of the big blind.

Luckbox: An incredibly lucky player.

Muck: The discarded cards. *To muck* is to fold your hand by pushing it toward the discard pile.

Raise: To increase the amount of a prior bet.

River (n,v): The final card to be dealt. Can also be used as a verb. *I rivered him*: He had me beat until the river, but the river card improved my hand.

Rebuy; re-entry: A style of tournament where you can enter multiple times, in contrast to a freezeout.

Set: Three of a kind, with the player holding a pocket pair and one matching card on board.

Shark: A skilled player.

Shove: To bet all-in or jam.

Showdown: When two or more players make it to the river and must show their hands to see which is best.

Six-max: A tournament format where no more than six players can sit at each table.

Straight: Five cards in a row.

Squeeze: To re-raise when one player has bet and at least one other has called that bet.

Suck out: To hit a miracle card after getting all of your money in with the worst hand.

Sweat: To see someone's hole cards. To buy a piece of someone's action.

Three-bet: To re-raise an initial bet. A *four-bet* is when a three-bet is raised. A *five-bet* raises a four-bet, and so on.

Tilt: To be emotionally involved in the decision process.

Trips: Three of a kind, with the player holding one of the three matching cards and the other two on the board.

Turn: The fourth card to be dealt on the board.

Under the gun: The first player to act before the flop.

Whale: A fish with a lot of money.

Acknowledgments

There's nothing that gives me quite as much anxiety as writing the acknowledgments section of a book. The book itself is long. If I forget to quote someone, I can be forgiven. If I forget someone in the acknowledgments, that's on me. This book especially has kept me up at night. For the last three years, it has been my life. And countless people have come together to make it a reality. I just know I'm going to forget someone crucial and never live it down.

So, let me start with the most obvious name: Erik Seidel. Without him, this book would not exist. It's hard to express enough gratitude to someone who was willing to take a complete flier on a random journalist who didn't know poker from blackjack, and open his life and mind to my never-ending questions. Thank you for letting me tag along on your journey and share in your wisdom. Thank you for your spirit, your generosity, your curiosity, the boundless love of poker that you've instilled in me. Thank you for becoming a true friend and mentor. Thank you for everything. I'm still waiting for those two jokers to pop out of the deck.

A profound thank-you, as well, to the Seidel family—Ruah, Jamie, Elian. You are all amazing and inspiring, and I'm eternally grateful to you for opening up your home to me for so many years. You've all made me feel like an honorary Seidel, and that's the greatest honor I could hope for.

I could have never imagined how welcoming and warm the poker world could be. Too many people to name have made it possible for me to be the player I am today, but I'd like to single out a few in particular: to Phil

Galfond, for hours of insight and support, Ike Haxton for all of your wise words and much laugher, Andrew Lichtenberger for my dose of Zen, Jared Tendler for opening my mind, and Blake Eastman for teaching me to read myself. Thank you all for contributing to this project and giving your time so selflessly. A big thank-you, as well, to Jason Koon, my Pio wizard; Krissy Bicknell, my endless inspiration; Celina and Randy, my Macau survival gurus, without whom I'd still be stuck in the back of a cab with a multi-tabling driver; and Liv, Igor, Vanessa, Fatima, Chris, Jen, and all of the Team Pros who made this journey so fun. And a final, immense poker thank-you goes to Eric Hollreiser for believing in me from the very start and bringing me onto the team. Thanks to Garry Gates, Mel Moser, and Moya Wilson for making the Team Pro journey smooth, fun, and fantastic. If I were to list every poker player who has helped me, I would have another book to write, so I'll simply thank you all for being so wonderful and making me feel like a true part of the poker community.

Thank you to Elyse Cheney and Adam Eaglin, who saw the promise in a tiny germ of an idea about luck and helped nurture it to its best possible shape, and to the rest of the team at the Cheney Agency—Isabel Mendia, Allison Devereux, Alex Jacobs, Danny Hertz, Claire Gillespie. My editor, Scott Moyers, has been absolutely incredible. Thank you for giving me the space I needed and for making this book the best it could be. I feel lucky to count myself as one of your authors. Thank you to the rest of the team at Penguin Press, including Mia Council, Sarah Hutson, Colleen McGarvey, Lauren Lauzon, Danielle Plafsky, Anna Dobbin, Alicia Cooper, Aly D'Amato, and Christopher King. And a thank-you as well to my UK editor, Nicholas Pearson, and the team at 4th Estate.

I couldn't have done this without my family and my friends, who've put up with me, been there when I needed them most, and believed in this project from the very beginning. Thank you for listening to me through countless lunches and dinners, for sharing many a bottle of wine, for helping me fight off the LA shower cockroaches and live to tell the tale. I'm very lucky to have you all in my life.

The final thank-you is reserved for Geoff. Thank you for inspiring me, for supporting me, for believing in me, for never complaining about poker sessions that end at three in the morning, and for always pushing me to be my very best self. Thank you for being as amazing as you are, always. You are what makes everything possible. I love you.

I now return to the land of nightmares, for I have certainly forgotten some Very Important People. But I promise, I treasure you all.

Index

Note: Page numbers in *italics* indicate glossary terms.

Index

Aria, 91, 122, 132, 156, 166, 168, 190, 233

Art of Scientific Investigation, The (Beveridge), 148

Art of War, The (Sun Tzu), 67, 76

Asch, Solomon, 198

Ashley, Maurice, 281

Asia Pacific Poker Tour (APPT), 296

astrology, 43

Atlantic City, 197

attentiveness
  and author's PCA title event, 273
  Bacon on, 137
  as key skill for successful poker, 10–11
  and nonverbal cues, 213, 217
  Seidel's emphasis on, 32, 142–52

Auden, W. H., 133, 142

Aussie Millions, 186, 256

avatars for online play, 71

baccarat, 296–97

backgammon, 46–48, 61, 181–83, 307–9

backing for poker players, 123. *See also* sponsorships; swapping

Bacon, Francis, 137

bad beats, 132–36, 147, 252, 314, *327*

Bally's, 132

bankrolls
  and author's first live win, 166
  and author's first Vegas play, 126–27
  and author's poker schedule, 122–23
  defined, *327*
  and goal of poker project, 237, 243
  and normal variations in poker, 124–25
  and World Series of Poker events, 230

Baron, Jonathan, 28

beaten dog syndrome, 262

Beauvoir, Simone de, 13

behavioral analysis, 211–15, 215–18, 218–26

Bellagio, 152–53

benefit-cost calculations, 270. *See also* game theory

betting
  bet size, 73, 79–80, 84–86
  and chess, 46
  continuation bets (C bets), 285
  and poker contrasted with other games, 36
  prop betting, 176–84
  side bets, 46
  and uncertainty, 38
  See also all-in bets (shoving); blinds; raising; three-betting

Beveridge, William, 148

Beyond Tells project, 212

biases
  awareness and vulnerability, 241–43, 270
  Dunning-Kruger effect, 242–43
  hindsight bias, 238
  and hot hand hypothesis, 106–9
  and self-assessment, 266
  status quo bias, 239
  and stereotypes and thin-slice judgments, 197, 200
  See also gender issues and misogyny in poker

Big Five personality traits, 45, 218–19

"big swinging dicks," 165, 169

Binion's, 125

Bird by Bird (Lamott), 275

Black Friday, 70

blackjack, 195

blinds
  author's first Main Event play, 246–47
  and author's WSOP play, 3
  and basics of Texas Hold'em, 53
  and charity events, 98–99
  defined, *327*
  and famous Seidel showdown, 83

Index

Index

Index

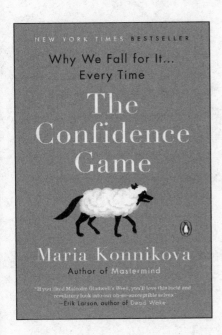
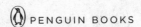

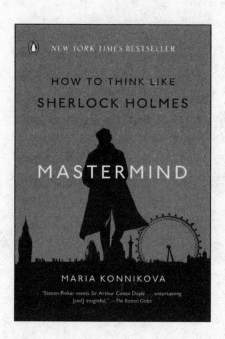